JESUS THE WISDOM OF GOD

Ecology and Justice
An Orbis Series on Global Ecology

Advisory Board Members
Mary Evelyn Tucker
John A. Grim
Leonardo Boff
Sean McDonagh

The Orbis Series *Ecology and Justice* publishes books that seek to integrate an understanding of the Earth as an interconnected life system with concerns for just and sustainable systems that benefit the entire Earth. Books in the Series concentrate on ways to:

- reexamine the human-Earth relationship in light of contemporary cosmological thought
- develop visions of common life marked by ecological integrity and social justice
- expand on the work of those who are developing such fields as ecotheology, ecojustice, environmental ethics, ecofeminism, deep ecology, social ecology, bioregionalism, and animal rights
- promote inclusive participative strategies that enhance the struggle of the Earth's voiceless poor for justice
- deepen appreciation for and expand dialogue between religious traditions on the issue of ecology
- encourage spiritual discipline, social engagement, and the reform of religion and society toward these ends.

Viewing the present moment as a time for responsible creativity, the Series seeks authors who speak to ecojustice concerns and who bring into dialogue perspectives from the Christian community, from the world's other religions, from secular and scientific circles, and from new paradigms of thought and action.

ECOLOGY AND JUSTICE SERIES

JESUS THE WISDOM OF GOD

An Ecological Theology

Denis Edwards

ORBIS BOOKS

Maryknoll, New York 10545

The Catholic Foreign Mission Society of America (Maryknoll) recruits and trains people for overseas missionary service. Through Orbis Books, Maryknoll aims to foster the international dialogue that is essential to mission. The books published, however, reflect the opinions of their authors and are not meant to represent the official position of the society.

Copyright © 1995 by Denis Edwards
Published by Orbis Books, Maryknoll, New York 10545, USA
All rights reserved.
No part of this publication may be reproduced or transmitted in any form or by any means, electronic or mechanical, including photocopying, recording or any information storage or retrieval system, without prior permission in writing from the publishers. For permissions write to Orbis Books, P.O. Box 308, Maryknoll, NY 10545-0308 USA.
Manufactured in the United States of America.

Library of Congress Cataloging-in-Publication Data

Edwards, Denis, 1943-
    Jesus the wisdom of God : an ecological theology / Denis Edwards.
        p.   cm. — (Ecology and justice series)
    Includes bibliographical references.
    ISBN 1-57075-002-5 (pbk.)
    1. Jesus Christ—Person and offices.   2. Human ecology—Religious aspects—Christianity.   3. God—Wisdom.   4. Trinity.   I. Title.
    II. Series: Ecology and justice.
    BT202.E274   1995
    232—dc20   94-38587
                                                                      CIP

Printed on recycled paper

For Peter Mark Edwards

Wisdom is radiant and unfading,
and she is easily discerned by those who love her,
and she is found by those who seek her.
She hastens to make herself known to those who desire her.
One who rises early to seek her will have no difficulty,
for she will be found sitting at the gate . . .
She graciously appears to them in their paths,
and meets them in every thought.

Wis 6:12-16

Contents

Preface

An important part of the work for this book was done when I had a sabbatical semester as a Visiting Scholar at the Center for Theology and the Natural Sciences, of the Graduate Theological Union at Berkeley. I am very grateful to Bob Russell, and to Mark Richardson and all at the Center. They were extremely hospitable, and their professional competence and friendly dialogue made it a great time of learning for me. I would like to express my thanks to all involved with the Graduate Theological Union. I owe a special debt of gratitude to Bill Stoeger, S.J., and to the Jesuit community of the Vatican Observatory in Tucson, for their hospitality and for the time and conversation shared so generously with me. This sabbatical was made possible by the Jordan-Kennedy Fund, and I offer my sincere thanks to the Jordan-Kennedy Committee and to Archbishop Leonard Faulkner.

The critical reaction of others has been of great importance to me as I have been working and reworking this material. I am particularly grateful for the precious time and energy given so freely by Zachary Hayes, Elizabeth Johnson and Kathleen O'Connor. They are each expert in areas I deal with in this book, and their encouragement and critical suggestions have been an essential part of the process for me. Others closer to home have given me very helpful responses to this work and support along the way. They include Michael Trainor, Patricia Fox, Alistair Blake, Robert Simons, Tony Kelly, Trudy Keur, Kevin O'Loughlin, Jan Bate, Trevor Bate and Anthony Kain. I am grateful to all of them and to the students and faculty of the Adelaide College of Divinity. I owe particular thanks to Bill Burrows, my friendly and encouraging editor, and to all at Orbis Books.

The love of my father and mother, Mark and Kath, and of Raelene, Mary, Kevin and our large extended family has meant much to me in the time of writing this book. It has been the time in which we have experienced the death of my young brother Peter. This book is dedicated to Peter, in the conviction that he now takes delight in the companionship of the God who moves the stars and gives life to trees, birds and us.

Introduction

Ecology and Theology

Australia, my homeland, is a beautiful and very ancient place, which has a diversity of landscapes from rain forests to deserts and a unique flowering of evolution in its flora and fauna. It is a land of great eucalyptus trees and yellow flowering acacias, of kangaroos, koalas, goannas and platypus. Much of its soil is fragile. The center of the country is desert. It is a country subject to droughts, bushfires, and floods. In the very short time since Europeans first arrived here, much of the land has been cleared and much of it has been badly damaged.

As a nation, we Australians have only recently begun to address the issue that this land was occupied for thousands of years by Aboriginal people and that it really was, and to some extent still is, their land. We are beginning to understand that Aboriginal Australians see the land as revelatory of the sacred and know much about how to live in this place. Belatedly, after decades of Eurocentric national policy, we are coming to embrace the idea that we are a multicultural society, with close links to South East Asia and with the Pacific.

My own experience is that of a male, middle-class Australian, with an Irish, English and Welsh family tree, living in a situation of relative wealth and privilege when compared to most of the Earth's people. It is obvious that my perspective can only be a limited and partial one, yet I believe that from our different perspectives, we need to be asking global questions about the state of the Earth. As an Australian Christian and theologian, I find myself needing to ask about the relationship between the land and a view of God. What is the relationship between the creating and redeeming God and human beings polluting the atmosphere, causing unpredictable changes to the global climate and damaging the ozone layer? What is the connection between ecology and theology? I hope that what follows can be seen as one partial glimpse, alongside many others, of some of the truths that may open up a way of healing for our Earth and its community of life.

The word *ecology* is related to the Greek word *oikos*, which means "house." It refers to the household of living creatures, the community of life, with its life-supporting systems. The word seems to have been coined by Ernst Haeckel, the German Darwinian, in 1866.[1] It always refers to the whole. Ecology is concerned with communities, with systems and with interrelationships. The pioneer of wilderness ecology, Aldo Leopold, has said that the basic concept of ecology is that land is a community. He writes: "We abuse land because we regard it as a commodity belonging to us. When we see land as a community to which we belong, we may begin to use it with love and respect."[2]

The word theology is related to the Greek word *theos*, meaning God. Christian theology is concerned with all things in the light of the God revealed in the Hebrew and Christian traditions, above all in Jesus of Nazareth. Christian theology finds in Jesus Christ the basis for an understanding of a fundamentally relational, trinitarian God. It sees all creatures, from quasars to koalas, as interconnected in one world of creation and salvation in God.

For a believer, ecology and theology can only be interconnected. The argument of this book is that there is a profound inner link between an adequate theology and an ecological stance. I will argue that theology is necessarily ecological. Many Christians have failed to acknowledge this interconnection, and Western civilization with its Christian heritage has made a terrifying contribution to the ecological destruction of the planet. Nevertheless, I believe that many ordinary Christians have an intuitive understanding that love and respect for God involves love and respect for God's creation. They know intuitively that theology involves ecology. This book is an attempt to reflect upon and to ground this intuition by making manifest the ecological significance of the central insights of Christian doctrine.

Movements of Hope

At the end of the twentieth century, the biological community which inhabits the Earth has reached a point of crisis. This crisis has been formed by a number of interrelated factors, including excessive exploitation and consumption by wealthy peoples, an economics of endless growth which takes no account of the limits of the Earth and exponential population growth. The damage to the ozone shield, climate change due to greenhouse gases, the pollution of the atmosphere, the rivers, and the seas, the degradation of land, the loss of wilderness and the extinction of species, all compel us to think again. Survival of life on Earth as we have known it will depend upon human behavior, above all in moving toward an economics of ecological sustainability, in acceptance of limits in consumption particularly by the wealthy and powerful, and in accepting limits to human population through freely chosen family planning.

This is an enormous challenge, perhaps the most difficult challenge the human community has ever had to face. The size and complexity of the issues involved can lead people of good will into a feeling of being completely overwhelmed, resulting in a sense of powerlessness and inaction. If this crisis is not to overwhelm us, we need to face it not only with intelligence, wisdom and creativity, but also with a basis for hope.

There is a basis for hope in the movements of consciousness and commitment that have emerged in the global community. It seems to me that three interrelated movements can be discerned at work in our world. First, there are movements of consciousness and movements of people committed to such values as democratic participation, social justice, human rights and access for all people to goods like food, housing and health care. As the philosopher Charles Taylor has shown, this is very much a development of modernity, with deep roots in the tradition mediated to us through the Enlightenment and Romanticism.[3] Second, there is the feminist movement, which offers a radical critique of patriarchal oppression and challenges the human community to new understandings of equality in gender relations, to new forms of mutual relationships, and to new participatory structures. Third, there is the ecological movement which unites people throughout the globe in a new understanding of the fragility of the life-systems of the planet, which enables human beings to see themselves in interrelationship with the ecological whole, and which is committed to a new global agenda that respects the integrity of the living systems of the planet.

These three movements interact at many levels. Those touched by feminism, for example, soon see how women bear the brunt of poverty around the world and find themselves committed to a search for global justice. At the same time, a feminist analysis, like that of Rosemary Ruether, shows the interrelationship between patriarchy, militarism and ecological destruction, and leads to a commitment to ecological integrity.[4] As Sally McFague points out, the ecological crisis affects people along class, race and gender lines. Poor women of color suffer the greatest impact.[5]

The ecological issue is not only about flora and fauna, but is also a people issue and a justice issue, since the ecology, the home we share, is a finite one. If our home is polluted, exploited and denuded, the poor of the Earth suffer and die along with fauna and flora. Ecology and justice are radically interrelated. An ethics for the third millennium will involve an intelligent and enduring commitment to the homeless and the hungry and to the ecological integrity of the Earth. In this book my focus will be on the attempt to develop an ecological theology, but this will involve attempting to be mindful of the interweaving of issues of ecology, gender and justice.

I would argue that, theologically, the ecological, feminist and justice movements can be seen as the movement of the Spirit in our times. They are the positive "signs of the times." They are resources for a period of crisis, the grace of this moment. These movements are not at all immune from human weakness and sin, but I believe that it is in them that the creative, liberating, healing Holy Spirit is revealed in a particular way for our age.

The Earth's Rain Forests

The loss of the rain forests is an ecological issue which encapsulates many others. It can be seen as a symbol of the crisis confronting the whole Earth. Rather than attempting to survey the range of ecological issues we face, I will focus on the rain forests as a starting point for the theological reflections of this book.[6]

My argument will be that the destruction of the rain forests is an issue for the global community. It has global effects and it has global causes, which include the lifestyles of the middle class in affluent countries and the structure of international finance. Theologically, I will argue that these rain forests are to be seen as a precious expression of the exuberant fecundity of God.

Around the world, forests are being cleared for agriculture and grazing, burned, cut for lumber, and flooded for dams and hydroelectric power. Seventeen million hectares of forest are destroyed each year. In one year, an area the size of Austria is cleared of forest.[7]

The great rain forests of the Earth are now found mainly in the Amazon basin, in Central Africa around Zaire, and in Papua New Guinea, Malaysia and Indonesia.[8] The Amazon basin, with its 2.1 million square miles of rain forest, has by far the biggest part of the world's 2.9 million square miles of rain forest.

At the current rate of deforestation, the tropical rain forests will have disappeared well before the middle of the next century. John Terborgh writes that "perhaps as much as half of the world's tropical forests had already been lost by 1990." This cleared land is now used for crops, plantations, and pasture, or it has been exhausted and abandoned as wasteland. Terborgh points out that, according to current estimates, 90 percent of what remains will be lost in the next thirty-three years.[9]

Among the first effects of deforestation are land degradation, compaction of soils and erosion. The abundance of life in a rain forest can lead to a mistaken view of the fertility of its soil. While forests in temperate areas can find up to 95 percent of their nutrients in the soil, and only 5 percent in the forest itself, in tropical rain forests the situation is reversed. Tropical rain forests often exist in very thin and nutrient-poor soils. In their case perhaps only 5 percent of the nutrients are found in the soil, with 95 percent coming from the forest.[10] The abundant, teeming, diverse life of the rain forest springs from the nourishment provided by the forest itself. James Lockman describes the process at work in the Amazon basin, where the soils are old, highly leached, lacking in nutrients and acidic:

> The entire nutrient reserves required by the forest are contained in the living and dead biomass. Since forest litter is mineralized so rapidly, and since the roots are never really dormant, nutrients present in decaying matter released into the soil are immediately taken up by the dense root mass near the surface of the forest floor. Virtually nothing is lost to leaching. Indeed, the mineral content of water in streams is close to that of distilled water. This sort of nutrient cycling is the opposite of the modern agricultural ecosystem, which depends on high annual inputs of nutrients in order to be sustained. Because of the rapid cycling of nutrients, the rain forest can grow on the same site for thousands, even millions, of years, despite the very poor condition of the soil.[11]

Al Gore notes that studies on the rain forests of the Ivory Coast have shown that the rate of soil erosion in forested land was as low as .03 tons per hectare, but after clearing this rose to ninety tons per hectare. Largely as a result of deforestation, a country like India loses an estimated six billion tons of topsoil each year.[12]

A second effect of deforestation is an increase in carbon dioxide, which will have a serious impact on global climate change. Trees take carbon dioxide out of the atmosphere and replace it with oxygen, transforming the carbon into wood. But when forests are cleared, this process is reversed. Deforestation adds to the greenhouse problem in a substantial way. The vegetation and soil of the Earth hold about a trillion tons of carbon, triple the amount stored in the atmosphere. Perhaps 50 percent of the carbon stored in plants is found in the rain forests. When forests are cleared, carbon from the trees and the cleared soil is oxidized and released into the atmosphere as carbon dioxide.[13] Carbon dioxide is released into the atmosphere slowly when cleared forests are left to decay, and very rapidly when forests are burned. In addition an open and burned forest floor becomes a new source of methane for the atmosphere, adding again to the greenhouse effect. We cannot predict the climate change which will occur as a result of this, but as Fearnside says, the very possibility of major, irreparable meteorological changes should give pause to those promoting massive deforestation.[14]

Deforestation also contributes to the breakdown of the protective ozone shield. Each year around September a large gap in the stratospheric ozone layer appears above Antarctica and the Southern Ocean, increasing ultraviolet radiation and the risks of skin cancer and long-term damage to vegetation in countries like Australia and Chile. There is the beginnings of a similar ozone problem above the Arctic, and a general thinning of the ozone shield, caused in part by chemicals such as chlorofluorocarbons. The destruction of forests adds significantly to atmospheric nitrous oxide, which catalyzes the breakdown of ozone molecules. This happens not only through burning, but also from the tendency of decaying organic matter in recently cleared areas to give off significant amounts of nitrous oxide.[15]

The destruction of the rain forests contributes to global crisis not only through increasing greenhouse gases that attack the ozone layer, but also by changing rainfall patterns. Al Gore notes that more water is stored in the forests of the Earth, above all in the great tropical rain forests, than in its lakes.[16] Forests themselves produce rain clouds through transpiration (the "perspiration" of vegetation). In this process the sun draws moisture up from the Earth and the trees, through the foliage of the trees. Moisture is swept up into the atmosphere in great banks of clouds before condensing into an afternoon downpour. This mechanism for water recycling is congenial to the growth of trees and the other organisms of the rain forest.[17]

When forests are destroyed, however, heavy rains continue for a while, wash away the now unprotected, fragile topsoil, and silt up nearby rivers. Then the rains themselves begin to bring less moisture. In Ethiopia forested land has decreased from 40 percent of the country to 1 percent in the last forty years, and declining rainfall has reduced much of the country to desert. It is feared that the burning of the Amazon rain forest will interfere with the hydrological cycle which carries rain to Peru, Ecuador, Colombia and Bolivia, creating future droughts in deforested areas. Lockman notes that "one of the great ironies in the debate on the future of the Amazon basin is that a rain forest can become a desert."[18]

Perhaps the most devastating effect of deforestation is extinction. The rain forest is thought to be the oldest land ecosystem on Earth. It represents an evolutionary process that has been millions of years in the making, a library of evolutionary history.[19] This heritage is being recklessly destroyed.

John Terborgh writes that before 1982 most biologists would have thought there was about two million species on Earth. Then came the discovery of the immense diversity of species in the canopy of the rain forest by Terry Erwin and his radically new estimate of the number of species at thirty million. Terborgh thinks this estimate too high and argues that we simply do not know how many species there are.[20] What we do know is that there is an exuberance of species in the rain forest— that a single tree may support 150 species of beetle, that a single hectare may contain two hundred different types of trees, and the same hectare may contain forty-one thousand species of insect, that a small area of forest may have twelve hundred species of butterfly, and a hundred hectares can provide habitat for 230 different species of birds.[21]

We do not know how many species there are in the rain forests, and we do not know how many species become extinct each year. Terborgh writes that "the number of extinctions the world is experiencing is unknown even to within an order of magnitude."[22] We know the status of only about 1 percent of all species. What we do know is that we are

recklessly destroying uncounted and largely unknown species of creatures forever.

The human community needs to come to terms with the fact that
extinction is irreversible. As Thomas Berry says, it is an eternal concept.[23] Ian Barbour points out that the obliteration of the rain forest
gene pool will distort the course of biological evolution on Earth. It
will extinguish not only countless species of plants and animals forever, but also the most complex and highly developed biotic community
to emerge in evolutionary history. This loss of biodiversity will mean a
radical impoverishment of biological life and a drastic loss of the Earth's
capacity for biological adaptivity.[24]

The destruction of the rain forest means the loss of potential new
forms of food, fiber, oil and fuel. It means the loss of resources for
human research and healing—a quarter of all prescription drugs have
their origin in such species.[25] It is from such plants that human beings
draw material for, among other medicines, analgesics, antibiotics, heart
drugs, enzymes, hormones, diuretics, anti-parasite compounds, ulcer
treatments, dentifrices, laxatives, dysentery treatments and anti-coagu-
lants.[26]

What is happening today in the Earth's rain forests may represent
the radical distortion of three and a half billion years of evolution. Since
the disappearance of the dinosaur sixty-five million years ago, we have
entered the Cenozoic period, characterized by an enormous variety of
life forms, many of which are now at risk. What makes this extinction
so horrifying is not just its scale, but the fact that human beings are
fully and solely responsible for it.

The effects of deforestation go beyond land degradation, the increases
of carbon dioxide in the atmosphere, climate change, damage to the
ozone layer, and extinction of species, to destruction of human beings.
Not only animals and plants suffer. The human beings who have lived
in peace with the forests for thousands of years are dislodged from
their homes and experience cultural disintegration, the loss of their lands,
their communities, and sometimes their lives. Whole populations are
forced into migration and end up in urban squalor.

The people of the Amazon had used their knowledge to sustain themselves from the resources of the ecosystem for several thousand years
without causing severe damage to the system as a whole. With the ar-
rival of Europeans in the early sixteenth century a new colonial era
began, which was characterized by an extractive approach to resources,

and by violence, slavery and cultural and ecological destruction. The Amazon became a resource for distant consumers and distant markets.

Since the 1960s Brazil has entered into a period of industrial and economic development, which has resulted in an enormous foreign debt. The Amazon was seen as a resource, and commitments were made to enormous road-building programs, along with the settlement of some of the country's poor in the Amazon region. Small-scale farming quickly collapsed, and big corporations took over the land for cattle ranching. The land of the poor tenants has been bought up, and the ranchers demand ever more land.

The forest is being cleared by heavy machinery, herbicides and burning. The rate of clearing has increased rapidly, particularly in areas opened up by government road-building, which has been financed in large part by the World Bank.[27] The result of clearing and running cattle on these huge areas is soil erosion and soil compaction. Grasses grow for a few years on the nutrients introduced by the burning of the forest, but, within five or ten years, the grasses deteriorate and the land becomes useless for grazing.

The reasons for the destruction of rain forest are many. They include rapid population growth in tropical areas, the desperate need for fuel of ordinary people around the globe, and misguided government development projects that attempt to "open up" rain forests for the lumber industry and for cattle grazing. Often government thinking is restricted to short-term goals by the desperate need for hard currency. Behind these problems and fundamental to any solution of them is the structure of international debt, whereby the powerful and wealthy countries hold poorer countries in the economic bondage of runaway debts.[28] The only human and ecological beginning to a solution is the writing-off or radical restructuring of dysfunctional and destructive debts.

What I want to address in this book is the issue of why it matters that we are destroying the rain forests. Of course, in any kind of ethical thinking, the destruction of the forests matters because it hurts human beings both now and in the future. The rain forest has long-term value for human beings (instrumental value), and clearly this value outweighs the short-term economic gain achieved by destroying it.

But is this all we can say? Is it simply a matter of weighing up the value to humans of destruction of the forest against the value to humans of its preservation? It will be the argument of this book that Christian theology suggests another position—that the rain forest, and each species that makes it up, has value in itself, intrinsic value, which human beings need to take into account and respect. I will argue that the central truths of Christian faith push us beyond anthropocentrism to an ethics of *intrinsic value*.

Cosmology

At the end of the twentieth century, we are beginning to see the Earth in its context of the universe. Because of space travel, we have been able to stand apart from the Earth and see it, at least in photographs, as a whole. We have become used to a new picture of the Earth, as a single, beautiful blue-green planet shared by all living creatures. Astronauts have noted that this picture inspires a sense of our common home on Earth. It gives imaginative force to the idea that we are one community and inspires the quest for global peace. It is a vivid image suggesting that the Earth is one biological community and that the systems of the planet are all interconnected.

It is precisely this interconnection, and the sense of biological community and of the ecological whole, which this book is about. This picture of the Earth requires that we pay some attention to the new understanding we have of its context in the universe.

Contemporary views of the universe spring from two interrelated sources, one that is largely theoretical and the other more observational.[29] The theoretical basis is Albert Einstein's General Theory of Relativity. Einstein depicted gravity as a stretching and a curvature of spacetime. The presence of mass or energy curves spacetime. Particles and light rays travel on curved paths because of the gravitational fields in their paths. Theorists who worked with Einstein's General Theory of Relativity and his field equations were soon able to use this theory to develop models of the universe. The standard approach to cosmology, which has emerged during the twentieth century on the basis of Einstein's insights, is that represented by the Friedmann-Lemaitre-Robertson-Walker models of the universe.

These standard models give rise to two startling and highly significant outcomes. First, these models are expanding, and they suggest that the universe is expanding and evolving. This so upset Einstein that he tried, in what he later called his greatest blunder, to avoid the outcome of an expanding universe by introducing an artificial "cosmological constant" into his theory. If the universe is expanding, and decreasing in temperature and density, as the models suggest, then this points back to a beginning of the universe of unthinkable smallness, density and heat. It points back to a singularity, to a beginning where the laws of physics as we know them would no longer apply. According to the theorists, the whole universe emerges and expands from the singularity in what is called the Big Bang. The Big Bang is not an explosion in an already-existing space and time, but the stretching and expansion of spacetime itself.

The second startling outcome of the standard models is that there are three types of models of the expanding universe: the open universe, the flat universe, and the closed universe. An open universe will expand forever. A flat universe will also continue to expand, but only just. A closed universe will eventually collapse back upon itself. The crucial issue is the amount of matter in the universe. The density which would make the universe flat is called the critical density. At present we do not know if the density of the universe is above the critical density, and is therefore open, or below the critical density and closed. A key issue here is the nature and the amount of nonvisible "dark matter" in the universe.

The second essential source for contemporary cosmology is astronomical observation. There are four strands of observational evidence which have given support to Big Bang cosmology. In the 1920s the great astronomer Edwin Hubble showed conclusively that many of the faint objects in the night sky are indeed other galaxies beyond the Milky Way. Furthermore, he showed that the absorption lines in the spectra of light coming from distant galaxies are shifted toward the red end of the spectrum. Redshifts indicate bodies moving away from us, while blueshifts indicate bodies moving toward us. Hubble found that not only are the distant galaxies moving away from us, but that the farther away they are, the faster they are receding. He had discovered the expansion of the universe, the expansion of space itself.

The second piece of observational evidence is the so-called helium abundance of the universe. Mathematical and theoretical models of the universe suggest that the high temperatures of the early universe would have produced a universe made up of about 75 percent hydrogen, about 25 percent helium, and tiny amounts of other elements. The rest of the elements, including the oxygen and carbon necessary for life on Earth, would be produced much later from hydrogen, in the process of nucleosynthesis operating at the heart of stars. In fact, what the theories predict is what the astronomers observe: The universe is made up of about 75 percent hydrogen, and about 24 percent helium, with small amounts of other elements.

A third and vital element in the observational evidence for the Big Bang is the discovery, made in 1965 by Arno Penzias and Robert Wilson, of the cosmic background microwave radiation. Theories of the Big Bang suggest that there was a period (thought to have begun when the universe was about 500,000 years old) when matter was freed from radiation. They suggest that the remnant of this original radiation should still be present in the universe, and that it would have a temperature a few degrees above absolute zero. The radiation discovered by Wilson and Penzias comes uniformly from all directions of the sky, and it has a temperature of about 3 degrees Kelvin. It seems that this is, indeed, the "afterglow" of the Big Bang. The discovery of this afterglow has established the Big Bang theory of cosmology against competing cosmologies, such as the Steady-State theory.

The fourth key observation is much more recent. Cosmologists had long pointed out that the existence of galaxies shows that matter has emerged in a "clumpy" fashion. This suggests that there would have been a precursor to this clumpiness in the early universe. There should be some variations in the background microwave radiation, which, when amplified by gravity, could account for the clumpiness of galaxies. Yet the background microwave radiation seemed remarkably even. Theory suggested that there should be tiny variations in it. In April 1992 researchers at Berkeley announced that very slight fluctuations had been detected by instruments on the COBE satellite.

The evidence for the general picture of the Big Bang theory, and for the worldview of an expanding and evolutionary universe, seems strong. There are important discussions about, and differences, over Alan Guth's concept of a period of "inflation" in the early universe. There are interesting attempts at a quantum theory of the creation of the universe, such as the Hartle-Hawking proposal for a finite but unbounded universe. But, for the purposes of this work, what is important is the worldview of an expanding universe. As Stephen Hawking writes, "The discovery that the universe is expanding is one of the great intellectual revolutions of the twentieth century."[30] It is this intellectual revolution, this new worldview, which must form an essential part of the context for a contemporary theology.

The universe we inhabit is probably between eight and eighteen billion years old. Our Sun and solar system had their origin about five billion years ago. We are situated near the inner edge of one of the spiral arms of the Milky Way Galaxy. This galaxy is about a hundred thousand light years across. The Milky Way rotates slowly, once every several hundred million years. It contains more than a hundred billion stars.

It was only in the mid 1920s that astronomy came to accept completely the existence of galaxies beyond our own group of stars. We now know that some of the faint smudges of light we see in the night sky are nearby galaxies. Light, travelling at 300,000 kilometers per second, takes two million years to reach us from the Andromeda Galaxy. The Large and Small Magellanic Clouds are much closer, at only 170,000 and 190,000 light years distance from us. These galaxies are linked with our own Milky Way as part of what is called the Local Group. There are more than a hundred billion galaxies in the observable universe.

The awareness that we are part of this kind of universe will shape the worldview of the next generation. An ecological theology, a theology of our interrelationships on the planet Earth, will need to be set against an understanding of Earth's place in the expanding universe. We will need to see ourselves as part of the Earth, as children of the Earth, but also as children of the universe.

Outline for a Theological Response

This book is an attempt to build an ecological theology which is radically theological in that it is based on a systematic understanding of the trinitarian God. It is my contention that such a trinitarian theology flows from a theology of Jesus Christ. It is intrinsically connected to Christology. More and more, it seems to me, there can be no theology of the Trinity which is not explicitly grounded in the event of Jesus and in the experience of the Holy Spirit, and no real Christology without a trinitarian theology of God. At the same time, there can be no theology of Jesus which is not at the same time a theology of human beings understood as interrelational creatures.

An ecological theology, then, will spring from an understanding of Jesus, of the God revealed in Jesus, and of a consequent understanding of humankind and other creatures. This means that this book will be concerned with areas of theology dealt with in Christology, trinitarian theology and theological anthropology. It will be, necessarily, a partial view of these theological specialities, and I will not be able to deal at all with other aspects of theology, such as the theology of church and the sacraments, which clearly are relevant to an ecological theology. My hope is to show in a systematic way the inner link between the theology of Jesus as Wisdom, the trinitarian God and human beings within creation, and the ecological praxis to which we are called in this generation.

This book is an attempt to develop an ecological understanding of the trinitarian God on the basis of a Wisdom Christology. Bruce Vawter long ago drew attention to the importance of Wisdom Christology and called for its recovery for a new context. At the end of one of his books he reflected back on the chapter in which Jesus was presented as the Wisdom of God:

> In this chapter, doubtless the most problematical of our entire book, we advanced the thesis that this most ancient christology, possibly the most ancient of all, but in any case representative of a respectable strain of biblical thought, cannot only continue to shed light on the meaning of the terms in which Chalcedon strove to formulize it, but can also beckon us to new ways and summon us to new voices. It can do this, perhaps, more easily than other New Testament christologies, which have produced other emphases. The fact that it can do this may also be an indication that it ought to.[31]

I believe that Vawter is right and that Wisdom Christology does "beckon us to new ways and summon us to new voices." Since Vawter wrote, scripture scholarship has done much to uncover the importance of Wisdom categories for early Christian understandings of Jesus. A systematic theologian who has set out on this "new way" with a "new voice" is Elizabeth Johnson, with her work on a "non-androcentric" Wisdom Christology; her recovery of Wisdom Christology is one of the foundations for the reflections of this book.[32]

I argue that Wisdom Christology is profoundly interconnected with trinitarian theology, on the one hand, and the theology of human beings in relationship to other creatures, on the other. This book is intended to be an ecological *theo*logy, an ecological theology of God, and its center is a trinitarian theology of God's interaction with creation.[33] It is a trinitarian theology which springs from a Wisdom Christology and leads to human ecological praxis.

PART 1

JESUS OF NAZARETH
AS THE WISDOM OF GOD

*Wisdom Christology as the Basis
for Ecological Theology*

1.

The Wisdom of God in Biblical Tradition

In Part One of this book, I will attempt to show how the recovery of a Wisdom Christology contributes to an ecological theology. The basis for this approach to ecological theology is found in the very nature of the biblical view of divine Wisdom. Wisdom is always closely associated with God's work of creation. Wisdom is concerned with the whole of creation, and with the interrelationships among human beings, the rest of creation and God. It is *this* Wisdom, radically associated with creation and with all creatures, who pitches a tent among us in Jesus of Nazareth. It is because Wisdom Christology is a creation theology, a cosmic theology, and a relational theology, that it can come to be understood, in our time, as an ecological theology.

I have suggested in the Introduction that one of the earliest theological approaches to an understanding of Jesus was through identifying him with divine Wisdom, and that this identification played a crucial role in the emergence of the church's theology of Jesus Christ. In this chapter, I will discuss the process whereby Jesus became interpreted in terms of Sophia within the Christian biblical tradition. This will mean first tracing the personification of divine Wisdom in the wisdom literature of Israel, and then considering key passages of the Christian scriptures where Jesus is identified with divine Wisdom.

The Wisdom Woman

In recent times biblical scholars have come to a new evaluation of the centrality of wisdom in the ancient tradition and scriptures of the Hebrew people. They have come, as well, to a new appreciation of the importance of the figure of personified Wisdom, particularly in the books of Job, Proverbs, Sirach and the Wisdom of Solomon.[1]

Divine Wisdom, Sophia, appears in the biblical literature as a woman, the Wisdom Woman. Wisdom is a feminine word in the ancient languages (*Hokmah* in Hebrew, *Sophia* in Greek, *Sapientia* in Latin), but Wisdom's personification as a woman means far more than simply that the language used to speak of her is feminine. She appears, speaks and acts as a fully developed personal being, an attractive, mysterious, powerful and relational woman. Kathleen O'Connor describes the Wisdom Woman and her communicative role:

> At the centre of the Wisdom Literature stands a beautiful and alluring woman. She is Lady Wisdom, or, as I prefer to call her, the Wisdom Woman. The primary mode of being of the Wisdom Woman is relational. In all the texts where she appears, the most important aspect of her existence is her relationships. Her connections extend to every part of reality. She is closely joined to the created world; she is an intimate friend of God; she delights in the company of human beings. No aspect of reality is closed off from her. She exists in it as if it were a tapestry of connected threads, patterned into an intricate whole of which she is the centre.[2]

Roland Murphy provides a minimal list of passages where Wisdom appears as personified: Job 28, Proverbs 1, 8, 9, Sirach 1:9-10, 4:11-19, 6:18-31, 14:20-15:8, 51:13-21, Baruch 3:9-4:4, and Wisdom 6:12-11:1.[3] I will focus on the key passages in Job, Proverbs, Sirach and Wisdom.

Job

It is difficult to say when Job was written, but scholars tend to place it between the seventh and fifth centuries B.C.E.[4] The figure of personified Wisdom appears in the poem in chapter 28, at the end of the long dialogue between Job and his three friends. The theme of this poem is "where shall wisdom be found?" (28:12, 20). It does not come from the earth (1-6). The birds of prey and the wild animals cannot point to it (7-8). Human beings do not know the way to it (13). The sea says, "It is not in me" (14). Yet its price is above all jewels and pearls (15-19). Finally we are told:

> God understands the way to it
> and he knows its place.
> For he looks to the ends of the earth,
> and sees everything under the heavens.
> When he gave to the wind its weight,
> and apportioned out the waters by measure;
> when he made a decree for the rain,
> and a way for the thunderbolt;
> then he saw it and declared it;
> he established it, and searched it out.
> And he said to humankind,
> "Truly, the fear of the Lord, that is wisdom;
> and to depart from evil is understanding."
>   (28: 23-28)

Only God knows the way to Wisdom. We do not find a description of wisdom in these verses, and her female character is not stressed. However, she already appears to be understood as related to the works of creation, yet distinct from them. Only God who made the wind, the rain and the thunderbolts can look to the ends of the earth and can see Wisdom. God established Wisdom and gave her a setting. Wisdom is presented as beyond any individual work of creation, but as present within creation.

The poem stresses Wisdom's transcendence. Wisdom belongs to God, and God alone knows the way to her. Roland Murphy comments that "within the context of the Book of Job, the poem functions as an indicator of the futility of human probing into the divine mystery." He notes that within the broader context of wisdom literature, "One may say that a mysterious figure of a personified Wisdom has made her initial appearance."[5]

Proverbs

The Book of Proverbs contains large collections of individual proverbial sayings (10:1-22:16; 25:1-29:27). Their purpose is training in the way of wisdom, to show what daily life before God is really like and to develop the capacity to respond well to it. A favorite approach is to comment on human life by making comparisons with other creatures. These proverbs embody a robust spirituality of the everyday, a creation spirituality. Some of them come from very early times, reaching not only back to the ancient temple administration and the royal courts of Israel, but also further back into family and clan wisdom.

The first nine chapters of Proverbs were probably written much later and have a different character. In them we find a series of carefully constructed longer poems and a vision of the pursuit of wisdom. The most common opinion is that these chapters are post-exilic.[6] The Wisdom Woman looms large in these chapters. She makes her appearance in 1:20-33, 3:13-24, 4:5-9 and 8:1-9:5.

In the first of these, Sophia suddenly appears as a prophet of God, crying out her message in the streets, at the town squares and the city gates. In the ancient world the main gate of a town was the hub of life. It "served as a market place where produce and products were sold and traded, as the place of justice where civil and criminal cases were tried, as the 'civic center' where gatherings of all sorts were possible, and as the social and intellectual center of the community where the elders and the leisured could sit, socialize and converse"[7] In such a public place Wisdom preaches her message, challenging her hearers to heed her warnings, and setting before them the choice between folly and disaster on the one hand, and the fear of God and life on the other.

In her second appearance the Wisdom Woman is first celebrated in vivid images. We are told that she is more precious than jewels (3:15), and that she is a "tree of life" to those who hold on to her (3:18). Then the great theme of her role with God in creation is announced: "The Lord by wisdom founded the earth; by understanding he established the heavens" (3:19).

This theme is taken up and developed in chapter 8, where Sophia appears again as a prophet at the town gate, crying out her message for all to hear. In an extraordinary passage, she describes her divine origin as the first of God's deeds:

> The Lord created me at the beginning of his work,
> the first of his acts of long ago.
> Ages ago I was set up,
> at the first, before the beginning of the earth.
> When there were no depths I was brought forth,
> when there were no springs abounding with water.

Before the mountains had been shaped,
before the hills, I was brought forth;
when he had not yet made earth and fields,
or the world's first bits of soil.
When he established the heavens I was there,
when he drew a circle on the face of the deep,
when he made firm the skies above,
when he established the fountains of the deep,
when he assigned to the sea its limit,
so that the waters might not transgress his
    command,
when he marked out the foundations of the earth,
then I was beside him, like a master worker;
and I was daily his delight,
rejoicing before him always,
rejoicing in his inhabited world
and delighting in the human race (8:22-31).

Sophia asserts several important things about herself in this poem. One is that God "begot" or "created" her as the first-born.[8] She was created "ages ago" (8:22). The Hebrew word translated here means "from everlasting." Wisdom existed before all natural things, before springs of water, mountains, seas and the sky above. She is older than the oldest thing known, the Earth itself.

The second important theological insight concerns the Wisdom Woman's presence with God and her cooperation with God in the creation of all creatures. Wisdom is God's child, companion and co-worker in creation. The sentence "I was beside him as an '*āmôn*" (8:30) can be translated in a number of ways, including "as an artisan" and "as a darling child."[9] It is quite possible that, as with some other riddles in this book, the author of Proverbs expects the wise reader to take more than one meaning.

Third, we find that Wisdom is God's delightful companion, and that she delights in the inhabited world and in the human community. Sophia is revealed as profoundly relational—interrelated with God, with all creatures, and with human creatures in a particular way. In fact, the Wisdom Woman has come into the midst of the human community in order to invite all to her great wisdom banquet:

> Wisdom has built her house,
> she has hewn her seven pillars.
> She has slaughtered her animals,
> she has mixed her wine,
> she has also set her table.
> She has sent out her serving girls,
> she calls from the highest places in the town,
> "You that are simple, turn in here!"
> to those without sense she says,
> "Come, eat of my bread
> and drink the wine I have mixed.
> Lay aside immaturity, and live
> and walk in the way of insight" (9:1-6).

These wonderful images of Wisdom building her house and inviting her hearers to a great banquet will influence the whole Wisdom tradition; they will give shape to Jesus' ministry in his meals and parables, and to the interpretation of this ministry. They will be a rich resource for the Christology of the early church and for Christian eucharistic theology.

Who is the Wisdom Woman in chapter 8 of Proverbs? Many scholars have argued that she may reflect female deities of Israel's neighbors. Roland Murphy suggests that her portrait may have been influenced by the Egyptian *Ma'at*, the abstract figure of justice, who could also be personified as a female deity.[10] It is clear, nonetheless, that the Wisdom Woman of Proverbs is thoroughly integrated within Israel's monotheistic faith in Yahweh. She is in some way identified with the God of Israel. She is the communication of God, the "voice of God." Roland Murphy insists that the Wisdom Woman of Proverbs is to be understood as "the revelation of God, not merely the self-revelation of creation." She is "the divine summons issued in and through creation, sounding through the vast realm of the created world, and heard on the level of human experience."[11]

Sirach

The Book of Sirach was written by Jesus ben Sira in Jerusalem about 180 B.C.E. and later translated into Greek by his grandson for the Jew-

ish community in Alexandria. Ben Sira wrote in a time of cultural up-
heaval. Israel was occupied by the Seleucid dynasty, and the pressure
to conform to Greek ways created diverse reactions within Judaism, as
some accommodated to Greek culture and others rejected all Hellenistic influences. Ben Sira's response is that of a traditionalist. Although
he is not against accepting what is good in Greek culture, his fundamental argument is that it is only in relationship with the God of Israel
that one can find true Wisdom.

The Wisdom Woman appears in three places in this book: the beginning (Sir 1), the middle (Sir 24) and the end (Sir 51). Kathleen O'Connor
speaks of Sophia holding up the structure of the book through these
three sections, like three walls holding up a house. She notes that the
figure of Sophia provides the basis and structure of Sirach's theology.[12]

In chapter 1 we hear of Wisdom's close connection with God (1:1-
10) and of the fact that Wisdom can be attained only through "fear of
the Lord" (1:11-20). In chapter 24, Sophia's great central speech is set
in the assembly of the Most High, in the heavenly court, and there she
proclaims her divine origins:

> I came forth from the mouth of the Most High,
> and covered the earth like a mist.
> I dwelt in the highest heavens,
> and my throne was in a pillar of cloud.
> Alone I compassed the vault of heaven
> and traversed the depths of the abyss.
> Over waves of the sea, over all the earth,
> and over every people and nation I have held
>   sway.
> Among all these I sought a resting place;
> in whose territory should I abide? (24:3-7).

Wisdom proclaims that she has come forth from God. She is born from
God's mouth, as a Word of God. She speaks of her role in creation, of
her exploration of the universe and of her sway over all nations in terms
usually reserved for God alone. She covers the earth like mist, as the
breath of God covers the waters (Gen 1:2). Like God (Jb 22:14) she
journeys through the vault of heaven, and has dominion over all things.
This prompts Roland Murphy to ask, "Is this really God in the figure of
travelling Wisdom?"[13]

But this transcendent Wisdom seeks a permanent home, a resting place. And the Creator chooses a place for her to dwell.

> Then the Creator of all things
> gave me a command,
> and my Creator chose the place for my tent.
> He said, "Make your dwelling in Jacob,
> and in Israel receive your inheritance."
> Before the ages, in the beginning,
> he created me,
> and for all the ages I shall not cease to be.
> In the holy tent I ministered before him,
> and so I was established in Zion.
> Thus in the beloved city he gave me a resting
>   place,
> and in Jerusalem was my domain (Sir 24:8-11).

Wisdom, who was with God in the beginning and shall not cease to be, has made her home in Israel. It is in the holy city that she has set up her tent and come to rest. From her home in Jerusalem she "grows tall like a cedar in Lebanon" and "like choice myrrh" spreads her fragrance, and like a vine her "blossoms become glorious and abundant fruit" (24: 13-17). Settled in the holy city, Wisdom, as in Proverbs 9, sends out a warm invitation to her great banquet:

> "Come to me, you who desire me,
> and eat your fill of my fruits.
> For the memory of me is sweeter than honey,
> and the possession of me sweeter than the
>   honeycomb.
> Those who eat of me will hunger for more
> and those who drink of me will thirst for more."
>   (24:19-21)

Here it is Wisdom herself who is the food and drink. She is the source of nourishment and life. This is language which will be echoed in the Christian gospels, but for Ben Sira it has a very concrete and very Jewish meaning. Wisdom is Torah.

> All this is the book of the covenant of the Most
>   High God,
> the law that Moses commanded us as an
>   inheritance for the congregations of Jacob.
>   (24:22-23)

Wisdom is found in God's gift of the Torah. Ben Sira thus incorporates the sacred traditions of Israel, the community's sacred history, legal tradition and spirituality, into the figure of personified Wisdom. As Kathleen O'Connor notes, "Sirach's identification of the Law or Torah with Sophia is his most radical and original innovation."[14] This identification of Wisdom and Torah is found also in Baruch (3:9-4:4). Sirach continues with a series of images which show that the Torah, Wisdom's presence and expression in Israel, is like the great rivers of the world, overflowing with abundance and life (24:24-29).

In the final poem in chapter 51, Ben Sira speaks as an old man, at times almost identifying himself with his beloved Wisdom:

> Draw near to me, you who are uneducated,
> and lodge at the house of instruction.
> Why do you say you are lacking in these things,
> and why do you endure such thirst?
> I opened my mouth and said,
> Acquire wisdom for yourselves without money.
> Put your neck under her yoke,
> and let your souls receive instruction;
> it is to be found close by.
> See with your own eyes that I have labored but
>   little
> and found for myself much serenity (51:23-27).

Sirach's theology would enable Judaism to understand true Wisdom in terms of the Torah and Torah piety. Sirach's language would be taken up and echoed in the early Christian writers, as they identified Jesus with divine Wisdom. They would understand Jesus as the one who provides living water and the bread of life. They would present Jesus as the one who invites the poor and overburdened to come to him, the one who invites his hearers to take up his yoke and to learn from him. For the first Christian communities, Jesus is understood as the one whose yoke is easy and whose burden is light, the one in whom they will find rest and peace.

The Wisdom of Solomon

This book seems to have been written in the second half of the first century B.C.E. or a little later, perhaps during Jesus' lifetime.[15] It was written in Greek by a learned Hellenistic Jew, who probably lived in Alexandria. The Wisdom of Solomon is a work which is both "intensely Jewish and, at the same time, thoroughly stamped by Greek culture."[16] It is written in the name of King Solomon, but its real author is unknown.

The first part of the book (1:1-6:21) is concerned with righteousness, wisdom and immortality. The centrality this book gives to the teaching of immortality represents a new emphasis in the history of the Jewish tradition, but as David Winston points out, "It must be seen as part of a continuous development in Hellenistic Jewish thought."[17]

The second section of the book (6:22-11:1) is a great celebration of divine Wisdom and of Solomon's love affair with Wisdom. Here Wisdom is closely identified with God and shares in an extraordinary way in divine transcendence.

Yet we are told in beautiful images that Wisdom is readily accessible to those who seek her: "One who rises early to seek her will have no difficulty, for she will be found sitting at the gate" (6:14). She goes seeking those worthy of her, appears to them in their paths, and "meets them in every thought" (6:16).

The author claims to have been led by Sophia to the knowledge of various sciences, including what are today called astronomy, botany, zoology, pharmacology and psychology. It is natural that all this knowledge would come from Wisdom, since she is understood as the divine Creator: "For wisdom, the fashioner of all things, taught me" (7:22). Wisdom is the *technitis* (7:22; 8:6), the divine artisan at work in creation. The author offers an extraordinary celebration of the praises of Wisdom:

> There is in her a spirit that is intelligent, holy,
> unique, manifold, subtle,

> mobile, clear, unpolluted,
> distinct, invulnerable, loving the good, keen,
> irresistible, beneficent, humane,
> steadfast, sure, free from anxiety,
> all-powerful, overseeing all,
> and penetrating through all spirits
> that are intelligent, pure, and altogether subtle.
> For wisdom is more mobile than any motion;
> because of her pureness she pervades and
> penetrates all things (7:22-24).

These twenty-one attributes (the perfect number seven multiplied by three) explain how it is that Wisdom can teach all these things. Wisdom is identified with spirit, a spirit which is utterly pure, pervades all things, and is thus utterly immanent. Yet, Roland Murphy notes, this immanence is balanced by transcendence, and Wisdom is portrayed as "holy, unique, all-powerful, and all-seeing."[18] The Wisdom of Solomon goes on to describe Sophia's relationship to God:

> For she is a breath of the power of God,
> and a pure emanation of the glory of the
>   Almighty;
> therefore nothing defiled gains entrance into her.
> For she is a reflection of eternal light,
> a spotless mirror of the working of God,
> and an image of his goodness.
> Although she is but one, she can do all things,
> and while remaining in herself, she renews all
>   things;
> in every generation she passes into holy souls
> and makes them friends of God and prophets;
> for God loves nothing so much as the person
>   who lives with wisdom.
> She is more beautiful than the sun,
> and excels every constellation of the stars.
> Compared to the light she is found to be
>   superior,
> for it is succeeded by the night,

> but against wisdom evil does not prevail,
> She reaches mightily from one end of the earth
> to the other and she orders all things well.
>
> (7:25-8:1)

Sophia is radically related to God. Now her divine character is expressed in a manner that goes beyond "begetting" (Prv 8:22) or "coming forth from God's mouth" (Sir 24:3). As Roland Murphy writes, "The general image is a sort of radiation from the divinity: vapor, effusion, reflection, mirror, image."[19] She is bathed in the divine light, and she is a mirror of divine energy (7:26).

Sophia is God's presence to the universe in continuous creation. The author goes beyond other biblical writers in this treatment of continuous creation, and in the attribution of this ongoing work to Wisdom.[20] So we find the author saying of Wisdom that "while remaining in herself, she renews all things" (7:27) and "she reaches mightily from one end of the earth to the other and orders all things well" (8:1). She is the "mother" of all good things (7:12), the "fashioner" of all things (7:22) and "renews" all things (7:27).

David Winston sees Wisdom in this book as "the Divine Mind immanent within the universe and guiding and controlling all its dynamic operations." Wisdom represents, he says, "the entire range of natural science, in addition to the arts, rhetoric and philosophy." She is "synonymous with Divine Providence." She is the "direct bearer of revelation."[21] Wisdom and Torah are not explicitly identified, and the author sees Torah as in need of further interpretation, which Wisdom can provide (9:17).

After celebrating the unity between Sophia and God in continuous creation, the Wisdom of Solomon goes on to describe her as "living with God" (8:3) and associated with all God's works (8:4). The Greek word used to describe this cohabitation of Sophia and God is *symbiosis*—the sharing of one life.

The book portrays a celebration of Solomon's love for Sophia. The relationship is described in personal and intimate terms. She is understood as friend (6:12-16), and friendship with her means friendship with God (7:14). She is very often seen as the beloved whom Solomon seeks as spouse (7:28; 8:2; 8:9; 8:16). She is mother to all things (7:12). David Winston suggests that the intensely personal description of the author's relationship with Sophia seems to allude to a mystical encounter with her.[22]

The theme of the unity between Sophia and God comes to a significant climax in chapter 10, in which she is presented as Savior. We are told explicitly that human beings are "saved" by Sophia (9:18), and in a remarkable way chapter 10 reinterprets Israel's history, attributing to Sophia the saving deeds normally attributed to Yahweh. Wisdom is accredited with God's work of salvation. It was Wisdom who was at work in the "deliverance" and "preservation" of Adam, Noah, Abraham, Lot, Jacob and Joseph. It was Wisdom who delivered the Hebrew people in the Exodus:

> A holy people and blameless race
> wisdom delivered from a nation of oppressors.
> She entered the soul of a servant of the Lord,
> and withstood dread kings with wonders and
>   signs.
> She gave to holy people the reward of their
>   labors;
> she guided them along a marvelous way,
> and became a shelter to them by day,
> and a starry flame through the night.
> She brought them over the Red Sea,
> and led them through deep waters (10:15-18).

Sophia is both Creator and Savior. To relate to her is to relate to God. Kathleen O'Connor writes of Sophia as she is portrayed in this book: "She is God, not a new god or a second god, but God poetically imaged as a woman. She is Sophia-God."[23]

The Identity of the Wisdom Woman

What is the origin of this female figure of divine Wisdom? There is general agreement among scholars that one or more female deities have influenced the biblical depiction of Sophia. A variety of possible influences have been suggested, including a Canaanite form of Astarte and Ishtar from Mesopotamia. Many think that, in the earlier period of the book of Proverbs, the prime influence was from the Egyptian figure of

Ma'at. In the later period of the Wisdom of Solomon, it seems clear that there is influence and borrowing from the cult of Isis.

Isis was a protector of sailors, and her cult spread from the port of Alexandria during the Ptolemaic period. Temples, inscriptions and coins of Isis are found in Rome, Pompey, Antioch, Corinth and Palestine. As her popularity grew, Isis assumed attributes and names of other female gods.[24] It is obvious that Isis could have been seen as a temptation to Jewish believers. It would seem that orthodox Judaism responded creatively with the figure of personified Wisdom. It is important to note that there is no evidence that the biblical writers thought of themselves as introducing a second deity into the tradition of Israel. There was no sense of conflict with Jewish monotheism and no alternative cult of Sophia.

What can be said about the theological meaning of Sophia?[25] Roland Murphy is surely right when he points out that the Wisdom Woman speaks with divine accents throughout all of the wisdom literature. Yet she is described in distinctive ways in the books of Job, Proverbs, Sirach and Wisdom. Sirach and Baruch identify her with the Torah, while in the Wisdom of Solomon she is a world principle, both immanent and divine.[26] The Wisdom Woman cannot be reduced to one simple reality. She escapes categorization. Roland Murphy concludes:

> The best one can say is that Lady Wisdom is a *divine communica-tion*: *God's communication, extension of self*, to human beings. And that is no small insight the biblical wisdom literature bequeaths to us.[27]

Wisdom is God's self-revelation. Kathleen O'Connor notes that there are times when there are clear indications that the Wisdom Woman is herself God. She comments that "in some of the poems about her, the Wisdom Woman remains a creature of Yahweh, though a privileged one, separate from God and delighting in the divine presence." In others, "the Wisdom Woman represents another way to look at God, another metaphor to speak of the beauty, power and attraction that God holds out to human beings."[28]

There is an extremely close relationship between Yahweh and Sophia as ways of speaking about God. Elizabeth Johnson writes on this inter-relationship: "Sophia is not Yahweh, understood in the specificity of that biblical name, but both female Sophia and male Yahweh express the one God who promises life upon being found." In certain texts "Sophia is in reality God herself in her activity in the world, God imaged as a female acting subject."[29]

Jesus as Divine Wisdom in the Christian Scriptures

Sophia, the Wisdom Woman, is the one in whom God creates the universe. She sustains all things. She is God's companion in creation, relating to all God's creatures and taking delight in them. Sophia is clearly a key figure in a biblical theology of creation and a key to the building of an ecological theology of Jesus Christ.

The early Christian community identified Jesus with Sophia, thus identifying Jesus with Sophia's care for the *oikos*, the household of living creatures. It was this identification between Jesus and Sophia that was to be the bridge whereby the community which believed that God had raised up Jesus of Nazareth came to see this Jesus as the pre-existent one. Wisdom Christology was the bridge to the theology of incarnation.[30] This identification of Jesus as divine Wisdom is found clearly articulated in Paul and in the gospels of Matthew and John. It can be traced back to an even earlier period, since it is implicit in quotations from early Christian hymns that we find in the Christian scriptures.

The Hymns of the Christian Scriptures

Scattered throughout the Christian scriptures are a number of texts that many scripture scholars consider to be pre-existent hymns or parts of hymns. They include Philippians 2:6-11, Colossians 1:15-20, Ephesians 2:14-16, 1 Timothy 3:16, 1 Peter 3:18-22, Hebrews 1:3, and John 1:1-18.[31]

Wisdom themes appear frequently in these hymns, which, it seems, were sung in liturgical assemblies well before the writing of the books in which they now appear. This suggests that the identification of Jesus with divine Wisdom must have occurred very early in the post-Easter community. Bruce Vawter has noted that the oldest Christology may well be the one based on these Wisdom categories.[32] These early hymns express the community's faith in Jesus Christ risen from the dead and attribute to him a cosmic role in both creation and redemption. Here is an important basis for a contemporary ecological approach to Christology.

Jesus is celebrated as the exalted and universal Savior, but as a Savior whose triumph comes by way of the cross.

When these hymns are considered together, a general pattern emerges of One who was with God in the beginning, was an agent in creation, became truly human, died on the cross, rose from the dead, is exalted above all powers and is the source of universal reconciliation.[33] Not all the hymnic texts include all these elements, but some of these elements appear in each hymn and the larger pattern appears in the great hymn to Christ in Colossians (1:15-20) and most elements are found in the Prologue to John's Gospel (1:1-18).

Thus, in the liturgical celebrations of the earliest Christian communities we find a highly developed Christology, a theological connection between God's action in creation and in Jesus, a cosmic role for the risen Christ, and, at least in John 1:1-18, an explicit theology of pre-existence and incarnation.

Wisdom categories lie behind these connections. In Hebrews 1:2-4, for example, we find these words:

> In these last days he has spoken to us by a Son, whom he appointed heir of all things, through whom he also created the worlds. He is the reflection of God's glory and the exact imprint of God's very being, and he sustains all things by his powerful word. When he had made purification for sins, he sat down at the right hand of the majesty on high, having become as much superior to angels as the name he has inherited is more excellent than theirs.

Jesus is presented as the one "through whom" the universe is created. Myles Bourke comments that this description of the Son as mediator of creation "assimilates him to the personified Wisdom of the OT (Prv 8:30; Wis 7:22)."[34]

Jesus is called the "reflection" of God's "glory," and the "imprint" of God's being. This is almost a paraphrase of Wisdom 7:26: "She is a reflection of eternal light, a spotless mirror of the working of God and an image of his goodness." The Greek word translated as "reflection" is *apaugasma*, and in the whole of biblical literature this word appears only in Wisdom 7:26 and Hebrew 1:3.[35]

We find in the Hebrews hymn that Christ "sustains all things," just as Wisdom "reaches mightily from one end of the earth to the other, and orders all things well" (Wis 8:1). Hebrews also celebrates Jesus' redemptive role as glorified Christ, and, as Myles Bourke notes, this again echoes Wisdom, whose role "is both cosmological and soteriological (Prv 8:22-36; Wis 9:9-18)."[36]

William Lane observes that there are three functions attributed to Jesus in this text: "He is the mediator of revelation, the agent and sustainer of creation, and the reconciler of others to God." And, he continues, "Each of these christological affirmations echoes declarations concerning the role of divine wisdom in the Wisdom of Solomon (cf. Wis 7:21-27)."[37]

A similar process occurs in the great hymn in Colossians:

> He is the image of the invisible God, the first-born of all creation;
> for in him all things in heaven and on earth were created, things
> visible and invisible, whether thrones or dominions or rulers or
> powers—all things have been created through him and for him.
> He himself is before all things and in him all things hold together.
> He is the head of the body, the church; he is the beginning, the
> first-born from the dead, so that he might come to have first place
> in everything. For in him all the fullness of God was pleased to
> dwell, and through him God was pleased to reconcile to himself
> all things, whether on earth or in heaven, by making peace through
> the blood of the cross (1:15-20).

I will be discussing this in detail later, and at this point need only point out its dependence on the Wisdom Woman of the Jewish Wisdom tradition. The one "in" whom all things are created is divine Wisdom. Elizabeth Johnson notes a striking dependence on personified Wisdom for what is said of Christ: "Not only the general pattern, but precise terms are transferred: Christ is the image (*eikon*) of God, the first-born, the one through whom all things were created."[38] Eduard Schweizer comments that "there is no passage in the New Testament, apart from the prologue to the Fourth Gospel and Heb. 1:3, whose roots can be traced so clearly to Jewish Wisdom Literature as the hymn in Col. 1:15-20."[39]

There is widespread agreement that the prologue to John's gospel comes from a pre-existent hymn. There is no agreement on exactly what belonged to the original hymn, but most would agree on at least the following verses:

> In the beginning was the Word,
> and the Word was with God,
> and the Word was God.
> All things came into being through him,
> and without him not one thing came into being.
> What has come into being in him was life,
> and the life was the light of all people.
> the light shines in the darkness,
> and the darkness did not overcome it . . .
> He was in the world,
> and the world came into being through him;
> yet the world did not know him.
> He came to what was his own,
> and his own people did not accept him . . .
> And the Word became flesh and lived among us,
> and we have seen his glory,
> the glory as of the Father's only Son,
> full of grace and truth (Jn 1:1-5, 10-11, 14).

The prologue uses the language of the Logos rather than that of Sophia. Yet what is said of the Logos here is thoroughly dependent upon what is said of Sophia in texts such as Proverbs 8 and Sirach 24. Raymond Brown sees a number of influences at work behind the Logos theology of the prologue, but he holds that the key influence is that of Sophia.[40]

Brown shows how the Logos hymn is structured like a Wisdom poem, and the functions of Sophia are attributed to the Logos. Like the Logos in the prologue of John, Sophia was with God in the beginning (Prv 8:22-23; Sir 1:1), was an active agent in creation (Prv 8:27-30; Wis 7:22, 9:9), reflects the divine glory (Wis 7:25-26), is the light and life of the world (Qoh 2:13; Prv 4:18-19, 8:35; Bar 4:1), delights to be with human beings (Prv 8:31) but is rejected by some (Sir 15:7; Bar 3:12), has set up her dwelling among human beings (Sir 24:8), and is one in whom we find glory and grace (Sir 24:16). Brown concludes:

> Thus, in the OT presentation of Wisdom, there are good parallels
> for almost every detail of the Prologue's descriptions of the Word.
> The Prologue has carried personification further than the OT did
> in describing Wisdom, but that development stems from the In-

carnation. If we ask why the hymn of the Prologue chose to speak of "Word" rather than of "Wisdom," the fact that in Greek the former is masculine while the latter is feminine must be considered. Moreover, the relation of the "Word" to the apostolic kerygma is a relevant consideration.[41]

It is an important question why not only the prologue but so much of the subsequent tradition replaced Sophia by the Logos. Elizabeth Johnson shows that the tendency of scholars to assume that a male term is more suitable goes back to Philo and mentions some comments of contemporary scholars:

> Eduard Schweizer proposes that it was in fact necessary for Christian thought to substitute the masculine designation for the feminine *sophia* because of the gender of Jesus. F. Braun argues that the masculine gender of *logos* is better adapted to the person of Jesus, while W. Knox comments that the fact the *logos* is masculine made it a convenient substitute for "the awkward feminine figure."[42]

It would seem that androcentrism may have played a significant role in the dominance of Logos language, probably in combination with other factors, including the usefulness of Logos language in a Hellenistic culture.[43]

It is important to note again the role that Wisdom language played in establishing the possibility of talking about the pre-existence of the divine Wisdom/Word that we meet in Jesus of Nazareth. It was only through identifying Jesus as divine Wisdom that the theological insight could be reached that the Wisdom who is God's agent in creation is made flesh in Jesus of Nazareth. Not just the theology of pre-existence but the emergence of the theology of incarnation and the theology of the Trinity are historically and structurally dependent upon the theology of Sophia and the identification between Jesus and Sophia.

Jesus Our Wisdom—First Corinthians

Apart from the hymns, our earliest source for the identification between Jesus and divine Wisdom is Paul's first letter to the Corinthians. In the opening chapter of this letter, Paul writes:

> For Jews demand signs and Greeks desire wisdom, but we pro-
> claim Christ crucified, a stumbling block to Jews and foolishness
> to Gentiles, but to those who are called, both Jews and Greeks,
> Christ the power of God and the *wisdom of God*. For God's fool-
> ishness is wiser than human wisdom, and God's weakness is stron-
> ger than human strength . . . He is the source of your life in Christ
> Jesus, who became for us *wisdom from God*, and righteousness
> and sanctification and redemption, in order that, as it is written,
> "Let the one who boasts, boast in the Lord" (1 Cor 1:22-24, 30-31).

I will be considering this text in some detail later in this book. At
this stage it is important simply to note this text as a major basis for a
Wisdom Christology. Elizabeth Johnson points out that scholars differ
in their interpretation of what Paul means by wisdom here. Some think
that Paul was simply taking over his opponents' Wisdom language
(Ulrich Wilckens), while others think that he was independently char-
acterizing Jesus as the new Torah (Martin Hengel, W.D. Davies). Some
think that Paul was explicitly identifying Jesus with personified Wisdom (A. Feuillet), while others think that Wisdom here means God's
plan of salvation (James Dunn).[44]

What is clear is that, first, Paul is identifying Jesus and Wisdom, and
second, Paul is deliberately using language that has a rich context in
the Wisdom literature. As a well-educated Pharisee, Paul was well aware
of this background. There is at least an implicit identification here between the Wisdom who was active in the creation of the world (Prv 8)
and Jesus crucified.

This becomes more obvious when, later in the same letter, Paul writes
of Christ's role in creation in a way which depends upon an understanding of Jesus as divine Wisdom:

> For us there is one God, the Father, from whom are all things and
> for whom we exist, and one Lord, Jesus Christ, through whom are
> all things and through whom we exist (1 Cor 8:6).

There are clear parallels with Wisdom texts (Prv 3:19), and scholars
conclude that Paul is here implicitly identifying Jesus with personified
Wisdom.[45] James Dunn insists, however, that at this point we cannot
say that Wisdom was, for Paul, a divine being, or that Christ was ex-

plicitly understood as pre-existent with God. What we can say is that Christ is the embodiment of divine Wisdom, the "climactic and definitive embodiment of God's own creative power and saving concern." Dunn suggests that in this text we see Paul's thought moving in a trinitarian direction, and he comments that "herein we see the origin of the doctrine of the incarnation."[46]

Wisdom's Prophet and Wisdom Personified—Luke and Matthew

In Luke's gospel the texts linking Jesus and Wisdom are found principally in four places. First, after the parable about the children sitting in the marketplace, and mention of the work of John the Baptist and Jesus, we find Jesus saying: "Nevertheless, wisdom is vindicated by all her children" (Lk 7:35). Second, in the list of woes uttered by Jesus, we find Jesus saying: "Therefore also the Wisdom of God said, 'I will send them prophets and apostles'" (Lk 11:49).

Third, there is Jesus' prayer of thanksgiving which celebrates that what has been hidden from the wise and intelligent has been revealed to infants, and his statement, "no one knows who the Son is except the Father, and no one knows who the Father is except the Son, and anyone to whom the Son chooses to reveal him" (Lk 10:21-22). Fourth is Jesus' lament over Jerusalem, which has long been identified as a Wisdom saying: "How often have I desired to gather your children together as a hen gathers her brood under her wings" (Lk 13:34).

It is worth noting that twice in these texts we find the Lukan Jesus speaking of God as Sophia. It seems clear, too, that in Luke 11:49 Jesus is being understood as one of the line of the prophets of Sophia. Joseph Fitzmyer writes: "The words of this saying suggest indirectly that Jesus himself is such a 'prophet and emissary' and even a spokesman of God's wisdom."[47]

This seems also to be the original thought underlying the idea of Wisdom's children in Luke 7:35. Scholars argue that behind Luke and Matthew's gospels there is a source they shared, which is often called the Q source. In this source, "Wisdom's children" would have referred to John the Baptist and Jesus. But Luke seems to be deliberately including the disciples in "Wisdom's children." Joseph Fitzmyer writes:

> Jesus and John were thus in the "Q" form the children of Wisdom, i.e., the representatives of God's own Wisdom. Wisdom is here

personified, and John and Jesus are her children. But whether that is still the identification of Wisdom's children in the Lukan context is another matter. By the addition of "all" in v. 35, Luke has included Jesus' disciples as well.[48]

It seems clear that for at least some parts of the early Christian community, Jesus was understood as Wisdom's child and Wisdom's prophet. This line of thought has been developed by Jack Suggs. He has argued that the circles connected to the Q tradition "tended to see Jesus' significance largely in terms of his function as Sophia's finest and final representative."[49]

Suggs's work has shown how Matthew takes this theology and transforms it by identifying Jesus and Sophia. In two separate instances we find Matthew putting Jesus in the place where the more original Lukan version speaks of Wisdom. Suggs summarizes the argument:

> Matthew used the Wisdom themes in his own way. Whereas there were those by whom Jesus was viewed simply as the last in the long line of Wisdom's representatives, Matthew daringly identified Jesus with Wisdom. For the evangelist, Jesus was not Wisdom's child but Wisdom incarnate. Nor was Jesus only a prophet sent by Sophia; he was, instead, the Sender of prophets and wise men and scribes. In relation to the law, Jesus transcended familiar categories: as he was the incarnation of Wisdom, so was he the embodiment of Torah.[50]

The evidence for these claims comes from the way Matthew has changed the original material. First, whereas in Luke we find Jesus saying, "Wisdom is justified by all her children" (7:35), Matthew changes the word "children" to "deeds," so that Matthew's text reads, "Wisdom is justified by her deeds" (11:19). This is a significant change. It is clear that the deeds in question are Jesus' deeds. Matthew had begun this section with John the Baptist hearing in prison about the "deeds of the Christ" (11:2). Matthew is clearly identifying the deeds of Sophia with the deeds of Jesus: "The blind receive their sight, the lame walk, the lepers are cleansed, the deaf hear, the dead are raised, and the poor have the good news brought to them" (11:4-5)—these are Wisdom's deeds. In identifying the deeds of Jesus with the deeds of Wisdom, Matthew is identifying Jesus with divine Wisdom.

Matthew's tendency to identify Jesus and divine Wisdom is confirmed by a second example. Where Luke reports Jesus as saying that the Wisdom of God would send prophets and apostles (Lk 11:49), Matthew simply changes the "Wisdom of God" to "I." His text reads, "Therefore I will send you prophets, sages and scribes" (Matt 23:34). Matthew puts Wisdom's words on the lips of Jesus. Jesus is thus understood as not simply a prophet of Wisdom, but as Wisdom herself, the one who sends the prophets. Jack Suggs comments: "In making this change Matthew has assigned to Jesus Wisdom's function as the sender of prophets—a function which belongs to no figure in pre-Christian Judaism except Wisdom and God."[51]

In Matthew we also find an important Wisdom passage not found in Luke. It occurs after Jesus' prayer of thanksgiving for revelation to the infants (Matt 11:25-26) and the claim to mutual knowledge between Father and Son (Matt 11:27). In this passage Jesus speaks as divine Sophia herself:

Come to me, all you that are weary and are carrying heavy burdens, and I will give you rest. Take my yoke upon you, and learn from me; for I am gentle and humble in heart, and you will find rest for your souls. For my yoke is easy, and my burden is light (Matt 11:28-30).

This is an echo of the invitation to come to lodge in Wisdom's house of instruction (Sir 51:53), to take up Wisdom's yoke (Sir 51:26; 6:24), and find with her light labor and rest (Sir 51:27). In Matthew, Jesus is the school of Wisdom we attend. As John Meier says of this text, "In Jesus the Wisdom of God, the teacher and the subject taught are one and the same."[52]

While not all scholars will speak with Suggs of Wisdom incarnate in Matthew, preferring to reserve this language for John's gospel, Suggs's analysis has made it clear that, for Matthew, Jesus speaks as personified Wisdom. John Meier is cautious about the danger of exaggerating the place of Wisdom Christology in Matthew.[53] Meier nevertheless writes that in Matthew we find "the meshing of the apocalyptic Son (of Man) and the figure of divine Wisdom," and that in Matthew's work, "the fusion of apocalyptic and sapiential themes in the service of high Christology could not be clearer."[54] According to Meier, Jesus, in

Matthew's gospel, is "not only the preacher of God's Wisdom; he *is* that Wisdom, revealed to the elect."[55]

Jesus as Wisdom Incarnate—The Gospel of John

In John's Gospel, it is evident at every point that Jesus is divine revelation descended from above and become incarnate. One way this is expressed is through the great "I am" statements, both those without a predicate (6:20; 18:5) and those where Jesus claims to be the bread of life (6:51), the light of the world (8:12; 9:5), the door (10:7,9), the good shepherd (10:11,14), the resurrection and the life (11:25), the way, the truth and the life (14:6) and the true vine (15:1).

Raymond Brown reflects that "in drawing this portrait of Jesus, the evangelist has capitalized on the identification of Jesus with personified Wisdom as described in the OT."[56] As Wisdom speaks in the first person in long discourses (Prv 8:3-36; Sir 24) so Jesus addresses his hearers in long discourses, often beginning with "I am." As Wisdom descended to dwell among us (Prv 8:31; Sir 24:8; Bar 3:37; Wis 9:10), so Jesus is the Son of Man who has descended from heaven to live among us (Jn 1:14; 3:31; 4:38; 16:28).[57] As Wisdom roams the streets, crying out her message, inviting all to hear her message (Prv 1:20-21, 8:1-4; Wis 6:16) so Jesus walks the streets, searching out women and men and crying out his invitation in public places (Jn 1:36-38, 43; 5:14; 7:28, 37; 9:35; 12:44). As Wisdom instructs disciples who are her children (Wis 6:17-19; Prv 8:32-33; Sir 4:11, 6:18), so Jesus gives instruction to disciples who are called his children (Jn 13:33). As Wisdom forms her disciples (Sir 6:20-26) and they come to love her (Prv 8:17; Sir 4:12; Wis 6:17-18), so Jesus forms his disciples (15:3, 17:17) and calls them his beloved friends (Jn 15:15; 16:27). As some accept and others reject Wisdom (Prv 1:24-25; 8:17; Sir 6:27; Wis 6:12), so some receive the message of Jesus while others reject him (Jn 7:34; 8:21; 13:33).

As Wisdom prepares a feast and calls out, "Come, eat of my bread and drink of the wine I have mixed" (Prv 9:5; Sir 24:19-21), so Jesus cries out, "I am the bread of life. Whoever comes to me will never be hungry, and whoever believes in me will never be thirsty" (Jn 6:35; 6:51); and so Jesus tells the Samaritan woman "those who drink of the water I will give will never be thirsty. The water I will give will become in them a spring of water gushing up to eternal life" (Jn 4:14).

In the light of all this, Raymond Brown can say that, in John, Jesus is "personified Wisdom," and "incarnate Wisdom." Jesus is Wisdom incarnate, Wisdom come among us in specific, individual, historical and human terms.[58]

This chapter has examined the biblical texts concerned with the figure of the Wisdom Woman, Sophia, and the Christian texts that identify Jesus and Sophia. I have been attempting to show the biblical foundations on which an ecological Wisdom Christology might be built: first, Sophia's role in creating, sustaining, and redeeming all things; and, second, the Christian identification of Sophia and her cosmic role with Jesus Christ.

2.

Jesus the Wisdom of God

Contemporary cosmology tells us that in the observable universe there are more than a hundred billion galaxies. It also tells us that the universe is in dynamic process—we live in an expanding and evolutionary world, with spacetime itself stretching and expanding rapidly. We know that we are enfolded within the curvature of spacetime, but we do not yet know whether we live in an open or a closed universe. This dynamic universe, which is our home, had its origin between eight and eighteen billion years ago in an expansion from an immensely compressed, dense and hot state in the process we call the Big Bang.

Christian believers point to a single human being who lived in Palestine two thousand years ago, a preacher in a village community, someone of little importance to the great Roman Empire and its history. This individual, who was Jewish, male, young and apparently relatively uneducated, at least in terms of Hellenistic culture, failed to win over his own religious leaders to his cause and was eventually executed as a troublemaker. Yet the Christian claim is that this clearly limited individual has meaning for the whole of human history, and not just for human history but for all other creatures, in fact for the whole universe.

How can we understand the significance of Jesus of Nazareth for all creatures? Liberation theology has struggled with the issue of the meaning of Jesus in the face of the structural poverty endured by many of Earth's citizens. Feminist theology has faced the issue of the meaning of the male Jesus for women in light of the experience and history of patriarchy. Alongside these theologies, there is a need to deal with questions about the relationship between Jesus and creation.[1] How are we to understand the relationship among his life, ministry, death and resurrection and the threatened species of today? What connection is there between Jesus of Nazareth and the great universe?

A recovery of the biblical theology of Jesus as the Wisdom of God can open up helpful perspectives on these questions and on other issues of our time. In this chapter, first, I look at Jesus "from below," as the human being whose preaching and practice profoundly embody the Wisdom of God; second, I consider him "from above," as divine Wisdom incarnate; third, in the light of this identification between Jesus and divine Wisdom, I outline some directions for a Wisdom Christology. In the following chapter I focus more directly on the relationship between Wisdom Christology and ecology.

The Wisdom of Jesus—The Preaching and Practice of Radical Compassion

Jesus can be understood as a great wisdom teacher, someone in the tradition of the sages of Israel, one who speaks in the Wisdom categories of proverbial saying and parable. But, at the same time, he is one in whom the Wisdom tradition is made radical by the anticipatory presence of God's Reign. The wisdom Jesus preaches is the wisdom of God, which challenges traditional human wisdom, shattering conventional worldviews and opening out on to the world of the Reign of God. *This* Wisdom demands not just new ways of thinking, but an ortho-praxis in the light of God's coming Reign.

The wisdom that Jesus preached and practiced is "radical" in the sense that it is based upon a familial relationship with a God of boundless, compassionate love.[2] This is encapsulated in Luke's gospel in the summary saying, "Be merciful, just as your Father is merciful" (6:36), and in Matthew's beatitude, "Blessed are the merciful, for they will receive mercy" (5:7). The centrality of compassionate love in the Christian tradition finds expression in the teaching of the unity of love of God and love of neighbor (Mk 12:30-31; Matt 19:19), the command to love the enemy (Matt 5:44; Lk 6:27), and the "new" command to love one another of John's gospel (13:34). Perhaps the strongest statement about the foundation of all things in compassionate love is found in the First Letter of John: "Beloved, let us love one another, because love is from God; every one who loves is born of God and knows God. Whoever does not love does not know God, because God is love" (4:7-8).

Wisdom's Teacher

Throughout the gospels Jesus is portrayed as a teacher of wisdom. At the beginning of Mark's gospel we hear the community's reaction to his teaching in the synagogue at Capernaum: "They were astounded at his teaching, for he taught them as one having authority, and not as the scribes" (1:22). His authority apparently comes from a different source to that of ordinary scholarship.

Jesus' parables are brilliant and engaging creations, the work of an artist with words. He opens up profound insight with poetic artistry in images and stories that are witty, playful and sometimes shocking. It is often noted that Jesus' method of teaching never coerces or dominates his hearers. His listeners are respected and left free.

Jesus is like other sages of Israel in teaching in proverbial sayings and in parables. He is part of the wider Wisdom tradition, as well, in that the content of his parables and proverbs echoes that tradition's concerns with day-to-day events. Like the other sages, Jesus finds God at the heart of everyday things—the world of nature and human experience. But, for Jesus, everyday experience is radically transformed by the anticipatory presence of God's Reign. His stories break open to reveal new insight into the liberating presence of God; they invite Jesus' hearers to new ways of acting.

The beauty of wild flowers, torrential rain, the sun shining on good and bad alike, a woman baking bread, seeds growing invisibly, children playing games in the marketplace, all open out into the challenge of the presence and action of God. As C. H. Dodd has written, "The sense of the divineness of the natural order is the major premise of all the parables."[3]

Jesus uses the wisdom forms of proverbial saying and parable to confront his hearers with the anticipatory presence of the God of compassionate love. God is revealed as boundless generosity. God is like the shepherd going in search of the lost sheep, the woman lighting the lamp and sweeping the floor in search of the lost coin, and the father running to embrace an errant son (Lk 15). The shocking story of the landowner who pays all workers a full wage, even though they have worked for different lengths of time, promotes the radical idea that God's compassion cannot be limited or constrained by human performance (Matt 20:1-16). The God of the parables is compassionate beyond comprehension and cannot be controlled by any human notion of what is appropriate.

Wisdom's Banquet

In the Wisdom literature, we find Sophia preparing a wonderful banquet of fine food and wine and sending out her messengers to invite all to her feast: "Come, eat of my bread and drink of the wine I have mixed" (Prv 9:3-5; Sir 24:19-21). Jesus' meals with outcasts and sinners, his great open air meals, and his parables about meals and banquets echo the banquet of the Wisdom Woman.

In Jesus' meals we are confronted with revelation into what Elisabeth Schüssler Fiorenza calls the "praxis of inclusive wholeness."[4] Jesus' celebratory meals witness to the inclusive graciousness of God. In a society where table fellowship is understood to create and express bonds of intimacy, Jesus welcomes the untouchables of society as friends to what are, in fact, anticipatory celebrations of God's coming Reign. These meals are a pledge and sign of divine forgiveness and an invitation to conversion. They provoke hostile reactions from the self-righteous: "Behold, a glutton and a drunkard, a friend of tax collectors and sinners" (Lk 7:34). But for the poor, the outcast and the public sinners they are good news. Being with Jesus brings healing and joy. As Edward Schillebeeckx has said, Jesus' dealings with people liberate them and make them glad.[5]

Matthew's gospel has Jesus defend his practice of eating with outcasts and public sinners by advising his critics to go and learn from the prophet Hosea: "Go and learn what this means, 'I desire mercy not sacrifice.'" (Matt 12:7). Jesus' inclusive meals are defended by reference to the inclusive nature of God. Eating and drinking with outcasts and sinners is an authentic witness to the God of Jesus. These meals are acts of fidelity to the God of boundless compassion and familial inclusivity. For Jesus, the practice of inclusive table companionship is fundamentally and immediately linked to the issue of what kind of a God God is. It is profoundly theological.

Wisdom's Praxis

Jesus' liberating and healing ministry is the presence in anticipation of the Reign of God (Lk 7:22). In this ministry we find that wise action, action in the light of God and God's Reign, is understood as the practice of inclusive compassion.

When Jesus is confronted with human need, the gospel writers use a Greek verb which refers to being moved in one's stomach or bowels. The ancient Jewish people regarded the inner organs as the seat of tender feelings like kindness and compassion, much as today the heart is regarded as the seat of these feelings. Jesus is "moved with compassion" by the plight of a leper (Mk 1:41), by the needs of the great crowd of people by the shore (Mk 6:34), by the hunger of the crowd (Mk 8:2), by the grief of the widow of Nain (Lk 7:13), by the crowds in the villages and cities (Matt 9:36), by the sick in the crowd (Matt 14:14), and by the blindness of two men (Matt 20:34). In each case the strong inner feeling of compassion leads to direct action: feeding, healing, teaching, liberating.

While Jesus' openness and generosity are universal and break through all boundaries, we find his ministry guided by an orientation of the "heart" toward, and an option for, three groups of people: the poor; the sick and the crippled; and the tax collectors, prostitutes, and public sinners. Jesus proclaims by deed and word that God's priority is with the poor, and that God's way is to go first in search of the lost one. The option for the poor reflects a theological truth, a truth about God. The practice of the Reign of God, Wisdom's practice, is made manifest in the praxis of a radically inclusive love, which involves priority for the poor and the outcast.

It is also made manifest in the formation of the community of disciples which Jesus calls and gathers. This group of disciples constitutes a new family. Jesus promises them that here and now, within his community, they will discover a new group of mothers, sisters and brothers (Mk 3:31-35; 10:29-31; Lk 11:27-28). No one is to play the role of the patriarchal father (Matt 23:8-12). All dominating forms of power are to be excluded, and leadership is to be exercised only as service (Mk 10:42-45). The new community is a place of equality and inclusivity. Women and men share in discipleship, and slaves and children are brought to the center of the new community, where they become models of discipleship, and of leadership. The community of disciples is called to a "solidarity from below" with the victims of patriarchal and feudal society.[6]

Jesus' Relationship to God

Jesus' preaching and practice of wisdom is grounded in his experience of God as boundless compassion. He is caught up in intimacy with the Holy One of Israel, dares to address this God in familial terms as *Abba*, and in this relationship knows the liberating power that can challenge all oppressive patriarchal structures and offer new possibilities for a profoundly relational way of life grounded in divine compassionate love.

The Wisdom of Israel was a particular kind of knowledge, a knowledge from experience, a relational knowing, involving, above all, relationship with God. At the heart of Israel's Wisdom theology is the conviction that the "fear of the Lord" is the beginning of wisdom.[7] Gerhard von Rad has said that this often-repeated saying "contains in a nutshell the whole Israelite theory of knowledge."[8] True wisdom is a knowledge that comes only through relationship with the living God. Kathleen O'Connor writes:

> Among the many meanings associated with fear of Yahweh, terror or fright are not included. The fear of Yahweh is a relational term which refers to overpowering awe and wonder, combined with powerful attraction humans experience in the presence of the Living God ... To live in the fear of Yahweh is to live in loving devotion, in close relationship, which makes humans feel small before such a being. Only those who have entered this relationship can recognise the wisdom and harmony pulsing through the universe. The fear of Yahweh is the summary virtue of the sages.[9]

The wise human person is a true seer, one who sees all things truly because he or she sees in the light of a relationship with the Creator.

Jesus' insight into life and creation springs from intimacy with the Holy One. He relates to God as one possessed by the Spirit of God. In the Spirit, Jesus addresses the Holy One in intimate and familial terms; knows in anticipation the coming of the liberating Reign of God, which will overturn all forms of oppression; and encounters God as the One who makes the sun rise, sends rain upon the just and the unjust, feeds the birds of the air and clothes the lilies of the field.

A Wisdom Christology sees Jesus as one in whom the "fear of the Lord," the relationship of loving knowledge, reaches such a profound depth that Jesus can be understood to be the human being in whom Wisdom is fully at home. Jesus, led by the Spirit, is caught up in radical openness to God and God's Reign. It is this relationship which constitutes Jesus not only as Wisdom's child and prophet, but as divine Wisdom. Jesus is so Spirit-led, so caught up in love with the God of boundless compassion, and so lives this compassion in liberating action, inclusive community and familial relationships, that it becomes clear, in the light of resurrection, that Jesus is divine Wisdom among us.

I have been arguing, in this section, that Wisdom categories can provide the basis for an authentic interpretation of the life and ministry of Jesus. During his lifetime Jesus was understood as a Wisdom teacher, and in the early Christian community he was understood as Wisdom's teacher and emissary and as Wisdom incarnate. Wisdom categories (alongside others) can help today's Christians gain authentic insight into the life and ministry of the historical Jesus.

"Wisdom Has Built Herself a Home"

Jesus, the prophet of divine Wisdom, was persecuted and killed (Lk 11:49). Wisdom was rejected, but the believing community, in the power of the resurrection experiences, saw God's saving purposes being accomplished even in, and above all in, the cross of Jesus. In the light of the resurrection the community of disciples went far beyond speech about Jesus as Wisdom's envoy and identified Jesus with divine Wisdom.

Wisdom categories thus create a link between the evaluation of Jesus in his lifetime and the evaluation of Jesus in the New Testament church. Jesus the great teacher of wisdom—one so closely associated with wisdom in his lifetime—is, after his death and resurrection, understood to be divine Wisdom.

Jesus Identified with the Wisdom of God

The identification that the Christian scriptures make between Jesus and the Wisdom of God has been discussed in the last chapter; at this point I will bring it to mind in summary form. The first Christian communities saw Jesus as Wisdom's envoy (Lk 7:35/Matt 11:19) and as Wisdom's prophet (Lk 11:49/Matt 23:34). Many scholars think that this is very early tradition about Jesus. It is found in the material that is common to Matthew and Luke, which is presumed to come from an earlier common source, usually identified as the Q source.

But the earliest communities also identified Jesus with divine Wisdom, sometimes implicitly and sometimes explicitly. We find Paul claiming that Jesus crucified is our Wisdom (1 Cor 1-2), the New Testament hymns speaking of Jesus in ways which implicitly identify him with Wisdom (Col 1:15-20; Heb 1:3-4; Jn 1:1-18), Luke showing Jesus to be a child and prophet of Wisdom (7:35; 11:49); Matthew portraying Jesus as the great teacher of Wisdom and having him implicitly claim to speak as Wisdom herself (11:19; 11:25-30; 23:34; 23:37), and John presenting Jesus as Wisdom personified and Wisdom incarnate (1, 6).

Two theological affirmations flow from this. The first of these is simply that in the early church, in its liturgical hymns and confessional writings, Jesus is understood as divine Wisdom, as Wisdom incarnate. Alongside other formulations and other titles, Christian faith can be expressed in the language "Jesus is the Wisdom of God" (1 Cor 1:24).

The second affirmation is that historically this ancient Wisdom Christology is the essential structural link in the development of the doctrine of the incarnation in the early church. It is in and through the identification of Jesus with pre-existent divine Wisdom that we find in the early Christian hymns the beginnings of a theology of incarnation, a theology which reaches a clear and unambiguous articulation in John's gospel. Here Jesus is the eternal Word made flesh. It is in the identification of Jesus with personified Wisdom that the insight has been reached that what is divine in Jesus (Wisdom) pre-existed his life and ministry and has become incarnate in him. Even in the prologue of John's gospel, as we have seen, the concept of pre-existent Wisdom lies behind the theology of the pre-existent Word.

It is the existence of the biblical tradition of divine Wisdom, with its understanding of Wisdom's pre-existence and presence with God in creation, that provides the conceptual framework which allows the theology of incarnation and pre-existence to emerge in the New Testament period. It is ultimately behind all Christian thinking about the Trinity. The historical dominance of the theologies of Jesus as divine Word of God and as Son of God has obscured the Wisdom Christology which was their origin.

Retrieving Wisdom Christology

Wisdom Christology remains the basis and framework for other theological approaches to Jesus of Nazareth. It has never been entirely lost in the life of the church. Wisdom theology has remained alive in different ways in the work of theologians and in the liturgy. Jesus was understood as the Wisdom of God in patristic theology and even in medieval theology, Wisdom was regularly attributed to the Second Person of the Trinity, and wisdom categories were used to speak of experiential knowledge of God, the knowledge that comes through love.[10] I cannot trace the emergence and decline of Wisdom Christologies here, but I will refer to some of the ways in which Origen, Athanasius and Pope Leo I used Wisdom categories.[11]

Perhaps the greatest Wisdom Christology of the early church was that of Origen (c.185-c.254). For Origen, Jesus Christ is the divine Wisdom who is the "emanation" of the glory of God (Wis 7:25). The structure of Origen's thought is that divine wisdom having had a cosmic role in creation is now made manifest in Jesus.[12] In this structure of thought Origen expresses the constant theme of all Wisdom Christology— what is revealed in creation is made manifest in Jesus.

Origen's great work of systematic theology, *On First Principles*, was written before he left Alexandria for Caesarea in 231. The first three chapters are on the Persons of the Trinity, and, in his second chapter, Origen's Christological vision is outlined in Wisdom categories. So, for example, he writes of the eternity of the Second Person of the Trinity:

> Wisdom, therefore, must be believed to have been begotten beyond the limits of any beginning that we can speak of or understand. And because in this very subsistence of wisdom there was implicit every capacity and form of the creation that was to be, both of those things that exist in a primary sense and of those which happen in consequence of them, the whole being fashioned and arranged before hand by the power of foreknowledge, wisdom, speaking through Solomon in regard to these very created things that had been as it were, outlined and prefigured in herself, says that she was created as a "beginning of the ways" of God, which means that she contains within herself both the beginnings and causes and species of the whole creation.[13]

All things are created in divine Wisdom, and every creature is contained implicitly in her. Here, in Origen's Wisdom Christology, is what Bonaventure will make explicit—every creature can be understood as the self-expression of the Wisdom of God.

It seems that Origen thought that the title of divine Wisdom encapsulated all other titles for Jesus. He wrote that "whatever then we have said of the wisdom of God will also fitly apply to and be understood of him in his other titles as the Son of God, the life, the word, the truth, the way and the resurrection."[14] In the later part of *On First Principles* Origen very often speaks of Christ as Word and Wisdom in the same sentence.

Origen used Wisdom Christology to respond to contemporary theological problems he faced. For example, he was convinced that God's power must always have been operative, and this suggested to him that in some way the world of creation must always have existed. He asked how this could be compatible with the fact that creatures were created. He suggested that the answer is in terms of biblical Wisdom Christology. All things have always existed in some way in divine Wisdom:

> God the Father always existed, and he always had an only-begotten Son, who at the same time according to the explanation we have given above, is called Wisdom. This is that Wisdom in whom God delighted when the world was finished, in order that we might understand from this that God ever rejoices. In this Wisdom, therefore, who was ever existed with the Father, the Creation was always present in form and in outline, and there never was a time when the pre-figuration of those things which hereafter were to be did not exist in Wisdom.[15]

Much later in his book Origen returns to ponder the mystery of the incarnation:

> But of all the marvellous and splendid things about him there is one that utterly transcends the limit of human wonder and is beyond the capacity of our weak mortal intelligence to think of or understand, namely, how this mighty power of the divine majesty, the very word of the Father, and the very wisdom of God, in which were created "all things visible and invisible," can be believed to have existed within the compass of that man who appeared in Judaea; yes, and how the wisdom of God can have entered into a woman's womb and been born as a little child and uttered noises like those of crying children; and further, how it was that he was

troubled, as we are told, in the hour of death, as he himself confesses when he says, "My soul is sorrowful even to death"; and how at the last he was led to that death which is considered by men to be the most shameful of all—even though on the third day he rose again.[16]

In this text Origen's Wisdom Christology finds wonderful expression. Divine Wisdom, in whom the heavens and the Earth are created, is now expressed in the cries of a newborn infant. Sophia, God's companion in creation, is revealed in the abandoned One on the cross. This inner relationship that Origen sees between God's self-communication in every creature and God's radical self-giving in Jesus' life and death is the basis for a truly Christian view of ecological issues, which will be developed in the next chapter.

Athanasius (c.296-377) thought of Jesus as the eternal Word and Son of God, but he could also think of him as divine Wisdom. In a lovely image he thinks of the role of divine Wisdom at work in creation as a musician bringing all creatures together into a beautiful harmony:

Like a musician who has attuned his lyre, and by the artistic blending of low and high and medium tones produces a single melody, so the Wisdom of God, holding the universe as a lyre, adapting things heavenly to things earthly, and earthly things to heavenly, harmonizes them all, and leading them by his will, makes one world and one world-order in beauty and harmony.[17]

Athanasius's image of Wisdom at work in creation, like a gifted musician, is a beautiful and apt one. It has been given new life by contemporary thinkers like Arthur Peacocke as a helpful image for God's work in continuous creation. Athanasius thinks of Jesus as Image, Expression, Word and Son of the Father, and also as Wisdom and Light. There never was a time when Wisdom did not exist:

If there be an Image of the invisible God, it is an invisible Image; nay, I will be bold to add, that, as being the likeness of the Father, never was it not. For when was that God, who according to John, is called Light (for "God is Light"), without a radiance of his proper glory, that a man should presume to assert the Son's origin of existence, as if before he was not? But when was not that Image of the Father's Ineffable and Nameless and Unutterable Subsistence, that Expression and Word, and He that knows the Father? For let him understand well who dares to say, "Once the Son was not," that he is saying, "once Wisdom was not," and "Word was not," and "Life was not."[18]

One of the most important documents in the history of Christology is the famous letter of Pope Leo I to Flavian of Constantinople (June 13, 449), sometimes called the *Tome of Leo*. This letter was crucial at the Council of Chalcedon and in subsequent theology of Jesus Christ.

At a central point in this letter Leo employs the text of Proverbs 9:1 ("Wisdom builds her house") alongside the text from John 1:14 ("the Word is made flesh") to affirm, against Eutyches, the human nature of Jesus Christ, the human flesh he took from his mother, and his human birth:

> But that birth, singularly wonderful and wonderfully singular, must not be understood as meaning that, because of the new type of procreation, the intrinsic quality of the birth was changed. Fecundity was given to the Virgin by the Holy Spirit, but the reality of the body was taken from her body; and with *Wisdom building a dwelling for herself* (Prov. 9:1), *The Word was made flesh, and dwelt among us* (John 1:14); that is, in the flesh which he took from a human being and which he animated with the breath of rational life.[19]

Leo's strong grasp of the doctrine of the incarnation can be expressed, and is usually expressed, in Word/Logos categories as "Word made flesh." But the same doctrine is expressed in Wisdom/Sophia categories as "Wisdom has built herself a home." This is not an isolated instance. In another letter Leo again addresses the theology of the incarnation. Speaking of Mary, the mother of Jesus, he writes:

> Only then, with *Wisdom building a house for herself* (Prov. 9:1) would *the Word become flesh* (John 1:14) within her inviolate womb. Then, too, the Creator of ages would be born in time and the nature of God would join with the nature of a slave in the unity of one person. The one through whom the world was created would himself be brought forth in the midst of creation.[20]

Leo here not only refers to the incarnation as "Wisdom building herself a home," but he shows the inner link in a Wisdom theology between God's work in creation and incarnation. When Wisdom builds her home among us, the one through whom the world was created is brought forth in the midst of creation.

It has always been appropriate to express faith in the incarnation by saying of Jesus that in him "Wisdom has built herself a home" (Prv 9:1). It has always been appropriate to sing in the Advent season:

> O come, now Wisdom from on high,
> Who orders all things mightily;
> To us the path of knowledge show,
> And teach us in her ways to go.[21]

It is also a venerable Advent custom to pray the "O antiphons," which are part of the Liturgy of the Hours:

> O Wisdom, you come forth from the mouth of
>   the Most High.
> You fill the universe and hold all things together
>   in a strong yet gentle manner.
> O come to teach us the way of truth.[22]

In these few lines we find a compendium of Christian theology in Wisdom categories: a trinitarian theology in terms of the procession of Wisdom from the mouth of the Most High; a theology of Wisdom's work in creation, in which Wisdom is understood as not only being present to all of creation, but as holding all things together; the suggestion of a theology of divine power as non-dominating, as Wisdom is at work in creation in a "strong but gentle manner"; the prayer "O come" as a plea for Wisdom's advent in Jesus of Nazareth; an understanding of Jesus as a Wisdom teacher, teaching us "the way of truth." This prayer is a summary of many of the themes of this book.

All of this suggests that we might once again take up the language of Wisdom to speak of the deepest mystery of Jesus Christ, and that this Christology, by continually making manifest the interrelationship between creation and incarnation, can form the basis for a contemporary ecological theology.

As Elizabeth Johnson has pointed out, Wisdom categories can express both Jesus' saving work and his identity. First, salvation in Jesus (functional Christology, Christ *pro nobis*) can be understood in Wisdom categories. Jesus in his life and ministry can be understood as prophet and child of Sophia, delighting to be with people, the one in whom "joy, insight and a sure way to God are found." And the saving work of Jesus' life, death, resurrection can be understood as "the deeds of Sophia reestablishing the right order of creation."[23]

Second, the ultimate personal identity of Jesus (ontological Christology, Christ *in se*) can be understood in Wisdom categories. Once Jesus is identified with Wisdom, the way is open to attribute to Jesus-Wisdom "preexistence, agency in creation, revelation of the knowledge of God, the giving of life, incarnation, and divinity itself, all patterned on Sophia's characteristics."[24] The Christological title of Wisdom can be given again to Jesus: *Hagia Sophia*, our Holy Wisdom, or Jesus, the Wisdom of God.

Directions for a Wisdom Christology

I believe that the retrieval of a Wisdom Christology can throw fresh light on a number of complex areas of contemporary theology. These are issues which not only create difficulties for many Christian believers today, but also, in many cases, are difficult to deal with in traditional "Son of God" Christologies. They include: pre-existence, the issue of the "person" of Jesus Christ, the maleness of Jesus in relationship to women, the doing of justice, Christology in relationship to other religious traditions, a theological approach to the possibility of extraterrestrial life, and the principal concern of this book, the relationship between God's self-revelation in Jesus and the created universe. The last of these will be pursued more fully in the following chapter. At this point I will say only a few words about the other important issues and attempt to show how a Wisdom Christology can throw light on them.

Pre-Existence

In discussion on pre-existence, it sometimes seems to be assumed that it is the human being Jesus of Nazareth who pre-exists. This needs to be understood as an inexact and exaggerated assumption. When it is taken literally, it is a serious and dangerous theological mistake.

The mistake is in the assumption that the created humanity of Jesus pre-exists. One of the dangers in attempting to communicate a theology of pre-existence in a Son of God theology is that the imaginative picture of the pre-existent divine Son tends to receive content from the life and historical figure of Jesus.

Another mistaken tendency is to project, consciously or unconsciously, one or more characteristics of the human Jesus (such as maleness) onto the pre-existent One. Such a concrete imaginative picture can make pre-existence and incarnation seem completely uncritical and incredible to our contemporaries. More important, this approach to pre-existence fails to respect the "not knowing" in our theology of the trinitarian Persons and their transcendence with regard to the characteristics we consciously or unconsciously attribute to them.

The great theologians of the church have always defended the incomprehensibility of God. Basil, Gregory of Nanzianzus, Gregory of Nyssa, John Chrysostom and John Damascene developed the theology of divine incomprehensibility. In the West, Augustine taught that God is better known through ignorance than through knowledge.[25] Anselm of Canterbury, Thomas Aquinas, Bonaventure and Duns Scotus stood firmly in this tradition. Above all, in Aquinas we find a profound understanding of the limits of analogical language, which can allow us to speak truly about God while at the same time preserving the divine incomprehensibility. In 1215 the Fourth Lateran Council declared that there is no similarity between creature and Creator in which there is not an even greater dissimilarity.[26] This tradition was continued by theologians like Nicolas of Cusa and his idea of "learned ignorance" (*docta ignorantia*), by the theology of the Dark Night of John of the Cross, and, in our own day, by Karl Rahner's theology of Holy Mystery.

This tradition is not simply one among many in the Christian tradition, but is an indispensable foundation for all theology. Yet in Christological discussion it is often forgotten that we need to remember the incomprehensibility of God in all our reflections on the pre-existent One.

What is needed is neither a denial of pre-existence nor an easy tolerance of it as a mythological statement, where myth is understood in a popular sense as having little connection with reality. In this view the theology of pre-existence would have little cognitive or metaphysical meaning for us today. On the contrary, I would understand myth positively as poetic insight into religious truth. I would argue that there are

wonderfully symbolic and poetic elements in the picture of pre-existent divine Wisdom, and that these poetic images point toward, and
offer insight into, the Holy Mystery of the trinitarian God. What pre-
exists is divine Wisdom within the trinitarian God. Pre-existence cannot be dismissed without dismissing the trinitarian God.[27]

What is needed is not the dismissal of the truth claims of the theology of pre-existence but a "negative theology" that points to the limits
of what we can know about the pre-existent One. Here, too, there is
need to recognize that we say more about what God is not than what
God is. The pre-existing Wisdom of God remains as abiding mystery to
us, even, or perhaps particularly, in the light of the incarnation.

Our scriptures speak of the "mystery" of God's purpose at precisely
this point (1 Cor 2:7; Col 1:26; 2:2; Eph 1:9; 3:2-6). It seems to me that
a Wisdom Christology is not only faithful to the biblical origins of a
theology of pre-existence, but can point us in the direction of a less
concrete imaginative grasp of the pre-existing One. It can involve a
helpful "negative theology" of the imagination. This great tradition of
divine incomprehensibility must be applied to the pre-existence of
Christ, and I believe that a Sophia Christology can help to preserve the
"unknowing" in our approach to the Second Person of the Trinity better
than a Son of God Christology.

The Human Person and the Divine Person

The use of Wisdom categories can help in a contemporary approach
to the teaching of the Council of Chalcedon that the divine and human
natures of Jesus Christ are united in one Person. In neo-Chalcedonian
thinking the one "Person" was normally understood simply as the divine Son of God.

But in the years since the Council of Chalcedon the word *person* has
continued to develop new meanings and resonances. For our contemporaries, a person is often thought of as a psychological center of consciousness and freedom. When the classical teaching is proclaimed today it is heard as if there is only one center of consciousness and freedom
in Jesus Christ, and this belongs to the divine Son of God. This leads to
thinking of Jesus in docetist and monophysite terms—as a divine being
who has taken on the appearance of a human being. The full humanity
of Jesus is denied. Such thinking ends up unfaithful to the doctrine of
the two natures in Jesus Christ, and denying the teaching that Jesus

possesses a human nature, which includes a human soul and a human consciousness.

It has become imperative for a contemporary theology to affirm that Jesus is a human person in the sense of being a human center of subjectivity.[28] At the same time, most theologians are not prepared to abandon the idea of the divine person. The only solution seems to be to speak, as Walter Kasper does, of a profound unity in Jesus between human person and divine person, so that "the indeterminate and open aspect that belongs to the human person is determined definitively by the unity with the Logos." In Jesus "it is through unity with the Logos that the human person comes to its absolutely unique and underiveable fulfilment."[29] In a related way, Edward Schillebeeckx speaks of a "hypostatic identification" of the human personal mode of being and the divine person in Jesus. He points out that while an identity between two finite persons is an inner contradiction, an identity between "a personal-cum-human mode of beings and a divine, infinite (and thus analagous) mode of 'being person' is no contradiction."[30]

The unity in Jesus is to be understood as a unity of the center of his human subjectivity and the "person" of divine Wisdom. It is important to remember, as Schillebeeckx points out, that the word *person* is being used in an analogous sense when it is applied to the eternal Word and Wisdom of God. The Wisdom of God is not a person in the same way that human beings are persons—there is an infinite difference between the two. There is need for a negative theology concerning the person of Sophia. We do not know much about such a divine Person. What we do know, from the incarnation, is that this divine Person is of such a kind as not to be opposed to human personhood, but its fulfillment. In Jesus we find human personhood flourishing in profound unity with the divine Person.

A Wisdom Christology helps us preserve the mystery and incomprehensibility of the divine Person. As I have said above, speaking of Jesus of Nazareth as the Wisdom of God incarnate can involve us in an appropriate negative theology of the imagination. Son of God Christology (in isolation) can tend to lead to an unreflective attribution of what we know of Jesus of Nazareth to the Second Person of the Trinity. Once this occurs there is no need for a human center of consciousness and freedom in Jesus.

We need to understand Jesus as a fully human person, a specific and concrete and historically limited human being with a human center of

consciousness and freedom. As a human being Jesus is a personal creature who is radically open to mystery and transcendence. This open
aspect of human personality is determined definitively in Jesus by his
unity with the Second Person of the Trinity, the divine Sophia. Jesus is
a fully human person precisely in being the person of Sophia. In thinking about the incarnation in Wisdom categories, it is possible to think
of Jesus' humanity, and his human personhood, flourishing in its profound unity with divine Wisdom.

A Feminist Christology

As I noted earlier, Elizabeth Johnson has led the way in the recovery
of a Wisdom Christology precisely as a "non-androcentric" Christology.
She points out how the gender of Jesus has been used to identify God
as male, and how it has also been used to identify males as normative
and exclusively capable of representing God. For these reasons, some
feminist scholars would see Christology as the doctrine most used to
subordinate and exclude women.[31]

The theological response to this issue has usually been by way of
reference to the historical Jesus and his liberating and inclusive ministry. Elizabeth Johnson has taken the discussion a step further through
her development of a Wisdom Christology. She makes a clear and strong
case that the early Christian identification of Jesus with holy Wisdom
can be the base for a contemporary non-androcentric and inclusive
Christology.

When the female figure of Sophia is identified with the limited, male,
Galilean Jew, Jesus of Nazareth, something powerful happens in
Christology. It creates a paradigm shift, as the field of meaning associated with the Wisdom Woman is brought together with the field of meaning associated with the gospel portrait of Jesus. This opens out into
new possibilities in an inclusive Christian vision of God's action in
Jesus of Nazareth. In this meeting of fields of meaning, there may be an
initial unease with the identification of the male Jesus with female
Sophia. The level of this unease reveals the degree to which the pre-
existing Word, the "Son of God," has been assumed to be literally male.

This unease can give way to new and liberating insight. It can lead to
a wisdom, which delights in the specific nature of divine self-communication in the limited, young, Jewish male Jesus, and yet finds revealed precisely in this historically conditioned individual that in Christ

there is neither Jew nor Greek, slave nor free, male nor female (Gal 3:28). The identification between Sophia and Jesus leads to a new appreciation of the inclusive and universal liberating love revealed in the specific and limited person, Jesus of Nazareth.

In fact, as I have already argued, the identification of the female figure of Wisdom and the male Jesus leads to an appropriate negative theology. It points to the incomprehensibility of God, and specifically to the incomprehensibility of divine Wisdom. Whether she is named Sophia, Logos, or Son, divine Wisdom is beyond male and female, and both male and female are images of her.

Elizabeth Johnson's study finds that in Paul, Matthew, John and the early Christian hymns, "the characteristics and roles of divine Sophia were applied to Jesus so that he came to be seen and confessed as the embodiment of Sophia herself, the focus of God's gracious presence in the world." She finds that this biblical Wisdom Christology "opens up a new avenue of thought for systematic theology grappling with the androcentric nature of its tradition."[32] A Wisdom Christology calls into question the distorted theological usage of the maleness of Jesus and "the combination Jesus Christ/Sophia leads to a healthy blend of female and male imagery that empowers everyone and works beautifully to symbolize the one God who is neither male nor female, but creator of both, delighting in both, saviour of both, and imaged by both together."[33] Elizabeth Johnson sees Wisdom Christology as an untapped resource of the tradition which can contribute to the redesign of Christology in the face of enormous cultural changes in the position of women.[34]

A Christology of Praxis

Wisdom categories can provide the basis for a theology of liberating praxis. There is an inner link between traditional Wisdom theology and practice. Wisdom is meant to be lived. It provides wise guidance in the ordering of one's life. It is linked to politics, and the concept of wise governance. Wisdom directs her followers to the practice of justice and mercy.

At the center of Wisdom theology is the concept of the "way," or the "path" of wisdom. In the opening chapter of the *Book of Proverbs* we are told that the goal of wisdom is "righteousness, justice and equity." Then in chapter 2 we find the great poem of the two ways, the way of wisdom and the way of folly. The way of wisdom is the way of fear of the Lord. Wisdom comes forth from the mouth of the Lord, "guarding the paths of the justice and preserving the way of the faithful ones" (2:8). Those who seek wisdom in God are told "you will understand righteousness and justice and equity, every good path; for wisdom will come into your heart" (2:9).[35]

In the teaching and practice of Jesus, traditional wisdom insight is made radical by the theology of the Reign of God. Jesus calls for a radical change of mind (*metanoia*) in the light of the Reign of God, the God who is *Abba*. This *metanoia* involves an orthopraxis. This right praxis finds expression in Jesus' own life and ministry in the option for the poor, the ill, the outcasts and sinners. In the wisdom of Jesus, relationship to God is intimately linked to the practice of mercy (Lk 6:36).

A Wisdom Christology is a theology of praxis.[36] A Wisdom Christology which is faithful to the gospel will be a theology of liberating practice. It will be a theology which springs from, and leads to, discipleship in the light of Jesus' life and message, his death and resurrection: "We proclaim Christ crucified . . . Christ the power of God and the wisdom of God" (1 Cor 1:23-25).

Like the Wisdom Woman of Proverbs 9, Jesus invites all to come to eat of his bread and drink of his wine. Like the wise person of Sirach 14, who encamps near Wisdom's house, and knocks tent-pegs into her walls and pitches a tent by her side, those who hear the message of Jesus are invited to choose lifelong companionship with him. This is the companionship of the disciple, the companionship of orthopraxis in the light of the coming Reign of God.

A Wisdom Christology involves the way of discipleship, a seeking of right action in daily life. It involves seeking the will of God in all circumstances and doing it. But this is discovered in relationship with Jesus-Wisdom, in the day-to-day practice of a discipleship.

Discipleship involves a relational knowing and a relational praxis— what the Christian tradition calls the discernment of spirits. Thomas Aquinas thought of the gift of wisdom as a "knowledge through love."[37] He saw this gift as a kind of affinity or "at-homeness" between our choices and the God who is present to us by grace. This at-homeness with divine things is the result of the love, the indwelling presence of the Holy Spirit, by which we are bound to God in grace.[38]

Relational knowledge, knowledge through love, is at the heart of discernment and the praxis of discipleship. As we face the ecological crisis, it is this kind of knowledge-through-love, a wisdom that is at-home with divine Wisdom's love for the Earth, which needs to inform our ecological praxis.

Jesus the Wisdom of God and Other Religious Traditions

One sun-filled morning in the northwest of Australia I had the privilege of meeting Hector Sundaloo, an elder, religious leader and painter of the Warmun Aboriginal community. He showed my companion and myself a painting he had just finished. When we asked about its meaning he told us with evident feeling that it represented the two Marys with the body of Jesus just taken down from the cross. As we talked he began to explain another level of meaning in the painting—its reference to his own "country" (the part of the land to which he is spiritually attached) and dreaming story.

He went on to explain that although he is a Christian believer, he is a "two-way" person. He is attached not only to Christian faith, but to his traditional faith. He sees Christian faith as building on the ancient wisdom which is his heritage. It seemed to me that his "two-way" view was not a facile syncretism, but an authentic capacity to draw on two interrelated but distinct sources of wisdom.

This issue of a "two-way" tradition is important for many people around the Earth. It is connected to another issue of contemporary theology—interreligious dialogue. Even granted the insights of contemporary theology and the teaching of the Second Vatican Council concerning the universality of God's gracious self-communication and offer of salvation, further questions remain: How do Christian believers speak of the meaning of salvation in Jesus Christ within the pluralistic context of interreligious dialogue? Does Christian theology continue to claim universal meaning for Jesus, or does he become one among many savior figures?

Raimundo Panikkar deals with the question through his theology of the universal Christ, who is not restricted to the historical figure of Jesus of Nazareth.[39] John Hick understands the incarnation as a myth that should be taken seriously, but not literally, and he abandons universal claims for Christ, adopting a pluralist stance which leaves room for other religions and other saviors.[40] Paul Knitter develops a "theocentric" theology of religions, based upon a reinterpretation of the uniqueness of Jesus, where Jesus is no longer understood as God's definitive or normative self-revelation.[41]

While I am sympathetic to Knitter's concern to move beyond exclusive and inclusive claims for Jesus vis-à-vis other religions, I believe that it is important to distinguish two contexts of meaning for the words *normative* and *definitive*. In the context of interreligious dialogue, as I will show below, I agree that Christians need not insist that Jesus is "normative" or "definitive," in the sense of being the prior norm and definition of other religions. On the other hand, these words have usually functioned within a Christian confessional commitment to bring out the decisive nature of what God has done in Jesus, and the radical nature of the praxis of discipleship. I believe that it is essential to maintain what these words pointed to in this context, that universal salvation comes to us and to our world in a decisive, unique, gratuitous and irrevocable act of God in the human being Jesus of Nazareth.[42]

I would differ further from John Hick, because of my conviction that the New Testament theology of pre-existence, richly couched in mythological language, proclaims a metaphysical truth—that what is revealed in Jesus pre-existed in God. Panikkar's position is closer to that of a Wisdom Christology, but it suffers from the difficulty that the word *Christ* (the "anointed one," the "Messiah") has a specific history within Judaism and a specific history within Christianity, where it quickly became a proper name for Jesus of Nazareth.

It seems to me that a helpful line of thought on this issue emerges from juxtaposing two theological insights. First, the Wisdom Christology developed here has something to offer in showing connections between Christianity and other religious traditions. Roland Murphy has pointed out how the Wisdom tradition of ancient Israel was always an open tradition, ready to learn from Israel's neighbors.[43] Wisdom was never confined to one tradition. Practically, the language of wisdom is used widely across many religious traditions, and provides a good basis for interreligious discussion. Theologically, Christians who see Jesus as the Wisdom of God can recognize that this same Wisdom of God may well find expression in other religious traditions.

Second, as Edward Schillebeeckx has stressed, reflection based on Christology itself, on the finite, limited and human Jesus of Nazareth, shows that what is revealed of the infinite mystery of God in Jesus is necessarily limited and partial and finite.[44] To deny this would mean effectively denying the true humanity of Jesus Christ. God is absolute, but no one religion is absolute, including Christianity.

These two insights suggest an approach which I will summarize in the following six points:

1. It is a central dimension of Christian faith that God's self-communication and universal will to save are decisively, uniquely, gratuitously and irrevocably expressed in Jesus of Nazareth, in his life, death and resurrection.

2. But in Jesus of Nazareth, we have a limited, historically conditioned, human expression of divine Wisdom. Jesus does not, and could not as a truly human and finite creature, reveal the totality of the Divine.

3. It is theologically appropriate for Christians, as they look to religions like Hinduism or the religious tradition of indigenous peoples, to be open to the discovery that these traditions contain reflections of the same holy Wisdom that Christians find in Jesus of Nazareth.[45]

4. This means that, from within Christianity, it will be understood that other religious traditions may possibly be institutional responses to divine Grace, expressions of divine Wisdom, which as in Christianity itself, will always be mixed with human limitation and sin. This is not to suggest that all religions are the same. Rather, it is to be expected that as well as sharing some things in common, they may well be extremely different and quite distinctive in their insights and their limitations.

5. Christians will need to recognize that divine Wisdom may well have something to say to them from within the other religious traditions which is not already said to them in Christianity.[46] Schillebeeckx writes that the "multiplicity of religions is not an evil which needs to be removed, but rather a wealth which is to be welcomed and enjoyed by all."[47]

6. In this context, the Christian conviction that Jesus can be seen as the incarnation of God's saving and universal love, the human face of divine Wisdom, can be put forward in interreligious dialogue, without imperialism or absolutism or any attempt to include other religions within Christianity. Christians need to face with openness and humility the possibility that other traditions may need to put forward their own convictions about what has universal significance for them.

Life in Other Solar Systems

A team from the Vatican Observatory reported recently that they had succeeded in identifying a planetary disk in the process of formation around a star. This was very significant by any standards, partly be-cause evidence of planetary formation around stars other than our sun keeps open the real possibility of life on other planets.

The media were extremely interested in this discovery, not so much because of its intrinsic scientific value, but because of the fact that it was made by an astronomical team linked to a Christian church. They seemed to assume that there was a sensational clash between the Bible and the existence of extraterrestrial life. In fact, of course, there is no such theological problem with life in another part of the universe. Chris-tian theology, on its own resources, can neither affirm nor deny the existence of other intelligent creatures on other planets.

Indeed, there is a Jewish-Christian tradition of extraterrestrial life, in the form of angels. Karl Rahner argues that it is not at all clear that Christians of today are committed to belief in angels either by the Bible or the history of doctrine. But, he argues, if angels do exist, they are certainly not "pure spirits" with no connection to the material world. If angels exist, they are part of the universe and have a cosmic function. In the vastness of the universe it is not impossible to think of evolu-tionary history as encompassing not only the emergence of human con-sciousness with its own inner relationship to matter, but also angelic beings with a different but real relationship to matter.[48]

It is also a real possibility that God's creation involves the evolution of other extraterrestrial life, self-conscious and free beings in other parts of the universe, called like human beings into a relationship of grace with their Creator. An Earth-bound theology cannot know any details about issues such as the relationship they have with God or their expe-rience of sin and redemption.

A Wisdom Christology, with its understanding of the inner link be-tween Wisdom's work in creation and incarnation, does open up a fur-ther line of thought. It suggests the probability that divine Wisdom would be revealed to such creatures not only through Wisdom's presence in creation, not only through the gracious presence of the Spirit of God, but also by some kind of free act of God by which divine Wisdom be-came present in their history.[49] However, it is entirely possible that in the wisdom and providence of God, their destiny and salvation history might be quite different from ours.

If divine Wisdom is present in other histories on other planets, this raises the following question: If there have been manifestations of Wis-dom on other planets, how would these relate to the risen Christ? It must be admitted frankly that for those who hold to the universal significance of Jesus Christ this remains a difficult question. If one believes, as I do, that Christian revelation does claim universal significance for Jesus Christ, then, if there are manifestations of divine Wisdom in other parts of the universe, there is an unresolved issue in the relationship between the risen Christ and these other manifestations of Wisdom.

What can be affirmed, I believe, is that other intelligent creatures may exist, and that if they do, then based on divine action with regard to us, we can only assume that what we know of God's saving will would hold true in some way in their case. It seems to me that with our present state of knowledge we have little grounds for further theological comment. What can be said is simply that Christianity is open on the issue of self-conscious life on other planets and regards this as an issue for science to establish one way or the other. Furthermore, Christian theology's understanding of the inclusive, compassionate and gratuitously saving nature of God suggests that if there are such self-conscious creatures, God may well reach out to them in the Holy Spirit and in some kind of presence or manifestation of divine Wisdom.

3.

Jesus—Wisdom and Ecology

The theology of Jesus as divine Wisdom can undergird a Christian approach to ecology and form the basis for a cosmic Christology. The figure of Wisdom is at the heart of New Testament theologies, which claim not only that all things were created "in" and "through" Christ (1 Cor 8:6; Col 1:16; Heb 1:2; Jn 1:3), but that all things will be transformed in the resurrection of the crucified and that this transformation has already begun (Col 1:20; Eph 1:10; Heb 1:3).[1]

I will argue that a Wisdom Christology can begin to show the interrelation between the expanding, interconnected and self-organizing universe and all its creatures, and the saving work of Jesus Christ. Wisdom was with God in the beginning, and all things were created in her. She is dynamically present in all creation, in the great cluster of galaxies, and in every sub-atomic interaction, in every tiny insect and flowering shrub, enabling them to be and to become. This same divine Wisdom became incarnate in Jesus of Nazareth. The crucified and risen Jesus is in his transformed humanity hypostatically united to divine Wisdom at the heart of all cosmic processes. The crucified and risen One has a new transforming and redeeming bodily relationship with the whole universe.

In this chapter, I will develop this argument by first showing the interrelationship between creation and incarnation in a Wisdom Christology, and then discussing what the cross tells us about the love that moves the universe, and what the resurrection means for the creatures of the universe.

Unity of Creation and Incarnation in Wisdom Christology

Roland Murphy has noted that it is practically an axiom of biblical studies that "wisdom theology is creation theology."[2] The Wisdom tradition is an approach to life and faith that is grounded in the experience of nature and of daily life. When Wisdom is personified, she is consistently presented as closely connected to the work of creation.

It is clear from the scriptures that divine Wisdom is to be understood as the self-communication of God in and through creation. As Roland Murphy has written, the biblical figure of Wisdom is "the divine secret in the created world," and "the divine summons issued in and through creation, sounding through the vast realm of the created world, and heard on the level of human experience."[3]

Wisdom is present with God at creation as a skilled co-worker (Prv 8:30; Wis 7:22; 8:6).[4] She "pervades and penetrates all things" (Wis 7:24); she "renews all things" (Wis 7:27); and "she reaches mightily from one end of the earth to the other, and she orders all things well" (Wis 8:1). She is present in all of creation, as the divine power of continuous creation.[5]

Yet Wisdom takes delight in the company of human beings (Prv 8:31). She "has built her house" among them and invites them all to her feast (Prv 9:1-6). In Sirach, we find Wisdom dwelling in the highest heaven, and travelling through the heavens, over the seas and all the earth, until the Creator chooses the place for her to pitch her tent. There, in the holy city of Jerusalem, Wisdom takes up her abode and issues her invitation: "Come to me, all you who desire me, and eat your fill of my fruits" (Sir 24:18).

These texts reveal a basic structure of thought in Wisdom theology, to which I have already referred: Wisdom revealed in the marvels of creation now makes her home among human beings. This biblical structure was a wonderful resource for the early Christian communities as they reflected on God's action in Jesus of Nazareth. They could see Jesus as the Wisdom of God, present and active in all of creation, pitching a tent among human beings on earth. This structure has great significance for a contemporary theology that wants to hold together creation and incarnation.

Many Christians assume that it is church teaching that the incarnation comes about only, or primarily, as a result of human sin and as a remedy for sin. In fact, of course, this represents only one school of theology, one of two traditional ways of seeing the relationship between creation and the incarnation. In one theological view (the so-called Thomist position—Aquinas's theology of redemption is broader and subtler than this) the incarnation is understood as coming about primarily to restore and redeem what was broken by human sin. In this kind of theology there can tend to be an extrinsic relationship between God's work in creation and the incarnation.

The alternative Christian theology sees the incarnation as flowing from God's free love for creatures. The incarnation is not dependent on the Fall. It was always part of God's plan. This is the Scotist position, identified with Duns Scotus, but also with Irenaeus in the early church and supported by Teilhard de Chardin, Karl Rahner and many other theologians today. Here the motive of the incarnation is simply the free self-communicating love of the divine will. Of course these theologians recognize the fact of sin and the need for redemption, but they see the incarnation of the Word of God as always intended by God. In this theological tradition there is the possibility of seeing a much more intrinsic link between God's action in creation and incarnation.

A Wisdom Christology lends support to the Scotist view and can help hold together a theology of creation and incarnation. A Wisdom Christology sees creation and incarnation as intrinsically connected in the one divine plan, while still insisting that the incarnation was a totally free act of God. In this view, there can be no separation of creation and redemption—no theology of creation independent of a theology of incarnation, and no theology of incarnation and redeeming grace not related to the created world. Rather, to borrow some words from Karl Rahner, "we can understand creation and incarnation as two moments and two phases of the one process of God's self-giving and self-expression, although it is an intrinsically differentiated process."[6]

The intrinsic connection is fundamental to the structure of Wisdom thought. Divine Wisdom is, by definition, God's presence and self-expression. God communicates God's self through divine Wisdom; Wisdom is present in all of creation and has built herself a home among us in Christ Jesus. Wisdom, God's companion and helper in creation, becomes incarnate in this one human being. God's self-communication in creation and grace reaches its irrevocable climax in Jesus.

This is the view of incarnation found in the prologue of John's gospel: "In the beginning was the Word . . . all things came into being through him, and without him not one thing came into being . . . And the Word became flesh and lived among us" (Jn 1:1-14). This hymn, along with the other great Wisdom hymns of the New Testament, supports a Christology in which creation and redemption are connected in the divine figure of holy Wisdom, who is God's self-expression in creation and who is made truly human in Jesus of Nazareth.

The Love That "Moves the Stars"— 1 Corinthians 1-2

In Paul's theology, divine Wisdom stands revealed above all in the incomprehensible mystery of the cross. I will argue that the identification between Wisdom and the cross has profound meaning for an ecological theology. It suggests that the love revealed on the cross is the very same loving Wisdom that is at work in, and manifest in, an ecosystem, a rain forest, and the Milky Way Galaxy. It is *this* Love that "moves the stars."

God's Foolishness

Paul is the first biblical writer to identify Jesus and the Wisdom of God. He does this in the context of dealing with divisions and factions within the Christian community at Corinth. There are those who claim to follow Paul himself, those who follow Apollos, those who follow Cephas, and, perhaps, another group who claim to follow Christ (1 Cor 1:11-12).

A key issue in the dispute concerns the possession of wisdom. Some of the community claim to possess a superior wisdom which makes them more mature than others, raising them to a spiritual sphere beyond concern about material things. These "wise" ones consider themselves as set above their fellow Christians. In the context of this situation Paul proclaims his theology of true wisdom:

> For Jews demand signs and Greeks desire wisdom, but we proclaim Christ crucified, a stumbling block to Jews and foolishness to Gentiles, but to those who are called, both Jews and Greeks, Christ *the power of God* and *the wisdom of God* (1 Cor 1:22-23).

This is a powerful statement that lies at the heart of Pauline theology. C. K. Barrett says of this text: "This is Paul's most brilliant epigrammatic description of the world in which the Gospel is preached, and of the Gospel itself."[7] What Barrett calls the "Gospel itself" is the radical identification between the crucified Christ and the power and wisdom of God. This crucified One, this extreme expression of human vulnerability, Paul tells us, is the power of God. This apparent foolishness is divine Wisdom.

Paul returns to the identification between Jesus and divine Wisdom at the end of the first chapter. Here he speaks of Christ Jesus, "who became for us *wisdom from God*, and righteousness and sanctification and redemption" (1 Cor 1:30).

What does Paul mean by "wisdom" in these texts? I have already indicated that there are differences among scholars on whether Paul is thinking precisely and explicitly of personified Wisdom at this point. But regardless of whether the figure of Sophia is explicitly in Paul's mind, it is clear that Paul is well aware of Wisdom theology and of its teaching about Wisdom's role in creation. In chapter 8 we find Paul connecting Jesus Christ with the work of creation; he writes of "Jesus Christ, through whom are all things and through whom we exist" (1 Cor 8:6). This connection between Jesus and God's work of creation could be made only on the basis of an implicit identification between Jesus and Wisdom's work in creation.

It is clear that when Paul calls Jesus "the wisdom of God" (1 Cor 1:24 and 1:30), "wisdom" has its general biblical connotations of God's work in creation. Wisdom theology is creation theology. But in Paul's mind wisdom means more than God's creative action. It also refers to God's plan of salvation. Paul speaks of wisdom as the mystery of God's saving plan: "But we speak God's wisdom, secret and hidden, which God decreed before the ages for our glory" (2:7). For Paul, divine wisdom is not only the plan, but also God's saving action in the cross of Jesus. As Barrett writes, wisdom is "not merely the plan but the stuff of salvation."[8]

The Pauline structure of thought is that the wisdom of God revealed in creation is now revealed in a staggering way in the cross of Jesus. This structure is made explicit when Paul writes: "For since, in the wisdom of God, the world did not know God through wisdom, God decided through the foolishness of our proclamation, to save those who believe" (1 Cor 1:21). Since the world did not recognize Wisdom revealed in the works in creation, God went much further, revealing God's self in the foolishness of the cross. Jerome Murphy-O'Connor comments that here Paul is saying that in the light of humanity's failure to accept the insight into God offered by wisdom already displayed in creation (v. 21a), "God just went ahead and did something really foolish (v. 21b)."[9]

God's wisdom is now revealed in the incomprehensible foolishness of the cross. Paul insists that it is precisely because God's wisdom is revealed in the cross of Jesus that he made no attempt in his ministry at Corinth to appeal to worldly wisdom or rhetoric: "I decided to know nothing among you except Jesus Christ and him crucified" (2:2). The Corinthians' faith was not to rest on human wisdom, but on the power of God (2:5). Real wisdom, God's kind of wisdom, can only be taught by the Spirit (2:13). Paul's own practice of ministry had been based upon the divine pattern of relationship with the world.

The divine way is to choose what is foolish and confound all worldly wisdom (1:27). In reflecting on this text, F. F. Bruce draws attention to the history of Israel, in which there are many instances where God deliberately chose "people or instruments that were foolish, weak, despised and mere nonentities by ordinary standards." Bruce argues that in this whole history, and above all in the cross of Jesus, "(God) annuls all conventional canons of wisdom, power, reputation, and value." He notes that nothing could be more subversive of these canons in the first century Greco-Roman world than the proclamation of the exaltation of a crucified person.[10]

God's self-revelation in the crucified One has overturned all standards. This points to the profound mystery at the heart of God's relationship with the world. This is expressed startlingly in one of Paul's key sentences:

> For *God's foolishness* is wiser than human wisdom, and *God's weakness* is stronger than human strength (1:25).

What does this verse mean? Hans Conzelmann points out that it stands out from the rest of Paul's text by its style, parallelism, and its chiastic relationship with verse 24. He writes that in its context in Paul's letter this verse is "a definition of the historic relationship which God establishes through the cross." But Conzelmann argues that it can be taken also as a larger comment about the God-creature relationship. It needs to be read as a maxim expressing "a timeless rule of the relation between divine and human power."[11] It expresses something about the nature of God, and about God's relationship with creation.

What is this "foolishness" of God? What is this divine weakness? Paul makes it clear that it is simply the revelation of the nature of divine love in the cross. It is the foolishness of love beyond understanding. It is the foolishness of divine compassion's vulnerability. Here in Jesus, and in him crucified, God's loving wisdom is revealed. This is God's "foolishness," which is wiser than human wisdom. This is God's "weakness," which is stronger than human strength (1:25).

It is easy today to hear these texts and to be insulated against their impact. It is helpful to attempt to hear them as the Corinthians would have heard them—as referring to someone recently tortured to death, in a manner which was extremely painful, degrading and ugly.

Paul would surely have approved of the theology of Mark's gospel, where Mark's readers are led at the end to look upon the tortured One and to say with the centurion: "Truly this man was God's Son!" (Mk 15:39). In 1 Corinthians Paul is having us confront the vulnerability and "foolishness" of the crucified One, saying, "Truly this is the Wisdom of God!"

The Love That "Moves the Stars"

This theology of Jesus as divine Wisdom has significance for a theology of God's interaction with creation. The cross expresses the passion of God for human beings and for all of creation. This kind of love between Creator and creatures is not only unpredictable to human reason but entirely unthinkable. Here divine Wisdom does something "really foolish." It is an extreme expression of identification between the Lover and the beloved—between God and suffering creation.

This kind of "wisdom" is excessive by any human standard. Wisdom stands revealed as compassion to the point of foolishness. If traditional wisdom is transformed in Jesus' teaching, in his death the Wisdom of God is revealed in an even more shocking way as radical compassion that knows no limits.

For believers, the great size and beauty of our universe reveal the wonder and artistry and the greatness of God. They see God at work in our expanding universe, in the great Milky Way galaxy with its more than a hundred billion stars, and in the more than a hundred billion other galaxies that make up our observable universe, sustaining all things, enabling creatures to break through to new levels of complexity and organization, and enfolding the whole curvature of spacetime within divine creative love. This is God's Wisdom at work.

Paul's theology of Wisdom confronts us with the fact that *this* Wisdom at work in the universe is now revealed in the vulnerable love expressed in the crucified One. The foolish excess of the cross reveals what is at the heart of the processes of the universe.

The last line of Dante's *Divine Comedy* tells of "the Love that moves the sun and the other stars." Karl Rahner has written that it is no mere pious lyricism when Dante regards even the sun and the other planets as being moved by that love which is God's self.[12] Dante's last line represents a fundamental theological truth.

It is worth noting that these are Dante's last recorded words. In the opening line of *Paradiso* Dante had written of the glory of the One "who moves all things." John Sinclair notes how the last line of the *Paradiso* and the whole *Divine Comedy* recall and expound this first line.[13] The glory of the One "who moves all things" *is* "the Love that moves the sun and the other stars"—"*L'amor che move il sole e l'altre stelle.*"

As Rahner was well aware, Dante's cosmology was that of the ancient world, a universe made up of the ten tiers of the Moon, Mercury, Venus, the Sun, Mars, Jupiter, Saturn, the fixed stars, the Chrystalline heaven and the place of the divine Trinity, the Empyrean heaven. Yet, Rahner could claim, in the expanding universe of late twentieth century, with its quasars, black holes, supernovas and its mind-numbing size, it is literally true that it is Love that moves the stars and the millions of galaxies of our universe.

What a Pauline Wisdom Christology means is that *this* Love is revealed in the foolishness of the cross. The divine Wisdom, at work creatively and continuously in the expanding universe and in our evolutionary history, stands revealed in the extreme vulnerability of divine foolishness of the cross. Here Dante's "Love that moves the Sun and other stars" is revealed at the heart of creaturely existence embracing creatures in all their finitude with the most extreme expression of divine vulnerable love. The Wisdom that shapes a word of more than a hundred billion galaxies reaches out to embrace struggling and suffering and sinful creatures in love which finds its final expression in death for us.

In their commentary on 1 Corinthians, William Orr and James Arthur Walther contrast Paul's arguments with the style of thought of the Greek mind, which developed elaborate arguments to demonstrate that a divine being must be free from distress and from any outside influences. In Greek culture, a divine being could not suffer as humans do.[14] Paul's theology challenges this line of thought. I will argue that his teaching of the "weakness" of divine wisdom is relevant in all discussions of God's relationships with the world, above all in considering the later Christian tradition of divine immutability and omnipotence. If God acts in the world through Wisdom, and Wisdom is revealed in the cross of Jesus in extreme weakness and vulnerability, then God's action in the world is to be understood in terms of freely chosen vulnerability.

This vulnerable and foolish love identifies with suffering creation in order to bring liberation and healing. The cross of Jesus is not only the foolishness of divine love but also the "power" of that love at work, filled with liberating resurrection life, with the promise of justice for the poor of the Earth and the transformation of all creatures. For "God's foolishness is wiser than human wisdom, and God's weakness is stronger than human strength" (1 Cor 1:25). It is this theme that I will take up again in considering the Colossians hymn, particularly its second stanza.

The Transformation of the Universe in Jesus the Wisdom of God—Colossians 1:15-20

If the Wisdom Christology of 1 Corinthians contributes to an ecological theology by giving insight into the love that is at the heart of evolutionary and cosmic history, the Wisdom Christology of the Colossians hymn (1:15-20) can be seen as contributing to an ecological theology by offering insight into the relationship between the resurrection of Jesus and the material universe.

The context for this hymn is the widespread New Testament celebration of Christ as the Wisdom of God. Part of this wider context is formed by the Pauline theology of mystery, where Christ is understood as the revelation of God's purpose of salvation, which had hitherto been hidden in God. In these texts the mystery of God's plan and God's wisdom are closely related concepts. Paul writes to the Corinthians: "But we speak God's wisdom, secret and hidden [literally, the wisdom of God in mystery], which God decreed before the ages for our glory" (1 Cor 2:7). This idea is taken up in Colossians (1:26-27; 2:2) and developed further in Ephesians (2:1-3:13). These texts make it clear that God's saving plan includes the gathering up of all things in Christ (Eph 1:10), things in heaven and on earth, and that God's saving will embraces all peoples and includes both Jew and Gentile. The mystery is the revelation of divine Wisdom. This is God's "mind" revealed. The mystery is

God's will to save all things in Christ. The mystery is Christ (Col 2:2; Eph 3:4).

The claim that *all things* are created "in Christ" or "through" Christ appears in many parts of the Christian scriptures in a variety of wisdom hymns and sayings: with Paul in *1 Corinthians* "there is one God the Father, from whom are all things (*ta panta*) and for whom we exist, and one Lord, Jesus Christ, through whom are all things (*ta panta*) and through whom we exist"(1 Cor 8:6); in *Colossians*, "he is the image of the invisible God, the first-born of all creation; for in him all things (*ta panta*) in heaven and earth were created" (1:15); in *Ephesians*, "a plan for the fullness of time, to gather up all things (*ta panta*) in him, things in heaven and things on earth" (1:10); in *Hebrews*, "in these last days he has spoken to us by a Son, whom he appointed heir of all things (*pantōn*), through whom he also created the worlds. He is the reflection of God's glory and the exact imprint of God's very being, and he sustains all things (*ta panta*) by his powerful word" (1:2-4); in *John's gospel*, "In the beginning was the Word . . . All things (*panta*) came into being through him, and without him not one thing came into being. . . . And the Word became flesh and lived among us" (1:1-14).

The supreme celebration of Christ's role in creation is in the hymn of Colossians (1:15-20). The majority of scripture scholars see this as a pre-existing Christian hymn—as "a quotation from a primitive Christian song."[15] They point out that this hymn is made up of two stanzas, both introduced by the words "He is . . . " (1:15 and 18b), both beginning by speaking of Christ as "first-born," both using similar constructions, and both including the phrases "in him," "through him" and "for" or "to" (*eis*) him.[16] Set out in two stanzas the hymn appears as follows:

> He is the image of the invisible God,
> the first-born of all creation;
> for in him all things in heaven and on earth were
>   created, things visible and invisible,
> whether thrones or dominions or rulers or
>   powers—
> all things have been created through him and for
>   him.
> He himself is before all things,

and in him all things hold together.
He is the head of the body, the church.

He is the beginning,
the first-born from the dead,
so that he might come to have first place in
    everything.
For in him all the fullness of God was pleased to
    dwell,
and through him God was pleased to reconcile to
    himself all things,
whether on earth or in heaven,
by making peace through the blood of the cross.

Scholars argue that the author of Colossians made two major redactional (editorial) changes to the pre-existing hymn, adding the reference to the church in verse 16 and the words "through the blood of the cross" in verse 20.[17] These changes are important because they give us a glimpse into the interests and priorities of the author of Colossians: first, to move from Christ's role in reconciling creation to his reconciliation of the church (the focus is on the church in the material that follows the hymn); second, to counter exaggerated enthusiasm by showing that the true basis for universal reconciliation is in the theology of the cross.

These redactional changes do not undercut the cosmic theology of the hymn. As Bruce Vawter comments:

The point we have been trying to make, however, is that this wisdom theology was deemed basically acceptable despite—or rather, precisely because of—it having been redacted. Implied in redaction, surely, is the presence of valuable material which, though improvable, is better kept as it is than let go, to be paraphrased away or nullified by parody. We cannot agree with the view of these christological hymns which holds that they were cited in the New Testament only to be purified of their heterodoxy . . . These hymns were cited, we believe, principally for what they were thought to have said well, therefore, and only secondarily, because by redaction they could be made to say it better. Redaction in other words, was first and foremost a sign of approval and adoption, the validation by a later generation of Christians of an initial christology that it judged to have been essentially right-headed.[18]

The author of Colossians obviously approved of the hymn, and understood the hymn in its new form as still referring to Christ's role in the universe. As Vawter says, "The christology of Colossians 1:12-20 has been accepted into the New Testament in all substance as it was first conceived."[19]

Creation of All Things in Christ

There is a clear movement of thought between the two stanzas: it flows from creation to redemption. The first stanza is concerned with the *creation* of all things in Christ, while the second stanza celebrates the *reconciliation* of the universe in Christ.

C.F.D. Moule has drawn attention to the fact that the "stupendous" words of this hymn apply to One who had been crucified just a few years before. He writes: "The identification of that historical person—the Nazarene who had been ignominiously executed—with the subject of this description is staggering, and fairly cries out for some explanation."[20] The explanation can only be found in the experience of the resurrection of the crucified, and the powerful light this event throws on all things. The resurrection sheds its light in both directions—forward to God's future transformation of all things, and back to God's creation of the universe.

The One who was crucified is now equated with the Wisdom who had been God's agent in creation from the beginning of time. I have already mentioned Eduard Schweizer's comment that the three texts of the Christian scriptures which can be most clearly traced to Jewish Wisdom literature are Colossians 1:15-20, Hebrews 1:3 and the prologue to John's gospel. He points out that it is striking in the Colossians text that "statements about the Pre-existent One are set directly alongside those about the human Jesus and his death on the cross."[21]

The first stanza of the hymn begins with a typical Wisdom expression, celebrating Jesus as the image of God. In the Wisdom of Solomon, we find Wisdom described as "a reflection of eternal light, a spotless mirror of the working of God, and an image of his goodness" (7:26). Just as Wisdom is the reflection, glory and mirror of God, so is Christ.

This theme is found not only in Colossians, but also in 2 Corinthians 2:6 and Hebrews 1:3.

And just as Wisdom was beside God in creation and was daily God's delight (Prv 8:30) and "reaches mightily from one end of the earth to the other" and "orders all things well" (Wis 8:1), so all things in heaven and earth were created "in," "through" and "for" him (Col 1:16), and "in him all things hold together" (Col 1:17).

Moule translates this last phrase as "the universe owes its coherence to him."[22] In this theology of Christ holding the universe together we find an echo of *Sirach*, where it is God's word which holds all things (*ta panta*) together (43:26), and the *Wisdom of Solomon*, where it is the Spirit of God that holds all things (*ta panta*) together (1:7).

In the light of the resurrection, and the identification between Jesus and divine Wisdom, it can be seen that all things were created "in," "through" and "for" (*eis*) Christ (1:16), and all things hold things together in him (1:17). He is the One who gives coherence to the universe and sustains all things— "He is the reflection of God's glory and the exact imprint of God's very being, and he sustains all things by his powerful word" (Heb 1:3).

Transformation of All Things in Christ

If the first stanza of the hymn in Colossians is concerned with the relationship between Jesus and the creation of the universe, the second is concerned with the role of the risen Christ in the reconciliation of the universe. The thought moves from God's work of creation to God's redemption of all things in Christ. Joseph Sittler, in a magnificent address to the General Assembly of the World Council of Churches at New Delhi in 1961, brought out the dynamics and power of the hymn's logic:

These verses sing out their triumphant and alluring music between two huge and steady poles—"Christ," and "all things." Even the Ephesians letter, rich and large as it is, moves not within so massive an orbit as this astounding statement of the purpose of God. For it is here declared that the sweep of God's restorative action in Christ is not smaller than the six-times repeated *ta panta*. Redemption is the name of this will, this action, and this concrete Man who is God with us and God for us—and all things are permeable to his cosmic redemption because all things subsist in him. He comes to all things, not as a stranger, for he is the first-born of all creation, and in him all things were created. He is not only the matrix and *prius* of all things: he is the intention, the fullness, and the integrity of all things: for all things were created through him and for him. Nor are all things a tumbled multitude of facts in an unrelated mass, for in him all things hold together.[23]

Against all false forms of dualism, Colossians insists that Christ has universal meaning. Against all errors which would trap the work of Christ in terms of a purely moral or spiritual role the author of Colossians "sets off a kind of chain reaction from the central atom, and the staccato ring of *ta panta* is the sounding of its reverberations into the farthest reaches of human fact, event and thought." Nothing is exempt— "all is claimed for God and all is Christic."[24]

Sittler brings out the meaning of the second stanza of the hymn, in relationship to the first, with his summary proposition: "A doctrine of redemption is meaningful only when it swings within the larger orbit of a doctrine of creation."[25] Colossians will not allow us to contain our theology of redemption within the narrower (although profoundly important) orbit of human sin and forgiveness. It must involve other creatures. The rest of creation cannot be seen merely as the stage on which the drama of human redemption is played out. The Colossians hymn insists that the whole universe is caught up in the Christ event.

This second stanza, like the first, begins with two affirmations about Christ—he is the "beginning" and the "first-born from the dead." Within Judaism, of course, Wisdom was called "the beginning."[26] In Proverbs, for example, we find Wisdom saying of herself: "The Lord created me at the beginning [or "as the beginning"] of his work, the first of his acts of long ago. Ages ago I was set up, at the first [the "beginning"], before the beginning of the earth" (8:22-23). But when the Colossians hymn claims, in this stanza, that Jesus is "the beginning," it does not mean simply that he is the beginning of creation, but that he is the "first-born from the dead," the origin and foundation of resurrection life for other creatures. In this sense he is before all things. All the "fullness" dwells in him. This seems to mean nothing else than the fullness of deity, for we hear in the next chapter of Colossians: "For in him the whole fullness of deity dwells bodily" (2:9).

The cosmic scope of the Colossians Christology is brought out sharply by the use of three different strategies to describe the universal meaning of Christ. First, there is the often-repeated expression "all things" (*ta panta*). All things were created in Christ according to the first stanza (1:16) and redeemed in him according to the second (1:20). Second, there is the use of the standard expression for the whole of creation: everything in "heaven and earth" is both created in Christ and reconciled in him. Third, there is the specification of the fact that the cosmic powers are created in him: thrones, dominions, rulers and powers. These are difficult to interpret. The first two of these were sometimes thought of within Judaism as belonging among the heavenly hosts of angels, while the second pair are sometimes named as beings and powers above the earth and the waters.[27] These powers seem to refer to what we would now think of as forces at work in human history as well as forces at work in the heavenly realm. Colossians is claiming that everything is "in Christ," and there are no exceptions.

In Romans we find creation groaning in labor pains, waiting to be set free from its bondage to decay (Rom 8:19-23). In Romans 8, as in Colossians 1:16, the forces of creation seem to be understood as created good and as directed toward redemption and reconciliation in Christ.

At other times in the Christian scriptures, the saving work of Christ is described as a victory which disarms negative cosmic forces and brings them into proper relationship (1 Cor 15:24; Phil 3:20; Col 2:15; 1 Pt 3:22). Ephesians understands Christ's resurrection as power over cosmic forces: Christ is seated "far above all rule and authority and power and dominion, and above every name that is named, not only in this age but also in the age to come" (1:21; cf 3:10). Christ is being envisioned as the power at work in the whole cosmos. This includes both earthly institutions and invisible powers, both politics and history on the one hand, and the heavenly realm on the other.[28]

In Ephesians we find a cosmic Christology like that of Colossians 1:15-20 expressed in a succinct and summary form in a one-sentence description of the mystery of God's plan: "A plan for the fullness of time, to gather up all things in him, things in heaven and things on earth" (1:10).

Christology, Ecology and Cosmology

The worldview of Colossians and Ephesians is very different from contemporary views of evolutionary history and from contemporary cosmology. There is a big shift from the "powers" of Colossians and Ephesians to ecosystems, global climate change, black holes, quasars and the choice between an open and a closed universe.

Yet, as Markus Barth points out, the theological principle at work in Colossians and Ephesians applies to both ancient and modern views of creation. He suggests that we need to understand the "principalities and powers" as time-conditioned language for what today we might call "the structures, laws, institutions, and constants of nature, evolution, history, society, the psyche, the mind." We do not need to reject this teaching about the powers as superstition, but reapply it in a new way within our own new worldview:

> Paul could not know what modern physics, biology, sociology, psychology, anthropology, and cybernetics were to elaborate. The recently coined scientific terminology for describing invisible and visible constants of creation, evolution, change, decay, and destiny was not available to him. But he showed concern for precisely the same fields. He did not despise or exclude the world of creation from his theology. Knowing that God had created heaven and earth, and that God "had made all things very good" (LXX Gen 1:31), Paul could not possibly endorse a dualism which ascribed creation to a split in the deity, or to the result of ever deteriorating emanations from the deity. A final dualistic tension between the worship of God and the scientific perception of the phenomena of nature and history, psyche and society, had no room in the minds of Israel's Wisdom teachers, nor in the mind of Paul who took up much of that tradition, as was shown earlier.[29]

When Colossians and Ephesians refer to Christ and the "powers," they are testifying to the relevance of Christ's work for everything in the created world. In taking up the thought of Colossians in today's world, it is both possible and necessary to reflect about the relationship between the crucified and risen Christ and the expanding universe, and the evolutionary biotic community of the planet Earth. What does the Wisdom Christology of Colossians say to our ecological and cosmological concerns? I would suggest seven points:

1. All of creation is directed toward Jesus Christ and will find its fulfillment in him. Colossians tells us that not only have all things been created "in him" but also "through him," and "for him" (1:16). Christ is

the mediator of creation, not only because divine Wisdom, which becomes incarnate in him, is God's creative power and presence, but because all things are created "for" Christ. The literal translation of the
Greek word *eis* is "toward" or "into." Lohse points out that there are no
parallels for this expression anywhere in Jewish Wisdom literature. All
things are created toward Christ—"In this way not only the statements
about the origin of creation are summarized, but also the goal of creation is indicated: creation finds its goal in no one save Christ alone."[30]

2. If Jesus is the Wisdom of God, then in him, in his limited human
words and deeds, in his life, death and resurrection, the mystery of
God's purpose and work in creation is revealed. If Wisdom is the divine Art at work in creation "luring" all things to be, and to become,
then the wonder of the incarnation is that this divine Wisdom has been
revealed in the human being, Jesus of Nazareth. Divine, cosmic Wisdom is revealed in this wise human being, filled with a sense of the
divine compassion, concerned with new familial relationships within
creation and with the Creator, and committed to radical inclusivity and
an option for the poor, the sick and the outcast. The Wisdom at work in
creation finds ultimate expression as compassionate love in the radical
vulnerability of the cross. *This* is the Wisdom of God, the Art of God at
work in creation and salvation.

3. Because of the resurrection of the crucified Jesus, it is no longer
simply divine Wisdom at work in continuous creation, but the risen
Jesus, Wisdom incarnate and the transforming power of his death and
resurrection that are at work in the universe. Jesus, now risen from the
dead, is identified with Wisdom's work of continuous creation and with
the reconciliation of all creatures. It is Wisdom who "orders all things
well" (Wis 8:1) and Wisdom made flesh in whom now "all things hold
together" (Col 1:17) and who now "sustains all things by his powerful
word" (Heb 1:3) and in whom all will be reconciled (Col 1:20).

4. This means that we must see the crucified and risen Jesus as achiev-
ing a radically new relationship with the universe. Karl Rahner has said
of Jesus: "When the vessel of his body was shattered in death, Christ
was poured out over the cosmos; he became actually, in his very humanity, what he had always been in his dignity, the very center of creation."[31] Jesus Christ, in the power of the resurrection, has become in
his humanity what the Wisdom of God always was, engaged with the
whole universe as a power at work shaping and transforming all things.
This means that the humanity of Jesus is eternally significant not only

for our salvation, but for the whole created universe. Jesus, like us a child of the universe, unlike us, the very Wisdom of God, is God's instrument in the transformation of the whole universe. Jesus of Nazareth, risen from the dead is (in the hypostatic union) one with the dynamic power which is at the heart of the cosmic process of galaxy formation and of evolutionary history on Earth.[32] It seems to me, that we have here, too, the basis for an understanding that our risen life in Christ will also consist of a new bodily relationship with the Earth and all its living creatures and with the whole material universe.

5. While the work of cosmic reconciliation has begun in Christ's resurrection, we live in a universe and a biotic community in which there is a good deal of ambiguity. It is a place of life and death, a place of goodness and suffering. It can be said that (nonhuman) creation needs redemption, not in a literal sense, as if creation had sinned and needed forgiveness, or was "fallen," but in the sense that it has not yet reached its goal, which is transfiguration in Christ. Meanwhile the power of resurrection is at work in creation, in a work which is not yet complete. The author of Colossians appears to have deliberately added to the great hymn to the cosmic Christ a reference to the blood of the cross (1:20). The cross is still at work, both in the world of human affairs and in the universe, which is reconciled in principle but still to be radically transformed.

6. The material universe, then, is neither simply a stage on which human beings play out their relationship with God nor a kind of launching pad for a more spiritual state of existence, a launching pad which will later become unnecessary.[33] The material universe itself will be transformed in the power of the risen Christ. The resurrection promise embraces not just human beings but the whole creation. The bodily resurrection of Jesus is the promise and the beginning of the reconciliation of "all things," whether "on earth or in heaven" through the blood of the cross (Col 1:20), of the "gathering up" of all things in Christ, "things in heaven and things on earth" (Eph 1:10), and of "a new heaven and a new earth" (Rv 21:1). As Paul said in Romans, creation "waits with eager longing," and "has been groaning with labor pains until now" in anticipation of liberation from the bondage to decay (Rom 8:18-23). Human beings form one universe with other creatures, and human bodiliness cannot be separated from the sphere of bodiliness—the physical universe. The whole universe itself will share in the consummation of all things in Christ.

7. At this stage science cannot predict whether the universe is "closed" and destined to end in fiery contraction, or "open" and destined for a cold and endless dissipation. Either way we seem to face extinction. It is possible that newer scientific paradigms will open up new possibilities. Ilya Prigogine and Isabelle Stengers point to the capacity for self-organization at the heart of the universe: "Instead of sliding into featurelessness, it rises out of featurelessness, growing rather than dying, developing new structures, processes and potentialities all the time, unfolding like a flower."[34] Science has hardly begun to explore this capacity for self-organization. But it must be admitted that mainstream cosmology puts before us a profoundly gloomy picture of the long-term future of the universe. What does a Christian theology have to say to this? I will return to this issue later in this book, but in the light of the Christian scriptures two affirmations can be made at this point: First, there is a promise in the resurrection that death does not have the last word either for individuals or for the universe, and that resurrection can transform not only individual bodies, but the universe itself; and second, the Christian scriptures do not suggest that this comes about simply through natural processes, but through an eschatological act of God in Jesus Christ (1 Cor 15:24-28; 1 Thes 5:1-10). Granted these affirmations, there is a further important question: Should we envisage this liberating eschatological action of God taking place in and through the processes of the universe, or should we think of the "old" creation coming to an end and being reconstituted by a new action of God from "outside"? I would argue for the first of these options. First, because it is far more congruent with everything we know of God's way of dealing with creation. Second, it respects the biblical teaching that divine Wisdom was always at work in creation, that all things were created "toward" Christ, and that through the risen Christ the reconciliation of the universe has already begun: "God was pleased to reconcile to himself all things, whether on earth or in heaven, by making peace through the blood of the cross" (Col 1:20). I find it difficult to believe that creation, which is the work of divine Wisdom and reconciled in Christ's blood, is to be put aside so that something new might be done.[35] Rather, if the risen Christ is already the secret heart and center of the created universe, then, through God's gracious act, the transformation of matter has begun from within the processes of the universe.

PART 2

THE TRINITARIAN GOD AND CREATION

*The Trinitarian God of Mutual Love
and Fecundity as the Center
of an Ecological Theology*

4.

The God of Mutual Love
and Ecstatic Fecundity

The focus of Part 2 of this book is on an ecological theology of the Trinity. It attempts to show how a Wisdom Christology can lead to an ecological understanding of God.

A theology of God which is faithful to the biblical tradition of Wisdom Christology outlined above needs to build on the following: the teaching of *the Wisdom literature* that Sophia is at work in all things, creating and sustaining them, and she delights in, and is revealed in, all creatures; the teaching and practice of *Jesus*, who, led by the Spirit, addresses God in familial terms as *Abba*, and shows God to be a God of radical compassion, a liberating and inclusive God, a God of intimate and familial relationships and a God who is imaged and revealed in the world of nature and daily life; the teaching of *the Wisdom Christologies* of the Christian scriptures, that the absolute foolishness and incomprehensibility of divine love for the world stands revealed in the horror of the cross, and that the whole universe is created in Christ and will be reconciled and transformed in the power of his resurrection already at work in creation.

This incomplete list is simply an attempt to bring to mind some of the key biblical insights that have been touched on in the development of a Wisdom Christology. It seems to me that an adequate view of God at work in the universe would need to include these insights in a creative and dynamic vision.

The main line of the Western theology of the Trinity runs through the work of Augustine and Thomas Aquinas and finds brilliant expression in this century in the work of theologians like Karl Barth and Karl

Rahner. This tradition obviously has much to offer our contemporary world. It has always been centered on relations and the divine communion. However, unlike the Eastern tradition, it has tended to focus on the *one divine nature* of God rather than on the salvific missions of the *Persons*. Its emphasis on the *being* or *substance* of God has sometimes obscured the ultimacy of *relationships*—although it must be said that for Aquinas, for example, relations remain central, and the being or substance of God is not at all static but radically relational. And its primary analogy or model is taken from the *psychology of an individual thinking and loving person*, rather than from the experience of *community*.[1]

In the light of contemporary individualism and the ecological crisis, and alongside the theology of Augustine and Aquinas, we need to retrieve a communal model of the Trinity. And, we need to attend particularly and consistently to the trinitarian relation with creatures. It is only through the self-expressive love of the Trinity directed toward us, and revealed in creation and the events of salvation, that we know anything about the Trinity at all. In much scholastic theology the emphasis shifted away from the Trinity's engagement in creation and salvation (the "economic" Trinity) toward abstract speculation on the Trinity in itself (the "immanent" Trinity). Catherine Mowry LaCugna has shown that this has meant a loss of the practical impact of the doctrine of the Trinity in Christian life.[2]

A number of contemporary theologians have developed trinitarian theologies that attempt to bring out more sharply the personal, relational and communal aspects of the tradition.[3] There is an important strand of the ancient tradition that can be a great resource for this contemporary work in the theologies of Richard of St. Victor and Bonaventure. In their different but related trinitarian models we can find approaches to the Trinity which are congruent with the tradition of divine Wisdom and of Wisdom Christology outlined above and which can speak to the ecological issues of today.

Both of these theologians stand in the tradition of Augustine, but they develop different approaches to Aquinas. Richard's model of mutual love and Bonaventure's dynamic model of a self-expressive goodness both offer useful and important insights for a contemporary theology of God's relationship with the world. In the following chapter, I will build on the theology of Richard and Bonaventure with six theses for a contemporary ecological doctrine of the Trinity.

The Trinity as Mutual Love—Richard of St. Victor

Augustine's theology, while giving primacy to the psychological model of the Trinity, contains reference to another more social approach to the Trinity, where the image is of the lover, the beloved and their love.[4] Neither Augustine nor his successors explored this approach. However, it was taken up in the twelfth century by Richard of St. Victor, who built his theology of the Trinity on the basis of reflection on the experience of human friendship. As Zachary Hayes had said, Richard "chose an element which was marginal in Augustine and placed it in the center of his own thought."[5]

Michael Schmaus is of the opinion that there are only two major trinitarian theories in medieval theology: that of Augustine, Anselm and Peter Lombard, which culminates in Aquinas; and the one inaugurated by Richard of St. Victor, which culminates with Bonaventure.[6] Within the whole Western tradition, William Hill observes, it is Richard who "opens the way for a social rather than a psychological model for thinking about the Trinity."[7]

It is difficult to read Richard today without being struck by the contemporary "feel" of his analysis. He was born in Scotland and joined the Canons of St. Victor in Paris soon after 1150, at a young age.[8] They were a vigorous and productive intellectual community, and Richard emerged as one of their leading thinkers, developing a unique theological style based upon faith, experience and reason.[9] He has been criticized for seeming to attempt to "prove" the necessity of the Trinity, a doctrine which, as all theologians agree, depends upon revelation and cannot be proved from reason.[10] There is no doubt that Richard speaks of "necessary reasons" for the Trinity, and that this language is misleading. It seems clear, however, that Richard is not interested in attempting a proof of the Trinity from reason, but that he is presuming the context of strong Christian faith and the doctrine of the Trinity, and then using reason and analogy to seek further understanding and to demonstrate the intelligibility of revealed doctrine.[11]

Richard's interest in human friendship and its interrelationship with divine love is part of a wider pattern of interest in friendship in the twelfth century. The new religious orders of this period, particularly the Cistercians, found recruits among adults who were intensely interested in questions of friendship and love.[12] In a recent study of the monastic experience of friendship, Brian Patrick McGuire argues that the twelfth century in Western Europe, particularly in England and Northern France, was uniquely "the age of friendship." It was a period in which friendships were cultivated in the monasteries, understood as part of the life of union with God, and discussed with intensity in conversations, letters and in major treatises.[13]

Ewert Cousins also notes that Richard lived in a century that marks a turning point in the history of love in Western culture.[14] He points out that at the end of the eleventh century the troubadours of southern France had created a new vision of romantic love in their Provencal poetry. In the twelfth century Christian theologians were exploring both Christian friendship and the love of mystical union with God. It was in this period that Bernard of Clairvaux composed his sermons on the Canticle of Canticles and his *Liber de Diligendo Deo*, Aelred of Rievaulx wrote his *Speculum Caritatis* and *De Spirituali Amicitia*, and William of St. Thierry his *De Natura et Dignitate Amoris*.[15]

Friendship and Mutual Love in God

Richard's uniqueness is in his application of this reflection on Christian friendship and love to the central mystery of the Trinity. He begins from an understanding of God as supreme goodness, which he establishes in the first two books of *De Trinitate*. Such goodness, he argues, must involve full and perfect love. But love which is centered on the self cannot be considered to be the fullness of love or charity. If there is the fullness of love in God, then it cannot be self-love or private love (*amor privatus*), but love which involves more than one person (*amor mutuus* or *caritas*).

Where there is the total fullness of goodness, true and supreme charity cannot be lacking. For nothing is better than charity; nothing is more perfect than charity. However, no one is properly said to have charity on the basis of the private love of oneself. And so it is necessary for love to be directed toward another for it to be charity. Therefore, where a plurality of persons is lacking, charity cannot exist.[16]

In this way Richard's thought moves from the fullness of goodness in God to self-transcending love, to the plurality of Persons. He supports this by a second argument, which is a reflection on the divine happiness. Arguing on the basis of human experience, Richard suggests that perfect happiness involves mutual love.

It is a characteristic of love, and one without which it cannot possibly exist, to wish to be loved much by the one whom you love much. Therefore love cannot be pleasing if it is not mutual. Therefore in that true and supreme happiness, just as pleasing love cannot be lacking, so mutual love (*amor mutuus*) cannot be lacking.[17]

To the arguments from goodness and happiness Richard adds a third, from the divine glory and benevolence. It is of the nature of divine glory to be benevolent in self-communication. How could we understand the benevolence of God, if God kept the abundance of divine fullness to God's self "in a miserly fashion" and refused to communicate this abundance?[18] Since God is no miser, Richard argues that in God there must be the mutual giving of interpersonal self-communication.

Richard reflects on what he takes to be supreme human experience of mutual interrelationship in friendship and love; he argues that if God is abundantly good, happy and glorious, then there must be in God a self-transcending love and real communication and profound interrelationship.

The Unity in God

Ewert Cousins points out that the reason Richard's position does not lead in the direction of tritheism, but to a deep sense of the unity of the Trinity, is because he is not thinking of human beings as isolated, autonomous selves, standing apart from others. His vision of the human person involves self-transcending love for others and a human degree of union with others. He sees human beings as communal beings. However, the human person, because of finitude, remains separate from others, in some degree of anxiety and fear about union with others.

But the trinitarian God is not restricted to the limited communal life possible to human beings. Richard sees the Trinity as "the ideal of interpersonal relations because here there is infinite self-giving and infinite reception of love." In the fullness of divine love the trinitarian Persons give of themselves infinitely without fear of losing themselves or of being rejected by the other.[19] The limited and imperfect human experience of self-transcendence in love points to the infinitely more profound experience of trinitarian communion.

Having argued toward an understanding of the plurality of Persons in God, Richard's second step is to insist that the love among them must not only be mutual but also a love between equals. Since "nothing is more glorious, more magnificent than to wish to have nothing that you do not wish to share," we can conceive of the Persons in God only as sharing equally from all eternity.[20] Supreme charity demands equality of Persons. For supreme charity, the beloved must be loved supremely and return love in the same way.

> And so in mutual love, fullness of charity demands that each be supremely loved by the other and consequently, according to the previously mentioned norm of discretion, that each ought to be loved supremely. However where each ought to be loved equally, it is necessary that each be equally perfect. And so it is necessary that each one be equally powerful, equally wise, equally good, equally blessed. So supreme fullness of love demands supreme equality of perfections in those loved mutually. And so in true Divinity, as the particular nature of charity demands a plurality of persons, so the integrity of the same charity requires supreme equality of persons in true plurality.[21]

This kind of supreme equality and mutuality can only be understood as involving profound unity. Every perfection is common to divine Persons who are mutually loving and loved. Divinity is one, and belongs to all the Persons.[22] The divine substance, which for Richard "is nothing other than Divinity itself," is common to the Persons. Richard thus concludes this stage of the argument by reference to the Athanasian Creed: "Therefore see by what a wonderful reasoning there is substantial unity in the plurality of Persons and a personal plurality in a true unity of substance, so that there is also 'individuality in persons and unity in substance and equality in majesty.'"[23]

The Generosity of Mutual Love Demands More than Two

The third step in Richard's argument is to establish the meaning of the third in the Trinity. He argues from a subtle psychological reflection on Christian friendship that mutual love demands a third. Ewert Cousins, interpreting Richard, writes that in friendship that is limited to two, "their personal encounter can shatter the wall of isolation, but their new-found union can set up new walls that will keep the rest of the world out."[24] In Richard's thought, this would not be mature or Christian love. In his thought, "the very dynamism that led to self-transcendence in uniting the two, now leads to a further transcendence from the sphere of the two alone to the third."[25]

For perfect love we look for one who can share in love for the beloved. Richard speaks of this person as the *"condilectus."*[26] This word seems to be his own invention. It refers to one who is "loved with," and to one who shares in love for a third. This analysis reveals an acute insight into the altruistic character of love. The lover wishes to share with a third the joy that the lover feels in the beloved. At the same time, the generosity of love is such that the lover wishes for the third to be loved by the beloved. Richard develops his understanding of *"condilectio"* in this way:

> When one person gives love to another and . . . alone loves only the other, there certainly is love (*dilectio*), but it is not a shared love (*condilectio*). When two love each other mutually (*mutuo diligent*) and give to each other the affection of supreme longing; when the affection of the first goes out to the second and the affection for the second goes out to the first and tends as it were in diverse ways—in this case there certainly is love (*dilectio*) on both sides, but it is not shared love (*condilectio*). Shared love (*condilectio*) is properly said to exist when a third person is loved by two persons harmoniously (*concorditer diligitur*) and in community (*socialiter amatur*), and the affection for the two persons is fused into one affection by the flame of love for the third.[27]

From this it is evident that the supreme form of love would have no place in the Divinity if there were not three Persons in God. For Richard, mutual love involves communal love. He speaks of "concordant love" (*concordialis charitas*) and "consocial love" (*consocialis amor*).[28]

The Supreme Mutuality of Trinitarian Love

This supreme form of love is beyond human beings, and is never found in any individual. In the Trinity, concordant love flows dynamically in all directions:

> Consider now how union with a third person establishes concordant affection everywhere and brings about consocial love through all and in all. If you direct your attention to any one among these three persons, you will see that the other two love the third concordantly. If you turn your attention to the second, there in like manner you will find that the remaining pair unite with equal desire in love for him. If you bring the third of these into consideration, without doubt you will see that the affection of the others flows in equal harmony to the third.[29]

There is no hint of subordination or hierarchy here, but completely communal mutuality. There is no relegation of the third in God to a passive role, but complete mutuality. In fact, in all of the crucial third chapter of *De Trinitate*, the emphasis is on mutuality, with no real attempt to account for what is distinct to the three Persons.

Richard reinforces mutuality in the Trinity by returning to the theme of supreme and total equality, and by showing how each Person must be understood as sharing equally and completely in divine simplicity. This equality and simplicity is of such a nature that "supreme and supremely simple being is common to all."[30] They share one and the same essence. The Trinity is thus unlike all other beings who are equal or similar to one another, and yet remain distinct and separate substances. Equality in the Trinity means far more than this. It means a unity of substance, so that "the supreme and supremely simple being which belongs to one person in this fullness and perfection also belongs to each other person in this fullness and perfection."[31] Sharing in the same substance means that there is a "coequality" of greatness in the Trinity, so that one Person in the Trinity cannot be greater or less than any other Person. All three Persons are coeternal and coequal.

Later in *De Trinitate* Richard does discuss the distinctions of the trinitarian Persons in terms of the processions of love: there is supreme love as freely given (the First Person), supreme love as received (the Third Person) and supreme love as received and given (the Second Person).[32] The Begotten One (the "nascible") both receives from the Unbegotten (the "innascible") and gives to the Third.

But in Richard the Spirit is not, as for Augustine, the love of the Father and the Son for each other.[33] There is no sense of a passive Spirit. Rather the Spirit is understood as a fully personal and relational existence of the divine Love.[34] Nor is there any kind of hierarchy of power or love. Richard points out that it is appropriate to attribute power to the First Person, wisdom to the Second and goodness or love to the Third.[35] But each Person possesses these attributes fully. The order of processions of love within the Trinity distinguishes the Persons but does not deny total equality and the supreme interaction of completely mutual love. Trinitarian life remains a completely mutual and equal giving and receiving of love. There is no difference in love or dignity.[36]

In his survey of social models of the Trinity, William Hill says of Richard's model that it is "possibly the most penetrating to be found anywhere."[37] It is significant for today's theology for a number of reasons. First, it faithfully reflects the biblical account of the economy of salvation. It reflects the love revealed in Jesus—both the divine "foolishness" of the cross and the love at work in creation through the power of the resurrection (1 Cor 1-2; Jn 3:16). It reflects not only the mission of divine Wisdom, but also the mission of the Holy Spirit who is love— "God's love has been poured into our hearts through the Holy Spirit that has been given to us" (Rom 5:5). It reflects Jesus' teaching and practice of a God who is boundlessly compassionate love, can be approached familiarly as *Abba*. It is faithful to the repeated biblical statement that "God is love" (1 Jn 4:8,16). It is also faithful to what the Scriptures suggest about the dynamic and overflowing love at the heart of divine interrelationships (Jn 14:10-11; 14:15-31; 15:9-17; 17:20-25).

Second, it can provide the basis for moving from a worldview and a metaphysics centered on being or substance to one centered on dynamic relationships. If mutual relationships are at the center of one's view of reality, then, as Catherine LaCugna says, an ontology of relationships can replace an ontology of substance.[38] In trinitarian thinking substance and relation are not opposed. The trinitarian tradition has always held that divine substance is relational. John Zizioulas writes that God's being is identical with an act of communion. This means that the ontological question (what something is) "is not answered by pointing to the 'self-existent,' to a being which is determined by its own boundaries, but to a being which in its *ekstasis* breaks through these boundaries in a movement of communion."[39] Ultimate reality centers on personhood and ecstatic, self-transcending communion. Reality is being-in-communion. This has important implications for thinking about creation. Big Bang cosmology reveals our common history and our interconnectedness with all other creatures of the universe. Quantum mechanics tell us that we live in reality, which is more a network of relationships than a world of substances. The ecological crisis forces us to begin to think relationally and to begin to see our own interconnectedness in the delicate web of life. Richard's trinitarian theology suggests that relationships of mutual love are the foundation of all reality. It argues that all creation springs from this dynamism of mutual love. Relationality is the source of creaturehood. An understanding of the Trinity as fundamentally relational can "breathe fire into the equations" of physics and provide the theological basis for an ecological ethics.[40] In such a theology human beings are challenged to see themselves in profound interrelationship with other creatures before a relational God.

Third, this communal view of the Trinity is a practical doctrine which offers a radical critique of the sinful structures of patriarchy and racism and all other forms of the oppressor-oppressed relationship.[41] It challenges all attempts at self-assertion at the expense of others, all patterns of domination, with a vision of a world built around mutual and equal relationships. The experience of genuine mutuality in relationship, central to much feminist reflection, is here named as the very center of reality and as its final meaning.

Fourth, this trinitarian theology can ground a theology of church as *koinonia* or *communio*. It provides a proper foundation for the worldwide movement of basic ecclesial communities and the rediscovery that real experience of community in face-to-face groups, meeting around the gospel and life, can lead to liberating praxis. It commits Christians to the fostering of communal and participatory life in the larger worlds of social interaction and politics. It gives ultimate meaning to our experiences of mutual friendship and places them in a profound context.

This friendship includes, of course, the friendship within Christian marriage. Ewert Cousins remarks: "Although drawn from the experience of friendship, Richard's thought here has special relevance to the love of husband and wife which overflows itself and expresses itself in their children."[42] I would suggest, as well, that this love can be seen as overflowing into hospitality, other relationships, work, community involvements and political action.

The Universe as the Self-Expression of God—Bonaventure

God as Dynamic, Ecstatic and Fecund

Ewert Cousins points out that while process theologians offer a critique of the God of classical theism, whom they see as the "Unmoved Mover," a God who is completely transcendent and unrelated to creation, "they have not taken into account the fecundity tradition of the Middle Ages, which proposes an image of God as dynamic and related to the world, not wholly unlike their own."[43]

The key figure in this tradition is Bonaventure (1221-1274). Bonaventure joined the Franciscans at an early age, was accepted as a Doctor of the University of Paris, and became Minister General of the Franciscan order in 1257. Zachary Hayes shows how Bonaventure's work reflects the interest of the early Franciscan movement in the theological implications of Francis's religious experience, above all in two key areas: the experience of the goodness of God, and the experience of creation as expressive of this divine goodness.[44]

Although he clearly stands in the Western Latin tradition, Bonaventure's thought owes much to the East, particularly to the concept of the dynamic fruitfulness of divine goodness. The first name of God is the Good (Lk 18:19), and goodness is self-communicative.[45] Bonaventure inherits from Pseudo-Dionysius the axiom that goodness is self-diffusive (*bonum diffusivum sui*), and this becomes one of the basic metaphysical principles underlying his theology of the Trinity and of creation. If goodness is self-diffusive, then the highest good will be most radically self-diffusive and fecund.[46]

Bonaventure's theology is built on the experience of God's action in the economy of salvation and in creation. His theological vision is determined by the missions of the Word and the Spirit. He sees creation as the expression of divine goodness. But he understands the divine self-expression in creation as pointing to a far greater self-expression within the life of the Trinity:

> For the diffusion that occurred in time in the creation of the world is no more than a pivot or point in comparison with the immensity of the eternal goodness. From this one is led to think of another and a greater diffusion—that in which the diffusing one communicates to another total substance and nature.[47]

With regard to creation, the Trinity is dynamic, self-expressive and fecund. But this dynamism, self-expression and fecundity in creation point to these realities existing in a boundless way in the Trinity itself.[48] As Ewert Cousins observes, "By placing absolute fecundity in the Trinity, Bonaventure has saved both God and the world."[49] He has rescued the transcendence of divine fecundity, which is such that it cannot be exhausted by creation. God is not swallowed up in creation. On the other hand, creatures are free to be their specific and limited selves, not overwhelmed by the divine power and immensity.

In the Trinity there is a procession of the Word by way of nature and a procession of the Spirit by way of liberality and love.[50] The first procession springs from the One who is the Principle, the "Fountain Fullness" (*fontalis plenitudo*) within God. The trinitarian God is the rich fountain from which the entire universe flows. But, as Zachary Hayes writes, "Bonaventure pushes beyond this to argue that the concept of primacy may be traced into the depths of the divine nature itself where it may be seen as the characteristic of the first person."[51] The First Person receives an emphasis which is foreign to the thought of Augustine and Aquinas and is similar to the classical Eastern theology. This One who is "Fountain Fullness" is central to Bonaventure's metaphysic of *exitus* and *reditus*, for the *fontalis plenitudo* is the source of all and the goal to which all returns.

This trinitarian vision brings with it a wonderful dynamism and a fidelity to the scriptures, but it also carries dangers of subordinationism (which Bonaventure avoids) and the hierarchies of neoplatonism. These dangers must be faced, and it is one of the reasons why I have given primacy to Richard of St. Victor's social model of the Trinity and its stress on mutuality and equality. Set in this context, Bonaventure's ecstatic understanding of the fountain fullness in God is a rich resource for a dynamic view of God and creation. In the context of Richard's theology, Bonaventure's dynamic vision can be understood within a theology of radical mutuality.

The Word is the self-expression of the divine fecundity, the self-expression of the good. The Word proceeds from the Fountain Fullness by way of *nature*, rather than by way of intellect, as in Augustine and Aquinas. This procession arises by way of nature from the fecund, ecstatic divine goodness. Goodness needs to communicate itself. The Word is the full expression of God's primal fruitfulness. Here we come upon a second crucial metaphysical principle of Bonaventure's trinitarian theology, that of exemplarity. Bonaventure sees the Word proceeding in an exemplary manner, which means that the Word is the self-expression of the Fountain Fullness, the unqualified Image of the First Person.

The Holy Spirit is Love. If the Word proceeds by way of the nature of self-diffusive divine goodness, then the Spirit can be understood as proceeding from the will, by way of liberality and love. Bonaventure also thinks of the Trinity in terms of mutual love, following Richard of St. Victor, and this line of thought is evident in his consideration of the procession of the Spirit.[52] He uses the concept of perfect love which is freely shared to show that in the Trinity there must be both *dilectio* and *condilectio*.[53] The intimacy between First and Second Persons is so great that the Spirit proceeds from them as from one principle.[54] The Spirit is the mutual love of the Word and the Fountain Fullness, and can be called Love and Gift, and the Bond (*nexus*).[55] Love is rightly attributed to all three Persons (essential love), and there is mutual love between the First and Second Persons (notional love) and from this mutual love there proceeds the Spirit who is Love (personal love).

Like Richard of St. Victor, Bonaventure insists on the supreme dynamic unity of the Trinity. He speaks of supreme "communicability," supreme "consubstantiality," supreme "conformability," supreme "coequality," and supreme "coeternity." All of this leads him to speak, in a way that is quite reminiscent of Richard, of supreme "cointimacy," and then, in an original move, to use the word "*circumincessio*" to describe this mutual interaction:

> Finally, from all that has been said, they must have supreme mutual intimacy, by which one person is necessarily in the other by

reason of their supreme being-in-one-another (*circumincessio*), and one acts with the other through the absolute indivision of the substance, power and action of the most Blessed Trinity itself.[56]

Bonaventure may have been the first in the West to use the term *circumincessio*, the equivalent of the Greek word *perichōrēsis*, which expresses the idea of persons in a profound and dynamic communion of interdependence and mutuality. He had earlier used this term in his *Commentary on the Sentences of Peter Lombard,* where he points to its scriptural foundation in the words, "I am in the Father and the Father is in me" (Jn 14:11).[57] As Congar says, this word *circumincessio* "points to a mysterious but admirable aspect to the life of the Trinity as a life of *Persons* in unity of nature."[58] It points to mutual interpersonal relations and mutual indwelling.

Thomas Aquinas used a parallel word, *circuminsessio*, from *circum-in-sedere*, to "sit around."[59] Bonaventure's term is far more dynamic. *Circumincessio* comes from *circum-incedere*, to "move around one another." It brings to mind the image of the divine dance, a dance of unthinkable intimacy and mutual love, a dance which freely overflows in creation and becomes expressed in the dance of the universe.

The Divine Exemplar

For Bonaventure, the life of the Trinity originates eternally from the One who is Fountain Fullness (*fontalis plenitudo*).[60] This Fountain Fullness expresses itself perfectly in the One who is Image and Word. This process reaches its consummation in the One who is the love between them, the Spirit.

The *Word* is Bonaventure's favorite title for the Second Person of the Trinity. He prefers it to Son because while Son expresses the relation of generation between First and Second Persons, Word expresses not only the relation with the First Person, but also the relation with creation, revelation and salvation.[61]

The Word expresses and represents the infinite creative power of the Fountain Fullness, and thus represents all possible things. The infinite variety of things is given unified expression in the Word. The Word is the locus of the divine ideas. These divine ideas give rise to the created world, in God's free choice to create. They are dynamic causes of creation.

In this theology, individual things in their distinctness, not just pla-
tonic universals, really are in God, in the divine Word.[62] The Word expresses and represents the ideas of all created things. These ideas, which
are contained in the Word in divine simplicity, are the exemplary causes
of all creatures. Thus the Word is called the eternal Exemplar. On the
one hand the Word is understood as the self-expression of the trinitarian
God, and on the other hand the Word is the Exemplar for every created
reality.[63] Here, in the eternal Word, is the "eternal Art" (*ars aeterna*) of
the trinitarian God.[64] From this eternal Art the truth and beauty of all
things flow.

While at one level the whole Trinity is exemplary with regard to the
world, this exemplary role is concentrated in the Second Person.
Bonaventure makes it clear that to speak of the Word as divine Exemplar is not simply an appropriation, but is proper to the Second Person.[65] It springs from the trinitarian processions: the Word is the Image
of the Fountain Fullness, and the divine Exemplar for creation.

Creation as God's Self-Expression

In Bonaventure's thought the dynamic goodness of the Fountain Fullness finds expression in the Trinity, and freely "explodes into a thousand forms" in the world of creation.[66]

The first cycle of emanation of Word and Spirit with regard to the
Trinity springs from the very being of God. But the second cycle of
emanation, exemplarity and consummation with regard to creation
springs entirely from the divine free choice to create.[67] Through free
choice, the Fountain Fullness of divine goodness "explodes" into what
is not God, into creatures which are not God, but are God's self-expression.

Bonaventure's view of creatures is that they exist by way of exemplary causality. An exemplary cause is the pattern, model or exemplar
according to which something is made. The Word is the Exemplar for
all things. This means that all creatures must be understood as revelatory signs of God. Bonaventure writes that creatures seem to be "nothing less than a kind of representation of the wisdom of God, and a kind
of sculpture." [68] They are the work of art produced by divine Wisdom.
He tells us that "every creature is of its very nature a likeness and re-
semblance to eternal wisdom."[69] This is not an accidental property of
creatures, but something that belongs to their very substance. It is an

intrinsic characteristic of creatures that they represent and give expression to the Wisdom of God.[70]

For Bonaventure, then, the universe is a book which can be read, a book whose words reveal the Creator:

> From this we may gather that the universe is like a book *reflecting*, *representing* and *describing* its Maker, the Trinity, at three different levels of expression: as a *trace* (*vestigium*), an *image*, and a *likeness*. The aspect of trace is found in every creature; the aspect of image, in the intellectual creatures or rational spirits; the aspect of likeness, only in those who are God-conformed.[71]

Human beings are made in the image of God, through the powers of memory, intellect and will, and when they turn toward God in conscious attention and love they are true images of God. When human beings are transformed by the Holy Spirit through grace, they are not simply images of God but the very likeness of God.

These human beings, if it were not for the distortion of sin, would be able to read the book of creation and come to know God: "In the state of innocence, when the image had not yet been distorted but was conformed to God through grace, the book of creation sufficed to enable humanity to receive the light of divine Wisdom."[72] In fact, fallen human beings are like illiterates with little appreciation of the book that lies open before them. They need the second book of the scriptures to read the book of the universe. Bonaventure insists that the book of scripture and God's gift of grace are both absolutely necessary for fallen human beings to reach a full understanding of what lies before them.

What is this vestige of the Trinity that we find in all creatures? It is the reflection in a creature of the Trinity as efficient, exemplary and final cause of the creature's inner structure. The First Person of the Trinity is reflected as the Power that holds the creature in being (efficient causality). The Second Person is reflected as the Wisdom, or the Exemplar, by which it is created (exemplary causality). The Third Person is reflected as the Goodness which will bring the creature to its consummation (final causality).

Leonard Bowman points out the important consequence of Bonaventure's linking of creatures and God by way of triple causality:

This sets his world-view apart from a Neoplatonic exemplarism which sees the universe as a hierarchical chain of being ordered by degrees of participation in being, so that the further down the hierarchy one goes the weaker and dimmer the reflection of being. For Bonaventure, every single creature from the angel to the grain of sand has its direct model and foundation in the Word . . . Each being is equally close to God, though the mode of relationship differs according to the capacity of the creature.[73].

This equality in degree of closeness with God, coupled with the teaching that every creature is the divine self-expression, provides a strong basis for an ecological theology.

The center of Bonaventure's thought about creation has to do with exemplary causality, because here we see, in the very form of a creature, its reference to the Exemplar. From exemplary causality comes the truth, form, species (intelligibility), number and beauty of a creature.[74] The truth of an eagle—its intelligibility, form, proportions and beauty—is constituted by the eagle's relationship to the exemplary cause, which is the eternal Art.

Bonaventure gives a special place to number:

Therefore, since all things are beautiful and in some way delightful, and since beauty and delight do not exist without proportion, and since proportion exists primarily in numbers, all things are subject to number. Hence number is the principal exemplar in the mind of the Creator, and in all things, the principal vestige leading to Wisdom.[75]

Beauty is understood as a matter of number, in the sense of being a matter of proportion between the whole and parts, of unity in multiplicity.[76] This unity in multiplicity points to the Exemplar, and in and through the Exemplar to the profound unity of the three Persons in the Trinity.

Bonaventure has a special word, *contuition*, to describe a way of seeing creatures in their relationship to God. It implies a simultaneous awareness of the reality of, for example, a giant sequoia tree, and of its eternal Exemplar. Contuition does not bypass the tree, nor is it limited only to the tree. It implies a real awareness of this specific sequoia tree *together with* a consciousness of divine presence. In fact, the tree itself is only known fully and ultimately when it is known in relationship to its eternal Exemplar.

In this life, the apprehension of eternal ideas is veiled, distorted by sin, and indirect, but it is real. Bonaventure tells us that the "First Principle created this perceptible world as a means of self-revelation so that, like a mirror (*speculum*) or a footprint (*vestigium*), it might lead the human being to love and praise God the artisan."[77] By gazing at a sequoia tree we can allow it to speak to us as sign, which points beyond itself to the Exemplar which it reflects and signifies.

> Therefore, whoever is not enlightened by such great splendour in created things is blind; whoever remains unheedful of such great outcries is deaf; whoever does not praise God in all these effects is dumb; whoever does not turn to the First Principle after so many signs is a fool. Open your eyes, therefore; alert the ears of your spirit, unlock your lips, and apply your heart that you may see, hear, praise, love and adore, magnify and honour your God in every creature, lest perchance, the entire universe rise up against you.[78]

Bonaventure's theology is relevant for a number of reasons. First, it is a trinitarian theology which is directly related to the economy of salvation. It springs from the biblical account of God's self-communication to us in Word and in Spirit. As Zachary Hayes says, Bonaventure's view is that of a "consistent economic Trinitarianism."[79]

Second, it is evident that the whole structure of Bonaventure's thought is consistent with, and expressive of, a biblical Wisdom Christology. His own preference for the expression *Word* reinforces this argument, because the Word is understood as the Image of the Fountain Fullness of God, as Exemplar for all creatures, and as God's self-expression in revelation and salvation. All of these concepts reflect the theology of the Wisdom literature, and the Wisdom texts of the Christian scriptures, which I have outlined above.

Third, Bonaventure's thought about God is dynamic and processive. In his theology, creation is the free self-expression of an ecstatic and fecund God. And this ecstasy and fecundity are located at the heart of the dynamic reality of the Trinity. Bonaventure cannot be fitted into the school of process theology connected with Whitehead, but I would argue that, in a more general sense, Bonaventure's theology is very much a process theology. The primacy he gives to the concept of the Fountain Fullness means that his theology of Trinity is dynamic and fruitful. Creation can be understood as the "free overflow of God's necessary, inner-divine fruitfulness."[80] This dynamic view of God is congruent with a worldview of emergence, with Big Bang cosmology and its understanding of the expanding universe, and with the evolutionary history of life on Earth.[81]

Fourth, Bonaventure's theology of the Holy Spirit's work of bringing the whole universe into consummation in God has great significance, but only when its neoplatonic view of consummation is radically corrected by a more biblical and Franciscan view. Bonaventure, under the influence of the *exitus-reditus* schema, saw created things as coming to their consummation in God mainly through human beings bringing with them elements of creation as they ascend toward God. He saw material creation as being mediated and transformed in the human eternal destiny with God.[82] This needs to be corrected by a more biblical vision of God's transformation of the created world itself. It is not that we ascend to God, leaving most of creation behind, but that God will be revealed as dwelling in the midst of creation, bringing healing and liberation to all creatures (Is 11:6-9, 65:17-25; 2 Cor 5:17; Rom 8:18-25; Col 1:15-20; Rv 21). The Christian theology of the resurrection challenges the neoplatonic schema at this fundamental point, asserting that the whole of creation matters to God and will share in the transforming power of the resurrection of Jesus. It will be this world that will be transformed. Karl Rahner insists that Christians who believe in the resurrection must take matter seriously. We should be the most "sublime of materialists," since "we cannot think of any ultimate fulfillment of the human spirit without thinking at the same time of matter enduring and reaching its perfection."[83]

Fifth, Bonaventure's trinitarian theology has profound ecological consequences. Every creature is an aspect of God's self-expression in the world. In its inner structure every creature reflects God's dynamic trinitarian presence as holding the creature in existence (the Fountain Fullness), as exemplary cause (divine Wisdom) and final cause (the Spirit of Love). Every creature in its form, proportion and beauty reflects the Word and Wisdom of God, the divine Exemplar. Every creature is a revelatory word written in the great book of creation. Every species, every ecosystem, the whole biosphere, every grain of sand and every galaxy, is a self-expression of the eternal Art of divine Wisdom. For Bonaventure, there is no simple identification between God and the world, no hint of pantheism. But his teaching could be described as a kind of panentheism. As Ewert Cousins writes, "In a most emphatic way for Bonaventure, God is in the world and the world is in God."[84] God is profoundly present to all things, and God is expressed in all things, so that each creature is a symbol and a sacrament of God's presence and trinitarian life. All creatures are like stained-glass windows, reflecting the divine: "As a ray of light entering though a window is colored in different ways according to the different colors of the various parts, so the divine ray shines forth in each and every creature in different ways and in different properties."[85]

5.

An Ecological Theology
of the Trinity

Some Theses

No one theology of the relationship of the trinitarian God to creation will ever say all that ought to be said. There is no one theology which can encapsulate the mystery. There is always need to say more and the need to say "but" to what has already been said. There is a need to recognize that here we come up against the limits of our theological models and analogies.

I have been suggesting that it may be helpful to borrow elements from both Richard of St. Victor and Bonaventure, and to see the trinitarian relations with creation in terms of both a model of mutual relationships and a model of dynamic and ecstatic self-communication. These different models allow different sides of the trinitarian relationship with creation to be stressed. They function in a complementary fashion, bringing out different dimensions of the relationship.

There can be a tension between an emphasis on mutuality, equality and the divine perichoresis on the one hand, and an emphasis on trinitarian dynamism, relationships of origin, the distinction of Persons and the dynamic relationship with creation on the other.

This tension has always existed in trinitarian theology. To some extent, it is reflected in the difference between the Western emphasis on the unity of the divine nature and the Eastern emphasis on the Persons. Both emphases are needed. The emphasis on unity and mutuality, when taken alone, can lead to a neglect of trinitarian dynamism and of the distinction of Persons and of their distinct role in creation and redemption. The emphasis on dynamism can lead to a neglect of mutuality and to an exaggerated concept of the primacy or monarchy of the First Person as the unoriginate origin of the other Persons. What is needed is to hold together radical mutuality, equality and perichoresis with a dynamic understanding of the distinct roles of the trinitarian Persons in creation and redemption.

In many circles today there is an understandable rejection of distinctions based on hierarchies. There is a well-founded fear that the claiming of such distinctions and differences can contribute to the legitimation of hierarchies of power and patriarchal structures. It has become obvious that those with an interest in preserving patriarchal structures appeal to the differences between men and women to keep women in their place. Racial supremacists stress the differences between races in order to establish their own dominance. It is clear that an uncritical emphasis on distinctions has been connected to attitudes of sexual, racial and national superiority. It has contributed to structures which have excluded some people from power and attempted to maintain them in dependency and poverty. But, of course, there is also the opposite danger to keep in mind—that an uncritical emphasis on equality can lead to intolerance of differences and a stifling of unique gifts. A trinitarian theology needs to be critically aware of the dangers of subordinationist and monarchical views of trinitarian distinctions, and yet not abandon its insights into the distinct Persons and their roles in creation and redemption.[1]

Authentic trinitarian doctrine is a constant reminder that mutuality and distinction are not to be seen as opposites, but as always requiring each other. Genuine mutuality of relationships will always involve dynamic distinctions. Both are essential for trinitarian theology. My argument is that for a contemporary theology of ongoing creation, and for a critically aware ecological theology, it is important to keep in mind two complementary trinitarian principles: the principle of mutual relationships on the one hand, and the principle of distinction, dynamism and process on the other. The first of these I find highly developed in Richard of St. Victor and the second in Bonaventure.

In what follows, I will attempt to build on these two principles to outline a contemporary ecological theology of the divine relationship with the universe. I will do this through a series of six theses. The earlier theses will encapsulate material discussed in the last chapter, and will need little comment here. The last two theses will need more discussion.

Thesis 1: The Trinity can be understood as Persons-In-Mutual-Relationship, in a communion of love which is radically equal and one; creation can be understood as this Trinity's free, loving relationship with a world of creatures.

This view of the Trinity reflects the experience of God's self-communication in the mission of the Holy Spirit and in Jesus the Wisdom of God. The Holy Spirit is experienced as the outpouring of love: "God's love has been poured out in our hearts through the Holy Spirit" (Rom 5:5). Jesus is the presence of divine love in human form, the very incarnation of love for creation (Jn 3:16), and in him, we are invited into divine friendship—"I call you friends" (Jn 15:15).

As Richard of St. Victor has made clear, our experience of mutual human friendship gives us a glimpse into what is at the heart of trinitarian life. His theology is based on the understanding that human friendship and love, in spite of all their limitations, point to, and in some way can already embody, divine love.

Richard's conviction that God is supreme goodness leads him to the idea that in God there must be the supreme experience of goodness, which he takes to be self-transcending, altruistic love. The experience of self-transcending love, of love which breaks out of the bonds of the self to reach out to another, must be in God. Such love longs to be shared with a third, the *condilectus*. This divine love of the trinitarian Persons reaches a communion, an intimacy, a unity which is so radical and profound that we can say that God is one. The experience of limited human self-transcending love points to the infinitely more profound experience of trinitarian communion and friendship.

According to Richard, this profoundly mutual friendship of the trinitarian Persons is the source of the perfect happiness that is at the heart of trinitarian life. This divine delight spills over into trinitarian relations with creatures. In Proverbs we find Sophia claiming that she was daily God's "delight" and that she "rejoices" before God always. She tells how with God, she "rejoices" in the inhabited world, and "delights" in the human race (8:30-31). A trinitarian theology, above all one informed by a Wisdom Christology, will be a theology of divine delight. Delight is at the heart of the communion in God and of the divine communion with human beings and with all creatures.

But if this model for understanding the trinitarian God's relationship with the world is to be understood in all its radicality, it must be understood not simply on the basis of human friendship, and not only in terms of divine delight in creation, but be seen afresh in the light of the absolute excess of love revealed in the cross of Jesus (1 Cor 1:22-25). It is the foolishness of love revealed to us in the cross of Jesus that stands behind the biblical claim that "God is love" (1 Jn 4:7-16).

It is this understanding of the love poured out on the cross that informs our understanding of the mutual love of the trinitarian Persons, of their invitation to human beings to enter into the mutuality of trinitarian friendship (Jn 15:15; 14:16-17; 17:20-26), and of their love for and delight in all creatures (Gen 1:31; 9:8-17; Is 11:1-9; Ps 104; Prv 8:39-31; Matt 6:26-30; Rom 8:18-23; Col 1:15-20; Rv 5:14, 22).

Thesis 2: If the Trinity is understood as Persons-In-Mutual-Love, then relationship, and not simply being or substance, can be understood as the primary metaphysical category. Ultimate reality is understood as Persons-In-Dynamic-Communion.

Ecology is about interrelationships. Ecological action and ecological ethics depend upon seeing all things as relational. Aldo Leopold has said that all ethics rests upon the premise that "the individual is a member of a community of interdependent parts." And, he argues, a "land ethic simply enlarges the community to include soils, waters, plants and animals, or collectively: the land."[2] The land is "a community to which we belong." It is not merely soil, but a "fountain of energy flowing through a circuit of soil, plants and animals."[3]

In 1914 J. Arthur Thompson first talked about the "web of life" to describe this interrelated world of interdependent creatures. In 1927 Charles Elton coined the term "food chain" as a way of referring to the nutritional dependency that has its origin in the sun's energy, and continues through plants, plant eaters and carnivores. The English ecologist Arthur Tansley, as an alternative to speaking of nature as a community, suggested the term *ecosystem*.[4] It was taken up to refer to the existence of interdependent and cooperative relationships between living creatures, their nonliving context and the sun's energy.

The ecological worldview is communal and relational. A theology of the Trinity as Persons-In-Mutual-Relationship offers theological support to this worldview by showing that reality is relational at the most fundamental level. In this kind of trinitarian theology, as Catherine LaCugna has said, "Person, not substance, is the ultimate ontological category."[5]

Every creature comes from and depends upon trinitarian relationships of mutual love. Catherine LaCugna argues that since all being originates in the personal God, then "all of reality, since it proceeds from God, is personal and relational." Creation itself is simply the relationship between God and the universe and each creature in it. The existence of a rain forest is dependent at every moment on the Trinity's relationship with the forest. For a thing to be, for it to be sustained in existence, means that it exists from the divine Persons-In-Communion.

There is nothing that does not have its origin in these Persons. The whole universe exists from within personhood.[6] It is always springing forth from ecstatic and fecund love. As Tony Kelly puts it: "The universe emerging in the long ages of time is ever coming into being out of such Love." The universe always exists from the trinitarian processions of the Word and the Spirit. It is the self-expression of the relational vitality of the trinitarian God. So, Tony Kelly continues, "The universe finds its ultimate coherence in as much as trinitarian reality draws it to participate in its own field of relationships."[7]

Where ultimacy is given to persons and relationships, then our whole worldview will be different. Walter Kasper writes:

> The development of the doctrine of the Trinity means a breaking out of an understanding of reality that is characterized by the primacy of subject and nature, and into an understanding of reality in which person and relation have priority. Here the ultimate reality is not the independent substance but the person, who is fully conceivable only in the relationality of giving and receiving.[8]

If we view relationships as the primary reality, then this means that we can begin to see all of creation, the universe itself, the biosphere on Earth, individual ecosystems, a living tree, a cell, or a proton, as fundamentally relational and part of a network of interrelationships.

We can begin to see ourselves as a part of the delicate web of life on Earth. We begin to see that Francis of Assisi was not being romantic and fanciful, but rigorously theological when he spoke of Brother Sun, Sister Moon, Brother Wind, Sister Water, and Sister Earth, our Mother.

Thesis 3: The trinitarian God is a God of dynamic, ecstatic and fecund self-communication; creation is the free overflow of this divine fecundity, the self-expression of the trinitarian God, so that each creature is a mode and a sign of divine presence.

The biblical witness and Christian experience both point to God embracing our existence in the outpouring of the Spirit and offering us salvation and friendship in Jesus of Nazareth. Experiences of Jesus and the Spirit point to the One who sent them, to the holy One, the One whose Reign Jesus announces in parable, in inclusive meals and in acts of healing and liberation, the One who can be addressed as *Abba*, the God of boundless compassionate love.

The Trinity revealed in the history of salvation, the economic Trinity, is the only Trinity we know. The dynamism of the work of the economic Trinity in the story of salvation points to the dynamism at the heart of the Trinity, to the processions of Divine Wisdom and the Spirit of Love from the One who is Source, Origin, and Fountain Fullness. This dynamic fecundity does not involve subordination or hierarchy but rather radical equality, mutuality and the being-in-one-another of the divine dance (*circumincessio*). The Trinity can be seen as the supreme instance in which distinction and difference are both preserved and embraced in the most radical communion and the most profound mutuality.

The trinitarian relations of ecstatic and fruitful love are understood to be the dynamic center of the unconditional outpouring of love in the missions of the Word and the Spirit. And the trinitarian God revealed in the story of salvation is the wonderfully fruitful source and origin of the abundance of creation.

As Bonaventure's theology makes clear, creation is the dynamic, exuberant overflow of the fecundity of trinitarian life. Divine Wisdom is the Exemplar, the divine Art, through which all things come to expression. Every creature, in its form, its function and its beauty, reflects the divine Wisdom. Every creature is the divine self-expression, a symbol and sacrament of God's trinitarian presence. Each creature is a work of art of the trinitarian God. Every species, each ecosystem, the

Earth's biosphere and the universe itself are the self-expression of divine fecundity and delight.

This means that the rain forest of the Amazon is to be understood as the self-expression of the divine Trinity. It is a sacrament of God's presence. Its vitality and exuberance spring from the immanent presence of the Spirit, the giver of life. They express the trinitarian love of life. The rain forest, in its form, function and beauty as a harmonious biotic community is the work of art of divine Wisdom. The species of plants and animals which are being destroyed forever are modes of God's self-communication and presence. As Thomas Berry has said: "We should be clear about what happens when we destroy the living forms of this planet. The first consequence is that we destroy modes of divine presence."[9]

Thesis 4: On the basis of the doctrine of the Trinity as Persons-In-Mutual-Communion, human beings can be understood not primarily as isolated individual subjectivities, but as persons-in-relationship, as persons who are both self-possessed and self-giving in communion.

The doctrine of the Trinity provides the fundamental basis for an understanding of the communal and mutual nature of human persons and provides the basis for a prophetic critique of all forms of sexism, racism, economic exploitation and dominating relationships.

On the one hand, authentic human friendship gives us a glimmer of insight into the life of mutual friendship in the Trinity. As Simone Weil has written: "Pure friendship is an image of the original and perfect friendship that belongs to the Trinity, and is the very essence of God."[10]

On the other hand, the trinitarian circle of friendship is a powerful challenge to our understanding of human personal and political relations. It suggests that the Christian vision of interpersonal life would place the highest value on mutuality-in-communion. It suggests that the Christian vision of social life would embody such values as mutuality, inclusivity, reciprocity, cooperation and unity in genuine diversity.

Elizabeth Johnson writes that in a model of Trinity based on a communion of mutual friendship there is no subordination and no domination, but "a community of equals, so core to the feminist vision of ultimate shalom." Trinitarian communion points to "patterns of differentiation that are non-hierarchical, and to forms of relating that do not involve dominance."[11] The doctrine of the Trinity is a practical doctrine, which, if we allow it, will have a radical and liberating impact on our structures and patterns of relationship.

The church is called to be a communion which lives from and represents the trinitarian communion. It is to be "a sign and instrument . . . of communion with God and of unity among all people."[12] This commits the church to effective witness in word and deed to the work of justice and peace. This theology of God calls the church to a prophetic critique of sexism, racism and all forms of domination and servility in social and political life. Above all, it calls the church to self-criticism and ongoing reform. It challenges the church to a search for new forms of participatory democracy and to an inclusive ministry. In my view, this calls for abandonment, not of the sacramental order of deacon, presbyter and bishop (which is what is often meant by the word *hierarchy*), but the abandonment of all practices and symbols of hierarchy understood as dominating power, and the seeking of communal, participatory and mutual styles of church structure.[13]

Thesis 5: Creation is the action of the whole Trinity, but it needs to be seen as involving the distinct roles of the trinitarian Persons, which are not only "appropriated" to them, but "proper" to them.

The self-expression of God in creation is properly trinitarian. The Augustinian teaching that "the Trinity's acts *ad extra* are one," has led to the common theological position that since creation is an action of the essence of God, there is no proper role for each Person. It has been the traditional view that when we attribute a particular role in creation to one of the Persons, we do so only by "appropriation." This means that we attribute to one Person what really applies to all three.

Contemporary theology has recovered the understanding that we must attribute a proper role to the trinitarian Persons in the salvific missions of the Word and the Holy Spirit.[14] It is proper to the Word to became incarnate, and proper to the Spirit to be poured out in Grace. My argument is that this attribution of proper roles needs to be extended to include a properly trinitarian notion of creation.

This would not deny the unity of the divine action in creation, but point to distinctions proper to the Persons within this common action.[15]

It would suggest that the universe is truly the self-expression of the *trinitarian* God.

How are these distinct roles to be understood? The Spirit of God can be understood as the immanent presence of God in all things. The Creator Spirit, the *ruach* of God, is the wind sweeping over the waters at creation (Gen 1:2; Ps 33:6), the breath of life which sustains all things and renews the face of the earth (Ps 104:29-30; Eccles 12:7). The Spirit is the One who nurtures things into life, the giver of life (the "*vivificans*") of the Nicene Creed. The Spirit is the indwelling of God at the heart of the processes of ongoing creation, empowering and luring all things into an unforeseeable future. The life-giving Spirit is also the gift of grace for human beings, the indwelling Love that is the transcendent depth to all our truly human experiences of love and commitment toward other persons and other creatures of God (Rom 5:5; 1 Jn 4:16). This indwelling Spirit is the same One who anointed Jesus to bring good news to the poor (Lk 4:18), who was poured out on the community of disciples at Pentecost, and who is at work in our lives when "understanding puts an end to strife, when hatred is quenched by mercy, and vengeance gives way to forgiveness."[16] The Holy Spirit is an inner teacher leading those who listen to all truth (Jn 16:13). This Holy Spirit, breathing through creation, is that which connects all created things in God, the web of unity, the basis of the community of creatures. The *koinonia*, the communion or fellowship of the Holy Spirit (2 Cor 13:13), unites not only Christian believers, not only the human community, but all creatures in a relationship of kinship. As Jürgen Moltmann has said, "*the community of creation*, in which all created things exist with one another, for one another and in one another, is also *the fellowship of the Holy Spirit*."[17] Through the indwelling Spirit, the One who raised Jesus from the dead will give life to our mortal bodies (Rom 8:11). This vivifying Spirit is the power of new creation at work in our world, bringing all things to their transformation in Christ.

Sophia, the Wisdom of God, is the One in whom all things are created. She is God's companion in creation and is daily God's delight, taking delight in the inhabited world and in the human race (Prv 8:31). She reaches out from one end of the Earth to the other and orders all things well (Wis 8:1). But Wisdom has made a home among us (Prv 9:1; Jn 1:14). In Jesus in his life and death for us we find the Wisdom which is at the heart of the universe revealed as boundless and unthinkably compassionate love. Jesus can now be understood as the Wisdom of God, the one in whom all things were created (Col 1:16; Heb 1:2; Jn 1:3). Jesus risen is the promise and beginning of the transformation of the universe. All things will be redeemed, reconciled and transformed in him (Rom 8:21; Col 1:20; Eph 1:20).

The experience of the life-giving Spirit, and of divine self-communication in Jesus, points to the One who is the Unoriginate Origin, the Ground of Being, the holy Mystery, the Source, the Matrix, the Spring of Life and Goodness, the One that Bonaventure calls the Fountain Fullness, the *fontalis plenitudo*. This is the One that Jesus addressed in familiar and intimate terms as *Abba*. This is the God of the poor, the sick, the sinners and the outcast. This is the One who can also be thought of as Mother, our Mother, the Mother of all creatures. The Book of Job asks the question: "Whose womb gave birth to the ice, and who was the mother of the frost from heaven?" (38:29). The God who is the mysterious and fecund Well-Spring from which all creation flows, and the God who will bring all to completeness, is like a parent teaching a child to walk, and lifting an infant to cheek (Hos 11:3-4). This God carries us from the womb to our old age (Is 46:3-4), comforts us as a mother nurses and comforts her children (Is 66:12-13) and will never forget the children of her womb (Is 49:15). All creatures are offspring of this One who can be imaged as Mother and as Father of the universe, and all of us are kin to one another.

Thomas Aquinas has an image of the trinitarian God creating like a craft-worker with an idea in the mind (Wisdom) and love in the will (the Spirit).[18] In Aquinas's thought, too, each creature bears traces of the Trinity:

> Because it is a definite and created substance it tells of its principle and cause, and so indicates the Person of the Father, who is the beginning from no beginning. Because it has a certain form and species, it tells of the Word, for form in a work of art comes from the artist's conception. Because it is ordered to others it tells of the Holy Spirit as Love, since the relation to other creatures is from the Creator's will.[19]

Aquinas would see the existence of a particular rock or flower or human person as pointing to its cause in the Unoriginate Origin. Its specific identity or form would be a manifestation of the Word. Its relationship with an ecosystem and an interrelated cosmos would manifest the bond of Love which is the Holy Spirit. But in Aquinas's system, these are understood as appropriations rather than as proper to each Person.[20]

I will mention three of the reasons which lead me to believe that we need to go beyond Aquinas to see the distinct roles in creation as proper to each Person. First, the theology of a "proper" role of each Person in creation seems more congruent with the scriptures than the view that the trinitarian roles are simply appropriations. Of course, it must be admitted that there is no evidence that any biblical writer ever had this issue in mind. But it seems to me that a theology of proper roles fits better than a theology of appropriation with a number of biblical texts. I am thinking particularly of the texts considered above, which identify Christ and cosmic Wisdom and stress creation "in" and "through" Christ. It seems to me that the whole biblical argument I have made for a Wisdom Christology supports the idea of a proper role for divine Wisdom in creation. I am also thinking of those texts which speak of the creative role of the Spirit of God (Gen 1:2; Jdt 16:14; Jb 33:4; Wis 1:7; 12:1; Ps 104:30; Rom 8:22; Acts 17:28), and the credal affirmation of the Spirit as "Giver of Life." There is no basis in scripture for the idea that these roles are to be considered as mere appropriations, and it seems to me that the more obvious interpretation of scripture is to take these texts as referring to proper roles.

Second, the inner logic of Bonaventure's system, which I have followed on the fecundity of the Trinity, suggests that the one trinitarian work of creation ought be understood in ways that are proper to each Person. For Bonaventure, it is precisely what is distinctive of each of the Persons (to be Fountain Fullness, Divine Image and Exemplar, and Bond of Love) that comes into play in the one work of creation. I am not claiming that Bonaventure makes this fully explicit, but rather that this is the implicit logic of his system. Bonaventure certainly does make it clear that to speak of the Word as Exemplar is to speak not merely of an appropriation but of a property.[21]

Third, the inner theological relationship between creation and salvation suggests a proper role for the trinitarian Persons in creation. Contemporary theology has already argued convincingly for proper missions of the Word and Spirit in the incarnation and the divine offer of Grace. But, as I have shown above, there is an inner theological connection between creation and redemption. As Rahner has said, creation and incarnation are two moments of the *one* process of God's self-giv-ing.[22] If this one process is properly trinitarian in the history of incarna-tion and grace, it seems that it must also be understood as properly trinitarian with regard to creation.

The universe, in this view, can be understood as the self-expression of the *trinitarian* God. The Fountain Fullness is the Unoriginate Ori-gin, the Well-Spring and Source of Being for all creatures. Jesus, the divine Wisdom, is the One in whom all things are created and the One in whom all will be reconciled. The Holy Spirit is the immanent pres-ence of God, the Giver of Life, who sustains and renews all things in the process of continuing creation, and is the Love which unites all creatures and will bring all to completion.

Thesis 6: The Trinity's interaction with creation is characterized by the vulnerability and liberating power of love. This trinitarian love respects both the freedom of human beings and the integrity of natural processes.

This thesis is meant to suggest that the trinitarian God enters radi-cally into the suffering of the world to promote liberation and fulfill-ment. It argues that God's action not only sustains and empowers the evolving universe at every point but also works creatively through the emergent processes of the universe and through the interaction of chance and lawfulness. God interacts with creatures in an evolving, expanding universe in a respectful and responsive manner.

In the Hebrew and Christian scriptures, God is portrayed as rich in emotional life, feeling love, delight, anger, jealousy and compassion. It is startling to see how soon Christian theology, as it engaged with Greek philosophical thought, stripped God of all feeling and declared God to be *a-pathos*, without suffering or vulnerability.[23]

In patristic and medieval theology, God was thought of as immu-table and invulnerable for many reasons. These include the fact that the Hellenistic ideal of divine perfection involved immutability, and the tendency of the Greek mind to perceive a close relationship between the eternity of God and immutability.[24] Two further reasons need to be kept in mind. Theologians rightly sought to preserve divine freedom, and the classical ideal of divine freedom meant self-sufficiency and freedom from dependency on creation. Hence, it was argued, God must be understood as immutable. Even the cross of Jesus was no exception, because it was claimed that the suffering of Jesus touched only the human nature and not the divine. Another important reason why medieval theology held to a doctrine of divine immutability was that God was thought of as "pure act" (*actus purus*), and if the divine being is pure act, there can be no movement from potency to act and hence no change in God.

This theology has proved radically inadequate in the century of the holocaust, of Hiroshima, of massive human suffering through war and famine, and of the violent assault on the life systems of Earth. These events of terror have demanded a radical rethinking of our theology of God.[25] Feminist theologians have analyzed the traditions of God's invulnerability and omnipotence and shown their relation with patriarchal culture and its horrific effects.[26] There is widespread agreement in contemporary theology that we need to return to a way of speaking that is more faithful to the biblical God. Ted Peters puts the issue well:

> At stake here is our understanding of God. Must we begin with a philosophically produced concept of immutable spiritual essence that dwells ineffably and eternally in metaphysical isolation from the physical world? Must we then pin that on the divine symbols whenever they appear in the New Testament discourse? Or, is God free to define divinity?[27]

I have argued above that central to Wisdom Christology is the fact that divine Wisdom is revealed in the shocking image of the crucified (1 Cor 1-2). This cannot be explained away as the suffering of only the human nature of Jesus. Paul is surely saying more than that. He is pointing to the cross and saying this is the revelation of God, this is the Wisdom of God. God suffers in the death of Jesus, and God suffers in the sufferings of our world. But this God not only shares the suffering of the world, not only stands with a suffering world radically in the cross, but offers a promise that resurrection, liberation and life are at work in our universe, and that our lives are part of that work.

In response to the concerns of classical theology it can be said, first, that when God is seen in terms of Persons-In-Mutual-Love then the ideal of freedom is not that of isolation and self-sufficiency. Rather, real freedom is understood as the freedom to enter into relationships, to risk oneself with another, to enter into love in openness to the other. This kind of freedom demands both self-possession and self-giving in vulnerability. And there is every reason to assume that the trinitarian

God is supreme in personal freedom, and free beyond comprehension to enter into the vulnerability of loving communion. This assumption is verified in a staggering way in the love revealed in the cross of Jesus.

Second, the basic metaphor for the trinitarian God, I have been arguing, is not *actus purus* but Persons-In-Mutual-Communion. This view of God removes the force of the theological argument that one who is pure act cannot suffer. Elizabeth Johnson expresses this with particular clarity:

> Classical theism models its notion of divine being on the root metaphor of motion adapted primarily from the nonpersonal, physical world. If one uses that model it is clearly the case that something purely in act cannot pass from potency into act, nor can something completely in motion be in any way passive or receptive. Hence, God cannot suffer. But this root metaphor is hardly adequate to God's holy mystery, which is utterly personal, transpersonal, source of all that is personal. A different interpretation becomes possible when the root metaphor is taken from personal reality that is constitutively relational. Then the essence of God can be seen to consist in the motion of personal relations and the act that is love. With this in view it is possible to conceive of suffering as not necessarily a passive state nor a movement from potentiality to act. Rather suffering can be conceived of ontologically as an expression of divine being insofar as it is an *act* freely engaged in as a consequence of care for others. The personal analogy makes it possible to interpret divine suffering as Sophia-God's act of love freely overflowing in compassion.[28]

What is called for in this theology is not less respect for God's mystery and transcendence, but more. God is the one in whom self-possession and self-giving, freedom and vulnerability, exist in a way beyond comprehension.

This means, by way of contrast to the view of Thomas Aquinas, that God must be understood as having a real relationship with the world. Aquinas, perhaps more than any other thinker, has a brilliant theology of creation as a relation. Creation is the intimate relation between each creature and God by which the creature exists. From the side of the creature, Aquinas argues, it is a *real* relation of dependence between the creature and God, by which God enables the creature to be. But, from God's side, Aquinas allows only a *logical* relation between God and the creature, since in his philosophical framework a real relation would seem to involve a necessity of nature.[29] And Aquinas could not allow that creation belongs by way of necessity to God's nature. God's relation to the creature cannot be thought of as constituting God's being. Aquinas rightly wanted to preserve God's freedom and to understand creation as a free act of God.

By contrast, in the relational metaphysics used here, I believe that it is possible and essential to affirm both that creation is a *free* act of God's love, and that through this freely chosen act of love God enters into a *real* relationship with creation, which means that God freely accepts the limitation and vulnerability of such relationship (Phil 2:6-11). God's supreme capacity for love is of such a kind as to be able to make space for others.[30]

Walter Kasper writes: "For the Bible, then, the revelation of God's omnipotence and the revelation of God's love are not contraries." Rather, Kasper suggests, God's omnipotence is precisely the supreme capacity to love. He argues: "It requires omnipotence to be able to surrender oneself and give oneself away; and it requires omnipotence to be able to take oneself back in the giving and to preserve the independence and freedom of the recipient."[31] As the mysteries of the incarnation and of Calvary tell us, the divine capacity for love involves an unthinkable vulnerability and self-limitation.

John Polkinghorne has often pointed out that God's love and faithfulness apply not just to human beings but also to the physical universe. God is the great allower and respecter of freedom, not only of human freedom, but also of the freedom of physical processes.

Polkinghorne suggests that part of the answer to the problem of evil and suffering may be found in God's respect for freedom. A traditional response to the evil caused by human beings has been what is sometimes called the "free-will defense." This points out that a God who is committed to respecting human freedom is vulnerable to the misuse of this freedom. To this argument Polkinghorne adds what he calls the "free-process defense." God also respects the freedom and integrity of physical processes. This "defense" appeals to "the divine gift of freedom to *all* of the creation, not just to humankind alone."[32]

If God freely creates in such a way as to be committed to the integrity of the processes of the universe, then God is not free to override these processes. God's freedom and power may well be self-limited in the very fact of creating a universe which unfolds by way of process.

This line of thought suggests that God, because of this free self-limitation, is not able to stop all suffering. It seems to me that this is the only line of thought on suffering which is congruent with what is revealed about God's compassion in the cross of Jesus. Here God is revealed as suffering with a suffering world in order to bring healing and liberation. This theological approach suggests that the reason that God does not intervene to stop immense suffering is because divine self-limitation in creating a finite, processive world means that God is not free to intervene. It suggests that the reason that God does not stop an earthquake which kills thousands of people is because God cannot.

Polkinghorne argues that we do not live in a universe in which everything is predetermined by God, although he certainly sees the divine purposes as being achieved through divine interaction with the universe and its processes. He points out that physical process at both the quantum and the macro levels is intrinsically unpredictable, being subject to the interaction of chance and necessity. He refers to a quotation from W. H. Vanstone, who writes: "If the creation is the work of love, then its shape cannot be predetermined by the Creator, nor its triumph foreknown: it is the realization of vision, but of vision which is discovered only through its realization."[33]

Edward Schillebeeckx, too, has argued that we need to give up the idea of divine "predestination." He writes:

We must give up a world history laid down "from eternity" and "manipulated" by God, without allowing God himself to be checkmated by our history. Nothing is determined in advance: in nature there is chance and determinism; in the world of human activity there is the possibility of free choices. Therefore the historical future is not known even to God; otherwise we and our history would be merely a puppet show in which God holds the strings. For God, too, history is an adventure, an open history for and of men and women. If I claim to believe in God who has taken the risk of creating the world, then my trust means that ultimately the world will be the expression of God's will in a way which is still not true and is even contradicted now by empirical experiences. So at this point we can never identify God's will in detail.[34]

I would differ somewhat from these theologians in arguing that we human beings cannot make any absolute claims about God's consciousness of future events. It seems to me that we are not in a position to declare that God cannot know the future. Theologically, we are not in a position to know exactly how our history is seen from the perspective of divine eternity. There is need for a negative theology, which respects what we do not know about the divine experience of time and eternity. In science, we find time treated as reversible in some contexts and as irreversible in others, and we find disagreement over whether the universe is to be considered fundamentally as a spacetime whole (the "block universe") or as a universe of flowing time.[35] Both theology and science suggest a need for caution in commenting on God's knowledge of future contingent events.

But it does seem to me that we have to give up the traditional view of the future unfolding according to a fixed and predetermined plan of God. I agree with Polkinghorne, Vanstone and Schillebeeckx that the future is radically contingent and unpredictable, and that we must abandon some traditional assumptions about divine foreknowledge and predestination. We need to think of God's resurrection promises being accomplished in ways that are unpredictable, contingent on future events, and responsive to both human freedom and natural processes.

The trinitarian God is adventurous in loving and freely depends on the beloved's response. This God is adventurous in creating and freely chooses to depend upon and engage with the process. This means that there are limits to divine power, limits set by love and respect for creation.

As Polkinghorne says, God is both loving and faithful, and this love and faithfulness are both expressed with regard to physical processes as God freely chooses to work through the interaction of contingency and chance on the one hand, and the regularities of lawfulness and necessity on the other.[36] This is not a contradiction of the biblical promise to bring all things to consummation but a conception of love's work as powerful and vulnerable and freely limited by respect for creatures. The divine saving purposes are achieved in a loving way, which means in a responsive way, as divine love responds creatively to contingent initiatives of human persons and to contingent outcomes in physical processes.

This theology offers a vision of the trinitarian God engaged in ongoing creation in the way that is consonant with radical love—not out of a static predetermined plan, but responsively, adventurously and inventively. This vision is congruent with the way of divine foolishness revealed in the cross of Jesus. The cross in itself represents a contingent and radical rejection of divine love, but this murderous response not only does not thwart love's purposes but becomes its most life-giving expression.

What is unchanging is God's fidelity to the resurrection promise. This promise is worked out in ways that cannot be predicted as the Wisdom of God, the divine Art, responds to creation with ingenuity and with constant envisioning of new possibilities, and as the Spirit of Love breathes life into these new possibilities. God's artistry is freely limited by God's loving respect for the dynamics of an emergent universe. But within the limitation set by love and respect for creation, the divine artistry is endlessly creative.

God engages with our universe as the great allower and respecter of freedom, and this means that the future of the universe is radically open. God's ongoing creative action (*creatio continua*) is through loving, faithful and fruitful interaction with physical process. This suggests that we need to think of the trinitarian God as responding creatively to the universe, as "improvising" on the theme of creation in the light of the interplay of chance and necessity.

One of the persons who has done much to show how the contemporary scientific account of chance and law can relate to Christian theology is Arthur Peacocke. He writes:

How can this understanding of God creating "in, with and under" the ongoing processes of the natural world be held in consonance with the recognition that new, and increasingly complex, forms of both inorganic and eventually living matter emerge by a combination of what we recognize as "chance" and "law"—and that this combination is inherently creative in itself and involves, for sound thermodynamic and chemical reasons, an increase in complexity? How can the assertion of God as Creator be interpreted in the light of this new and profound understanding of the natural processes by which new organised forms of matter appear, both non-living and living? . . . I have earlier tried to express this situation by seeing God as Creator as like a composer who, beginning with an arrangement of notes in an apparently simple tune, elaborates and expands it into a fugue by a variety of devices.[37]

Like Athanasius before him, Arthur Peacocke images the Creator as a musician. But Peacocke's awareness of the contingency of physical process leads him to stress the improvisation of the musician. He sees the Creator as unfolding the potentialities of the universe as an *Improviser of Unsurpassed Ingenuity*. Alongside the image of the improvising musician, Arthur Peacocke suggests another helpful image for creation—that of the divine dance. In a later book Peacocke refines the analogy of the divine improviser in an important way. He suggests that we move beyond the image of a composer writing improvisations at a desk and think of someone like Johann Sebastian Bach improvising a three-part fugue on a given theme at the keyboard.[38] Here the highest creativity is both responsive and improvised. Bach at the keyboard creates beautiful music that responds to the limits set by the theme, the instrument, and the laws of musical composition as Bach understood and developed them.

Arthur Peacocke also discusses another image—that of jazz musicians improvising on a theme in Preservation Hall in New Orleans.[39] This image is appealing because here a group of artists responds not only to a theme but also to each other's free and unpredictable responses to the theme. Of course God cannot be thought of as simply one player amongst others. But granted the limits of the image, it can help to bring out the spontaneity and responsive creativity of the divine work. In this kind of music the greatest moments are those of group improvisation, when a group of musicians together creates an exciting musical whole that depends on the interaction between the unpredictable creative responses of players to one another. So the trinitarian God creates in a way which is responsive to freedom and process.

In terms of musical analogy, the Fountain Fullness, Divine Wisdom and the Spirit of Love are all involved in the one musical improvisation on the theme which is the emergent universe. Like brilliant musicians, they respond creatively to each other, to the material presented by the processes of the universe, and to the laws of nature and chance. In the image of the dance it is possible to imagine the trinitarian dancers in mutual communion and delight weaving and flowing through the whole universe, taking delight in each creature, drawing each into the dance of the whole, responding with creativity to the rhythms set by the processes of chance and law.

From the trinitarian theology outlined above, there flow two fundamental principles for an ecological theology:

1. The trinitarian God is to be understood as Persons-In-Mutual-Communion. Relationships of mutual love undergird the expanding universe

and hold all things together. The God of mutual relations freely and reciprocally interrelates with all creatures in ways which respect their identity. Reality is fundamentally interrelational, and human beings are called to see themselves as in some way kin with all other creatures.

2. The trinitarian God is a God of dynamic and fecund self-expression. Every species and every creature is God's self-expression, a word of God, a sign of the trinitarian God, a mode of divine presence.

The consequences of these principles for human life and for ecological praxis will be explored in the next two chapters.

PART 3

HUMAN BEINGS IN THE COMMUNITY OF CREATURES

A Theological View of Human Beings in Relationship to Other Creatures as a Basis for Ecological Praxis

6.

Human Beings and Other Creatures

One of the issues the ecological crisis brings into sharp focus is the way we humans see ourselves in relationship to other creatures. At the base of exploitative Western attitudes to nature there has been a concept of the human person as the individual conscious self, usually a male self, understood over against other persons, bodiliness and other creatures.

This individualistic concept of the self finds religious expression in a private view of Christian faith. It receives cultural expression in the value that our society places on individual human fulfillment—exemplified above all in advertising.

An ecological theology needs to challenge this view and ask: Are we human beings fundamentally individual conscious beings, or are we fundamentally communal and inter-subjective? Are we the measure and meaning of other creatures, or are we radically interrelated with them within a larger pattern of meaning? Is the Christian view of salvation simply a matter of individual justification before God, or does salvation in Jesus Christ involve other creatures and the universe itself?

In this chapter I argue that the theology of the trinitarian God revealed in Jesus leads to a view of human beings which is inter-subjective, and interrelated with the Earth, the universe and all its creatures, and I suggest that it leads to a theology of salvation which embraces the universe.

From Individualism to Persons-In-Mutual-Relationship

Western culture, shaped in large part by the Enlightenment, brings with it some real gains in our understanding of the human person.

Charles Taylor has shown how the modern concept of the self involves a number of positive values which have not been taken for granted in earlier cultures. He discusses the notion of the importance of the affirmation of everyday life (as opposed to hierarchies of birth or wealth), the value of human life, the dignity of the human person, the concept of equality of rights and the moral autonomy of the individual.[1] The modern turn inward, with its emphasis on individual moral autonomy, has led to great gains in our sense of what it is to be human and in our understanding of basic rights.

But, as Taylor points out, there is another side to this story. The internalization of moral resources, achieved by the Enlightenment thinkers, was achieved at a great price. The human being became the thinking subject over against a world which was understood in mechanical terms. Descartes argued that we need to take a disengaged stance toward other objects in the world and also toward our own bodily experience. He was largely responsible for introducing the subject-object split into modern thought through his fundamental distinction between the *res cogitans* (the thinking subject) and the *res extensa* (the objects of experience characterized by their extension in space).

In Descartes's view, human reason objectified the world and also human bodily experience, and controlled both as instruments. He understood the world as a mechanism, and this mechanistic world was to be subject to the instrumental control of human reason. He was interested in a "practical philosophy," which would encourage the control and use of nature:

> Instead of that speculative philosophy which is taught in the Schools, we may find a practical philosophy by means of which, knowing the force and action of fire, water, air, stars, heavens and all other bodies that environ us, as distinctly as we know the different crafts of our artisans, we can in the same way employ them in all those uses to which they are adapted, and thus render ourselves the masters and possessors of nature.[2]

Descartes's philosophy, which Charles Taylor characterizes as a philosophy of "disengaged reason," leads not only to a radical dualism of body and soul and to an exaggerated individualism, but to the conviction that human persons can be understood as "masters and possessors" of the rest of creation. This view of the human as master and possessor of nature has lent legitimacy to the pollution of the atmosphere, the rivers and the seas, the degradation of the land, the destruction of ecosystems, the extinction of species and the exploitation of the Earth's resources without regard for ecological sustainability. It seems to me that a primary task for an ecological theology is to offer an alternative, more relational view of the human person.

A theological view of the human person is one that is faithful to Jesus and to the trinitarian God. This God, I have argued, can be understood as Persons-In-Mutual-Communion, and the universe can be seen as this relational God's fruitful and ecstatic self-expression. The theology of God as Persons-In-Mutual-Relationship suggests that human beings, made in the image of God, are to be understood as persons-in-mutual-relationship rather than as disengaged subjects. It suggests that inter-subjectivity, which is at the heart of the universe, may also be central to a proper understanding of the human.

In the Bible we find human persons understood as unique individuals with their own importance and dignity before God, but not as self-contained and isolated individuals. The scriptural view is that human beings are fundamentally relational and constituted by relationships. They are part of a community, a people called by God. Ian Barbour has pointed out that in the Bible "we are who we are as children, husbands and wives, parents, citizens and members of a covenant people."[3] In the Christian scriptures, as I have said above, we find Jesus calling people into a new familial relationship with God and into a community of equals, a "new family" of brothers and sisters.

Ian Barbour shows that the theological claim that community is essential to the human is both consistent with the insights of contemporary science and supported by reflection on everyday experience. In science we find that genetic and cultural evolution are understood as group processes.[4] Evolutionary history is a history of communities. We evolve as social beings. Furthermore, sociology and linguistics make it clear that our intellectual and cultural development depend upon our interactions with others. We depend upon others in order to develop the capacity to participate in language, symbolic thought and the culture of the human community.

Reflection on experience supports the theological claim that human beings are fundamentally inter-subjective. A baby is dependent on parents and extended family not only for language and culture, but also for a sense of self. The process of becoming a self occurs only in community. An infant becomes an interacting person only by being treated as a person, by being surrounded by a warm and loving human community. Where this process is distorted, human beings suffer extreme damage and deprivation. As adults, our sense of self and our happiness are still determined to a large extent by our interrelationships. The whole process of growing as a person and growing in wisdom, which Aquinas describes as "knowledge through love," occurs in and through the loves, the friendships, and the other interrelationships of our lives.

Jürgen Moltmann suggests that what he calls the "livingness of life" comes into play "in the reciprocity between word and answer, action and reaction, the discovery of other and the discovery of oneself in relationships." He argues that our experience of ourselves is always mediated by relationships with others. It is only those who go out of themselves who come to themselves. We experience ourselves in the experience of other people. From the time we are born, Moltmann writes, "being human means being-in-relationship" and "human subjectivity is only possible in inter-subjectivity."[5] Self-awareness is constituted through social experience.

Moltmann goes on to suggest that the experience of God's Spirit is also always the experience of the God who is sociality, the God who binds together the I and Thou and Us.[6] This is a theme that has been strongly argued from a different perspective by Karl Rahner. Rahner shows that our experience and love of God occur in, and are dependent on, our going out of ourselves in relationships with others, so that it is ontologically true that we can only love God in loving our neighbor.[7] Experience and love of God, like so much else that is essential to the human, depend on our being persons-in-communion-with-others.

The theological view that human beings are radically inter-subjective can be supported by all of these considerations. But the most fundamental basis for this relational view of the human is the theology of the trinitarian God as Persons-In-Mutual-Relationship. What I am suggesting, as faithful to this trinitarian view of God and faithful to the scriptures, is not a collapse into a collectivism which would deny individual autonomy, rights and freedom and which would put aside the genuine gains of the Enlightenment. It is not a matter of community at the expense of the individual or of an individualism which disregards community. Rather, I am advocating a concept, based on the Trinity as Persons-In-Mutual-Relationship, whereby both individuality and mutual community coexist in mutual interdependence. The trinitarian image of Persons-In-Mutual-Relationships leads to a communal and relational understanding of the human person without denying the value of the individual and without absorbing the individual into the group.

Human Participation in the Community of Creatures

To say that human beings are beings-in-mutual-relationship with each other is only a partial description of human relationships and human identity. Human beings are interrelated not only with each other but also, in differentiated ways, with all other creatures and with the trinitarian God. They are not only inter-subjective, but also interconnected in networks of relationship which in some way embrace every other creature on Earth and the universe itself.

I will attempt to develop this line of thought by first borrowing from Karl Rahner's concept of the sphere of bodiliness and by then turning to science to listen to the story it tells of human interrelationship with other beings in an evolutionary universe. This leads to some principles for a theological view of the human person in relationship to other creatures.

The Sphere of Bodiliness

The ancient biblical view of the human being was generally bodily and holistic. This was true not only of the Hebrew scriptures but also of the Christian biblical writings, with their conviction that the Word was made flesh in Jesus of Nazareth and their central doctrine of the resurrection of the body. On the basis of these doctrines, the early Christian community resisted the dualism of the Gnostic and Manichaean movements and the teaching of these movements that matter was evil. But Christianity did not escape the subtler influence of neoplatonism, which tended to suggest that bodily existence is inferior to a higher world which is the soul's true home. In spite of positive attitudes to creation in the scriptures and in great theologians like Irenaeus and Aquinas, the inculturation of the gospel within a Hellenistic neoplatonic world has led to distortions in the Christian tradition, resulting in negative and demeaning approaches to the body, to creation and, as feminist analysis has shown, to women.[8]

Karl Rahner has sought to combat this line of thought by arguing that human beings are fundamentally and intrinsically bodily. Without denying in any way that there are the two dimensions of body and spirit in the human, Rahner holds that the human being is a unity of such a kind that there can be no separation of the two. There are no separated souls. What, then, happens in death? In his early work Rahner argued that when a body dies, the human spirit opens out into a wider, but still bodily, relationship with the material universe. Far from becoming non-bodily it becomes bodily in a new way. Far from becoming acosmic at death, the human person becomes pancosmic.[9] Rahner thought that a person who achieves a real relationship with the physical universe in death could be understood to have a real influence within our world, as part of what the tradition calls the "communion of saints."

I believe that this concept of death, and the entrance into resurrection life as a new relationship with the physical universe, has much to offer. From a different "process" perspective, John Haught has also argued recently that we can "understand the act of dying not as a person's separation from the earth and the universe, but as a unique occasion for entering into an even deeper relationship with them."[10]

Perhaps equally important is Rahner's concept of the "bodily sphere."[11] By this he means not only that we are fundamentally bodily and communal, but also that we are always interconnected in a sphere of bodiliness. Through our bodies we reach out into a sphere which does not belong to ourselves alone. Bodily existence involves us with a world of other creatures. There is no inwardness in us that is not touched by what comes from without. At the very center of our beings we always have something to do with other human creatures, with the food we eat, the air we breathe, the flowers we smell, the wind which brings rain. And we necessarily have something to do with Jesus, whose death two thousand years ago took place in a bodily sphere which is still ours today.

We are part of the whole, directly connected with the rest of creation. Rahner can say that "through bodiliness the whole world belongs to me from the start in everything that happens." If this is true, then the environment in which we live can only be a matter of great importance to us. There can be no retreat into indifference to physical reality. Indifference to the physical world might be consistent with some dimensions of Hellenistic thought, but it is completely unchristian.

Rahner sees that the human person is something of an open system. He writes: "Of course we must not get the impression in this connection that our body stops where our skin stops, as if we were a sack containing a number of things, which clearly ceases to be where its 'skin,' the sacking, stops."[12] He points out how dependent our bodies are on the physical realities like the sun. If there were no sun or moon, our bodies would be radically different. In fact, of course, if there were no sun of any kind, we would not exist at all.

We live in a common sphere, a common space that makes all communication between creatures possible, a space which is in one sense our common body. This sphere of bodiliness has a future. The resurrection of the dead will involve not only the transfiguration of the individual, but the transfiguration of the common sphere of bodiliness. Rahner suggests that our eternal destiny may have something to do with our acceptance of this transformed bodily sphere, in which we always necessarily are.

Made from Stardust

Part of the data for theological reflection today is our new understanding of the emergence of human beings, together with all other creatures, in our common story of the Big Bang and the expanding universe. This story makes manifest our interdependence not only with the creatures of Earth but also with the whole universe.

The universe began between eight and eighteen billion years ago, in an extremely rapid expansion from an unthinkably dense, hot and compressed state. The Big Bang was the origin not only of matter but also of space and time. The expansion of the universe is understood as the stretching and expanding of spacetime itself.

Much happened in the fierce temperatures of the first second of history. Many cosmological theorists speculate that in a tiny fraction of this first second the early universe ballooned out in a period of rapid exponential inflation, expanding in size by a factor of 10^{80}.[13] Within this second the four forces of the universe emerged in their differentiated forms as gravity, electromagnetism, and the strong and weak nuclear forces. Photons and particles were able to interact in equilibrium. Once quarks and antiquarks ceased their mutual annihilation, the strong nuclear force enabled surviving quarks to link up to form protons and neutrons, the components of all future atomic nuclei.

The reconstruction of what happened in the first second remains speculative, but there is a good deal of agreement among cosmologists about what happens after the first second. Stephen Hawking writes:

"We can be fairly confident that we have the right picture, at least back to one second after the big bang."[14] Between three and four minutes after the Big Bang the temperature had dropped to a level at which the first atomic nuclei could be formed. It was still far too hot for atoms to form, but it was cool enough for protons and neutrons to link up to form the nuclei of helium and hydrogen.

For the next half a million years the universe expanded and cooled. But the temperature was still too hot for the formation of atoms, and the universe existed in the form of a glowing plasma of ionized hydrogen and helium. Matter was opaque to radiation and remained coupled to it.

By the end of this period the temperature of the universe had dropped to something like the temperature of the sun's surface. Particles and photons became decoupled, leaving electrons free to combine with nuclei to form stable atoms. The universe's radiation, now separated from matter, formed the origin of what we call the cosmic background radiation, which was to be discovered by Arno Penzias and Robert Wilson in 1965 and to have its fluctuations charted by researchers using data from the COBE satellite in 1992.

As radiation went its own way, matter came into its own. Clouds of hydrogen and helium took shape, and the long process of formation of galaxies began. Density built up as the clouds of hydrogen coalesced under the influence of gravitational forces. Temperatures rose and nuclear reactions ignited in the emerging galaxies, fuelled by the conversion of hydrogen into helium. The universe lit up as the first stars were born.

Successive fusion processes in these stars enabled the light elements, hydrogen and helium, to be converted into heavier elements like carbon, oxygen and neon. As a star ages, heavier elements can be synthesized up to iron. Elements heavier than iron can be forged in supernova explosions. Some of these elements flow out into space through stellar winds and are catapulted out into the galaxy through nova and supernova explosions of spent stars. In this way the galaxy is enriched with the elements necessary for the formation of planets like Earth and the bodies of living creatures.

We are made from stardust. All the elements in the human brain and heart were forged in the furnaces of stars. Paul Davies writes, "We are built from the fossilized debris of once-bright stars that annihilated themselves aeons before the Earth or Sun existed."[15] The most abundant elements in our bodies are oxygen (65 percent), carbon (18 percent), hydrogen (10 percent), and nitrogen (3.3 percent). With the exception of the primordial hydrogen, all the atoms which make up our bodies have been produced in stars. The atoms thrown off into space by aged stars have been recycled into new stars, planets, and living creatures. Every creature on Earth has its origin in stardust. This is our common story and our communal history. We are made from the stars.

In a reflection on this story, Robert John Russell has written:

> I am also a child of stardust, whose story can be traced back to a time before the earth was formed, back to a generation of stars now gone forever, but whose violent deaths in supernovas transformed stellar hydrogen into the dust that eventually became our planet—and my flesh. Hence, alive now and in this place, I am connected to earth and sky by biology and cosmology. I breathe in the universe and give it out again.[16]

Our sun is a second or third generation star. It had its origin about 5 billion years ago, formed from a cloud of gas and dust in one of the spiral arms of the Milky Way Galaxy. The fossil record dates life on Earth back to about 3.5 billion years ago, with the appearance of unicellular micro-organisms, known as prokaryotes (with no cell nucleus), which were similar to modern bacteria. When the process of photosynthesis became oxygen producing, about 1.8 billion years ago, it allowed aerobic (oxygen-loving) bacteria to increase and diversify. The eukaryotes (advanced unicellular organisms with a cell nucleus) appeared about 1.5 billion years ago. This kind of cell has been basic to the structure of other organisms up to now. Multicellular organisms (such as forms of algae and tiny primitive animals) arrived on the scene about a billion years ago. About 670 million years ago the first macroscopic animals appeared in the form of marine invertebrates like flatworms and jellyfish. At the beginning of the Cambrian period, 570 million years ago, there was a very rapid expansion and diversification of life in the sea, and the emergence of the fundamental branches of the animal kingdom known as phyla. The vertebrates emerged in the sea during this Cambrian period, and these would give rise to amphibians, followed by the reptiles, and then the birds and mammals.

The first land plants appeared about 425 million years ago, and the first land animals (amphibians) about 350 million years ago. This was followed by a great expansion of plants and animals on land in the Late Palaeozoic period (345-225 million years ago), the age of the reptiles in the Mesozoic period (225-65 million years ago) and the Cenozoic period (from 65 million years ago), in which mammals and flowering plants have come in to their own. The first mammals appeared about 200 million years ago. There is evidence of *Homo erectus* from about 1.7 million years ago to half a million years ago, *Homo sapiens* from about 500,000 years ago, and widespread flourishing communities of modern humankind 40,000 years ago. Modern humankind may have been in existence from about 100,000 years ago.

Human beings share one evolutionary story that embraces every species and every living creature. However, it is far from being a story of steady upward progress. Rather, as Stephen Jay Gould points out, evolutionary history is more like a bush with many branches, most of which end in extinction. Evolutionary history is a story of dead ends, of the loss of countless species. It is a story of chance and unpredictability and small adaptations to local environments, which bring about the wonderful diversity of life on Earth.

It is also a story of increasing complexity and self-organization. The work of researchers like Ilya Prigogine and Manfred Eigen points to a widespread tendency in the universe for far-from-equilibrium open systems to move toward higher levels of complexity and self-organization.[17] It is possible that self-organizing principles in nature will help to explain the origin of life as well as the increasing complexity of living creatures.

In and through this whole process, through the workings of chance and law, through the process of natural selection, what has evolved is a wonderful diverse, exuberant community of living creatures. Human beings are part of this process, interdependent with every other part of the process of the biotic community of Earth.

Two Principles for a Theological Anthropology

Human beings share in this common story of creation. We have a communal heritage with all other creatures, in being born from the Big Bang, made from stardust, and brought to life within an evolutionary community. It is because of supernovas far out in space that our carbon based life-forms can exist. We are intimately interconnected with the whole life-system of the planet and the complex interaction between living creatures and the atmosphere, the land and the water systems.

But human beings are not only radically interrelated with other creatures, they have a particular place in the system. Carl Sagan describes human beings as "the local embodiment of a Cosmos grown to self-awareness."[18] Arthur Peacocke writes that in human beings "part of the world has become conscious of itself and consciously and actively responds to its surroundings."[19] Teilhard de Chardin echoes Julian Huxley in describing human beings as "evolution become conscious of itself."[20] Paul Davies describes the sequence from the Big Bang to atoms, stars, planets, life and human beings and concludes: "Thus, the universe became self-aware."[21] Many scientific thinkers agree in describing the human person as the universe come to self-consciousness in a particular place and time.

The common story of the universe suggests two basic principles for a contemporary anthropology: 1) the human person is profoundly and intrinsically interconnected with every other creature as a child of the Earth and a child of the universe; and 2) the human person has the particular dignity and responsibility which come from being one in whom the universe has come to self-awareness. These two principles emerge from the story that science tells. They arise from a contemporary scientific worldview.

Christian theology, listening to science, can recognize here the pattern of God's action in creation and embrace these principles not only on philosophical but also on theological grounds. First, theology supports the conviction that we are kin to all other creatures because it teaches that we share with them a common origin in God's creative action; we share a common journey in the ongoing story of creation, as God is present to every part of the universe dynamically sustaining and empowering it; and we share a common destiny in the New Creation.[22] Second, it supports the particular dignity and responsibility of human beings because of its conviction that human beings are made in God's image, that they are called as self-conscious beings into relationship in grace with the trinitarian God, that they are called to love other creatures as they are loved by God, and that they are invited to be God's partners in the ongoing history of creation.

Christian theology sees human beings as interconnected with all other creatures who are made from the stars and part of one evolutionary history, and as self-conscious beings called to relationship with the trinitarian God.

In our time human beings have the power and the freedom to decide between life and death for themselves and for other species on Earth. We have reached a new stage in evolutionary history, where cultural evolution is at least as important as natural selection.

Christianity is part of this evolutionary history, and it offers an inclusive principle which runs counter to the tendency of natural selection. As Sally McFague writes: "Once evolutionary history reaches the human, self-conscious stage, natural selection is not the only operative principle, for natural selection can be countered with the principle of solidarity."[23] She sees the central Christian praxis of solidarity with the oppressed as going beyond human beings to include all life-forms. She sees this as "a democratizing tendency that counters the fang and claw of genetic evolution as well as its two basic movers, law and chance."[24]

Sally McFague suggests that a Christian commitment to solidarity with the oppressed can be seen as in some ways consonant with and in other ways as in defiance of the evolutionary principle. It is consonant in that it can be argued that there is a new stage in evolutionary history, a primarily cultural stage, where it becomes imperative for all life-forms to share the basic goods of the Earth. She points out that Christian claims for inclusivity and solidarity with the oppressed run counter not only to general evolutionary tendencies, but also to tendencies in cultural evolution, since we so "naturally" construct our worlds to benefit ourselves.

In a Christian view, human beings refuse to share the Earth because of sin's hold over human lives and over the social and political order. Liberation from sin is found in God's love and forgiveness expressed in Jesus Christ, and it involves the far-from-obvious step of "identification with the vulnerable and the needy through the death of the self."[25]

We human beings, then, are called to the awesome task of being God's partners in creation. We cannot avoid this role. We help to bring life, or we will bring death. We depend thoroughly on our biological history and the life-systems of the planet, yet we are altering the course of evolutionary history. We no longer see ourselves as the center of the universe, and we recognize that God's love and purposes embrace creatures that we will never see or even be able to imagine. As Sally McFague has said: "We have been *decentered* as the point and goal of creation and *recentered* as God's partners in helping creation to grow and prosper in our tiny part of God's body."[26] Humbly and truthfully, we know ourselves as called to partnership with God.

Salvation and the Universe

This chapter has been centered on a theological understanding of human beings in relationship to other creatures. It has been arguing for a view of human beings as intersubjective, communal and interrelated to all other creatures as creation come to self-consciousness.

Some readers may wonder at this stage why I am not dealing fully with the traditional themes of Christian anthropology, sin, redemption from sin and the life of grace. I can only affirm that the doctrines of sin and salvation remain for me as fundamental as ever, and if anything, more desperately important at the end of the century of the Holocaust, of Hiroshima and Nagasaki, of global warming, acid rain and a damaged ozone layer. I have dealt with these fundamental doctrines in other places and need to take them for granted in this work, which cannot be a complete theological anthropology.[27] My main concern at this point is to argue that salvation is a bigger concept than simply the forgiveness of sin. Nonhuman creatures, and the universe itself, do not sin. Yet they will be transfigured by the saving love of God revealed in Jesus in what the scriptures call the New Creation. Salvation, redemption and reconciliation include the forgiveness of sins, but they are larger concepts embracing the transformation of the universe.

As Christian believers today ask about the meaning of salvation, they face all the ancient fundamental questions—about sin and forgiveness, the suffering of the innocent, death and life beyond death, and the meaning of who they are and what they do before God. But they also ask the questions: What does salvation in Jesus Christ have to do with the ecological crisis? What does it have to do with the universe?

Science and Theology on the Future of the Universe

There is a distinct difference between scientific predictions of the future of the universe and Christian hope in the New Creation (2 Cor 5:17). According to much of science the long-term future of the universe is bleak. Either the universe is open and its future will be to go on forever, becoming "cold, dark, empty space, populated at an ever decreasing density by a few isolated neutrinos and photons, and very little else."[28] Or the universe is closed, in which case the expanding universe will slow down, reverse its motion and begin to contract, so that in time the entire universe "shrivels into less than the size of an atom, whereupon spacetime disintegrates."[29]

Many scientists, and many other people as well, find these scenarios profoundly depressing. A famous example of this is found on the last page of Steven Weinberg's *The First Three Minutes*, where he writes that the universe faces a future extinction of either endless cold or intolerable heat; he comments that "the more the universe seems comprehensible, the more it also seems pointless."[30] In his recent book *Dreams of a Final Theory*, Weinberg reflects on reactions to this much-cited comment and admits that it was a nostalgic saying—"nostalgic for a world in which the heavens declare the glory of God."[31] For Weinberg and many others, the scientific predictions of the end of the universe seem to make implausible the Christian claims for a New Creation, life beyond death, or belief in God.

It seems to me that this perceived implausibility is a matter of "feel" and "fit" rather than one of logic. It "feels" implausible within a contemporary culture to imagine the Creator of the universe acting to transform the universe in a way that cannot be predicted by contemporary science. Yet Christian theology needs to affirm that there is nothing illogical or improbable about divine action that brings the universe to its consummation—if one is prepared to accept the existence of a Creator and such "counter-intuitive" (to contemporary scientific culture) concepts as the incarnation, the love of God revealed in the crucifixion of Jesus, and the resurrection.

Weinberg has some critical things to say about a liberal theology, which all too easily accommodates itself to any prevailing position, and he is even more critical of dogmatic fundamentalist views. It seems to me that a Christian theology ought not accommodate itself to contemporary culture and ought not avoid speaking about resurrection and the New Creation. Nor should it reject scientific predictions about the future in a fundamentalist isolation from contemporary culture. Both these options end in infidelity to the gospel and in intellectual dishonesty.

I believe that a more appropriate stance for Christian theology with regard to the future of the universe is to hold in tension both the scientific predictions about the future of the universe and Christian belief in the resurrection and the New Creation, and to live with this tension.

At the end of his life Karl Rahner pointed out that with the increasing complexity of human knowledge in areas like science and theology, we have no guarantee that we will always be able to reach a synthesis of affirmations coming from different sources. But, he argued, we should not see our inability to reach a synthesis as itself a sufficient reason to reject either affirmation. There are times when the only option is to live with the lack of synthesis.[32] It may well be necessary to accept that the tension between scientific views of the end of the universe and the affirmations of Christian eschatology cannot be resolved at present. This may change as science and theology develop. But it may mean that, for the time being, Christians will find themselves in a "cognitive minority" within a contemporary scientific culture on issues such as the resurrection and the promise of the new heavens and the new Earth.

John Polkinghorne points to the relationship between the death of individuals and the predicted death of the universe. We human beings are certainly going to die, and yet Christians affirm faith in the resurrection of the body. A little thought makes it clear that a God who would bring humans to new life beyond death can also bring the universe to new life.[33] It is no more difficult to believe in God's power at work in the resurrection of one person than it is to believe in the transformation of the universe. Perhaps it is true to say that belief in neither is supported by contemporary scientific culture. But this is no reason to abandon what is central to Christian faith nor to abandon the insights of science. The invitation is to live creatively with both until a new synthesis can be found, confident that the God of truth is behind our faltering and limited achievements in both science and theology.

Perhaps such a new synthesis may emerge from changes in both science and theology. In science, the old mechanistic concept of the universe, which seemed so antagonistic to Christian faith, has gone and been replaced by the unpredictability of quantum mechanics, chaos theory and the self-organizing universe. It may be that the sciences of complexity and self-organization, and new developments in cosmology, will also open up new ways of thinking about the long-term future of the universe.[34] In theology, theologians like Karl Rahner have shown how God's action in the universe need not be thought of as an extrinsic action which overthrows the old creation. Rather, God's work of New Creation can be thought of as coming from within creation itself. God's future for the universe, the New Creation, may come, by God's salvific action, from within the expanding universe itself in ways which we are unable to imagine and cannot predict.[35]

The Salvation of the Universe

Much has happened to extend our understanding of the theology of salvation in the second half of the twentieth century. Gustavo Gutiérrez is a key figure in contemporary liberation theology and in the development of a theology of salvation. Doing theology from the side of the poor of Latin America, he asks the question: What relationship is there between salvation in Jesus Christ and the historical process of liberation? Gutiérrez finds three interrelated dimensions of a theology of liberation: 1) human actions aimed at political liberation; 2) the broader movement toward full human liberation; and 3) liberation from sin for communion with God.[36]

These three dimensions are all part of a single salvific process. Jesus Christ is the liberator whose saving action embraces all dimensions of human existence. The three levels are distinct, and each is necessary. They must not be collapsed into one another. Yet they are interrelated, so that one cannot exist fully without the others. Human political actions which are truly liberating can be understood in this theology as a partial and limited realization of God's salvation. But they are not all of God's salvation and cannot be simply identified with it, since God's future transcends all our projects, which are always to be understood as subject to human error and sinfulness.

Gutiérrez succeeds in developing a theology of salvation which embraces both our experience of forgiveness of sin and our participation in movements aimed at justice and liberation. He lays the basis for an integral theology of salvation or liberation, one that is faithful to Jesus' own preaching and praxis of the liberating Reign of God. Paul VI, in his 1975 work on evangelization, stressed this integral nature of salvation when he wrote that a theology of liberation must envisage the whole human person, in all his or her aspects, right up to and including openness to the divine.[37]

Edward Schillebeeckx has been another major contributor to an integral theology of salvation. Based on a very careful exegetical study of the Christian scriptures, he arrives at a theology of salvation which embraces the whole person. It includes liberation in seven "constants" of human existence: in our relationship to human corporeality, nature and the ecological environment; in our relationship to other persons; in connection with social and institutional structures; in the conditioning of people by time and place; in the mutual relationship of theory and practice; and in the religious or "para-religious" consciousness of the person. The seventh constant is that all of the other six form an irreducible synthesis in any adequate notion of the human person and of salvation. A theology of salvation which focuses on some to the exclusion of others leads to a distorted view of religious life as, for example, only about I-Thou relationships, or only about personal relationship with God, or only about ecology. All are necessary. God's salvation is to be understood as embracing all dimensions of the human.[38]

How are our actions and experiences connected to God's final salvation? Schillebeeckx suggests that we may see in our lives "fragmentary anticipations" of God's future Reign. In our everyday experiences that "all is grace" we already experience partial anticipation of final salvation. Our earthly actions aimed at human liberation can be understood as a part of salvation coming from God, even though they also include elements of human weakness and sin. We cannot simply identify our human projects with God's salvation. This would be idolatry. Our projects are historically conditioned and limited, and always subject to distortion from human frailty and sin. God's final eschatological salvation transcends our experience and our actions, and cannot be foreseen or controlled. Yet in our everyday lives we already experience the presence of God's salvation in partial and anticipatory ways.

Schillebeeckx has indeed forged an inclusive and integral theology of salvation, one that has been widely appreciated because it is so inclusive. It is important to notice, however, that it remains in this formulation a notion of *human* salvation. It is an integral notion of human salvation, which embraces human relationships with all dimensions of life.

It seems to me that we need to go beyond this formulation, which is centered on the human, and deliberately set it within a broader ecological and cosmic framework of salvation. God's new creation will be a transformation of all creatures, and integral human liberation needs to be seen within this context. Such a theology of salvation needs to situate human liberation, including individual, ecological, interpersonal, political and religious dimensions of liberation (Schillebeeckx's contribution), within the context of the redemption of all creation (Rom 8:21; Col 1:20). In schematic form, such a theology of salvation would involve:

1. *God's transformation of the whole universe.* Salvation in Christ embraces the great clusters of galaxies and the interactions of subatomic particles; it touches every plant, insect, animal, human being, and eco-system on Earth. The risen Jesus is the beginning of the New Creation, and in his resurrection, the transfiguration of the material universe has begun, a process which will reach its conclusion in God's final eschatological act of salvation.

2. *God's self-offering in saving grace to human beings, and the invitation to them to participate in a human way in the divine work of on-going creation and redemption.* God's liberating grace, and our call to participation, involve all the dimensions of human existence:

- our interrelationships with other persons and our life in community
- our relationship to our selves, our bodiliness, minds and feelings
- our participation in social and political structures and our engagement in transforming action aimed at justice and peace
- our relationship to other living creatures, to ecosystems, the Earth and the universe
- in and through all of this, our relationship with the living God in the forgiveness of sin and the life of grace

Salvation then becomes a concept that embraces the whole of creation. Within this overarching concept it also involves our own human attitudes and praxis with regard to interpersonal relationships, our bodily selves, politics and social systems, the Earth's biological community and God.

What will God's future look like? Christian theology has to admit that it can provide little explicit detail for its affirmation about the future. It calls us to trust in the divine promise about resurrection, New Creation and eternal joy in interrelationship with the trinitarian God and with all God's creatures. We are promised a future of unending exploration of the fecund abundance of the divine Persons, and of unimaginable fulfillment of our heart's longing for loving relationships, in company with all God's creation.

Beyond this, it is a matter of speculation and projection on the basis of what we know of divine action in creation and incarnation. Jurgen Moltmann completes his recent Christological theology with a great vision of final redemption. His vision of final salvation and new life seems to include literally *all* creatures that have ever existed in a New Creation.[39] In a recent work John Polkinghorne argues that "the vast tracts of the cosmos are not to be considered as merely disposable accessories to the local human story," but he does not see this as necessarily involving the recreation of everything that ever existed: "The anaerobic unicellular life of early Earth was a staging post of biological evolution and we do not have to suppose that it, as such, must reappear somewhere in the new heavens and the new earth."[40] Its value would be preserved in the destiny of that to which it gives rise.

As this difference between Moltmann and Polkinghorne shows, the details of the transformation of creation are far from clear and are a matter of legitimate theological speculation.

The future of creation is in the trinitarian God, and it remains profoundly unpredictable. Just as Christian faith cannot tell a person the detail of what lies on the other side of death, and death remains a handing over of ourselves to God in unknowing and in radical trust, so the end of the universe remains for believers a matter, not of foresight, but of radical trust and Christian hope based on the promise of God made manifest in Jesus of Nazareth.

A Christian theology of salvation, based on God's action in the death and resurrection of Jesus, tells us that we have reason for hope that our actions directed toward love, justice and care for the Earth and its creatures have meaning in terms of God's final transformation of all things in Christ. The resurrection teaches us that even what appears to be terrible failure can have final meaning. Cleansed of sinful elements and transfigured in Christ, our contributions do matter in terms of God's New Creation. As Pope John Paul II has said with regard to our human actions and efforts, in God's final salvation "nothing will be lost or will have been in vain."[41]

In this section, I have been arguing that Wisdom Christology and a trinitarian theology of mutual relations and fecundity lead to a view of human beings as persons-in-mutual-relationship and as kin to other creatures in an Earth community. We are all children of the universe, made from stardust, sharing a common journey and directed toward a common future in God. Salvation in Christ will embrace the whole universe and every creature in it, and every dimension of human life, and this saving, transforming action has already begun in the resurrection of the Crucified.

7.

Ecological Praxis

I have been arguing that when Jesus is understood as the Wisdom of God, it becomes possible to glimpse the unity between God's self-expression in each creature and in Jesus of Nazareth. In a Wisdom Christology it becomes clear that the Wisdom revealed in a rain forest is revealed in a new and staggering way in the crucified One. The resurrection of Jesus crucified can be grasped as the beginning of the transformation of the whole universe.

The God revealed in Jesus is a trinitarian God—a God revealed not only as Wisdom incarnate, but also as the Spirit at the heart of life and as the incomprehensible Fountain and Source, who can be addressed with familial trust and confidence as *Abba*. This trinitarian God is a God of dynamic mutual interrelationships. At the same time, the trinitarian God is revealed to be a God of ecstatic fecundity and boundless generosity, so that creation can be understood as the free self-expression of divine goodness. From this trinitarian theology two principles for an ecological theology flow. First, the fundamental understanding of reality is relational, and the universe is understood as always springing from dynamic trinitarian relationships. Second, the whole universe and each creature of the universe, from the Andromeda Galaxy to a wild orchid, are to be understood as God's self-expression.

In the last chapter I argued that a Christian anthropology understands the human person as essentially interpersonal and as intrinsically interrelated with other creatures in one community of life on Earth. Human beings can be understood as self-conscious creatures invited into conscious interpersonal relationships with the Creator and to partnership

153

with the Creator in care for creation. In this final chapter I conclude these reflections by making explicit seven directions for ecological praxis which emerge from this theology.

The Intrinsic Value of All Creatures

Christian ecological praxis is founded on the understanding that creatures have ethical value not just because they may be useful to human beings, but because they have intrinsic value—value in themselves.

Any worldview that places human beings at the center of the universe, whether physically, spiritually or ethically, can be called an anthropocentric view. In the context of ecological discussions, anthropocentrism is usually understood to refer to the view that human beings have ethical value in themselves ("intrinsic value"), while other creatures are not seen as having value in themselves. In an anthropocentric ethics the value of nonhuman creatures comes only from their relationship and usefulness to human beings ("instrumental value").

It would be anthropocentric to argue that a rain forest should be cleared because of the economic benefits that clearing would bring to a logging company or to potential farmers. It would also be anthropocentric (and legitimate) to argue against clearing a rain forest because of future benefits the retained rain forest would have for the human community.

It is another thing altogether to argue that a rain forest has value in itself (intrinsic value), and that this value must be taken into account in any decision about logging.

The argument of this book is that a Christian trinitarian theology leads to an ecological ethics of intrinsic value. It is not an ethical view in which everything is centered on human beings (anthropocentrism). Nor is it simply the alternative view, which would see everything centered on living creatures (biocentrism). It is not even simply a view which would see the whole Earth or the universe as the center of ethical discussion (geocentrism or cosmocentrism).

Rather, the argument here is that all things have value in themselves because of their relationship with God. I am in agreement with the position articulated by James Gustafson, who writes that we must "relate to all things in a manner appropriate to their relations with God."[1]

It is the dynamic trinitarian Persons-In-Mutual-Relationship that give meaning and value to all things in the universe. This is a thoroughly theocentric view. It is the direct result of a Wisdom Christology, which sees all things as created and transformed in Jesus-Sophia, and of a trinitarian theology like that of Bonaventure's, which sees each creature as the free act of divine self-expression.

Things have value in themselves because they are the self-expression of God. They are the created articulation of the eternal Word, divine Wisdom, the Art of God. Modern science has shown us *how* this articulation has occurred. It explains the process—the interaction of chance and lawfulness, the expanding universe, and biological evolution on Earth. We are becoming very aware that this process involves evolutionary dead ends and false starts and countless extinct species. Yet for the Christian this is the way of divine Wisdom—the way of respect for the integrity of created processes.

The contemporary Christian, faced with this extraordinary evolutionary story and with the wonder of a tropical rain forest, cannot but see this diversity and vitality as the Book of God, the ecstatic self-expression of divine fruitfulness. Wanton destruction of this divine self-expression is deadly sin, unparalleled in human history.

As Thomas Berry has written:

> There is an awe and reverence due to the stars in the heavens, the sun, and all heavenly bodies; to the seas and the continents; to all living forms of trees and flowers; to the myriad expressions of life in the sea: to the animals of the forest and the birds of the air. To wantonly destroy a living species is to silence forever a divine voice.[2]

Birds, plants, forests, mountains and galaxies have value in themselves because they exist and are held in being by the divine Persons-In-Mutual-Communion, and because they are fruitful expressions of divine Wisdom. They are indeed the voice of the divine, and to destroy one of them irresponsibly is to stop arbitrarily a mode of divine self-expression. To destroy a species is, as Berry writes, to silence a divine voice *forever*.

Human Value

A Christian ecological praxis respects the unique value of human persons and gives priority to the poor of the Earth.

Some Christian thinkers have never transcended anthropocentrism, and their basis for judgment on all ethical issues is the dignity of the human person. My argument is that the dignity of the human person is not the only criterion for ethical decision-making. The human person needs to be understood within a community of creatures, which have their own intrinsic value.

On the other hand, some ecologists give no unique place to the human person. Some, like deep ecologists Arne Naess, George Sessions and Bill Devall, argue for an "ecological egalitarianism" and a "democracy of the biosphere."[3] Others, like J. Baird Callicott argue that the whole carries more weight than any individual part.[4] A forest or a wetland has more value than an individual. Thomas Berry can speak of human beings as "the most pernicious mode of earthly being" and as "the affliction of the world, its demonic presence."[5]

Ecofeminists stress the interconnections between creatures. They often reject hierarchical ordering, and some refuse to assert the rights of human beings over other creatures.[6] There are those, however, like Marti Kheel, who believe overemphasis on the ecological totality undervalues the individual. An abstract identification with the whole can fail to recognize and respect the individual and the need for individual self-identity within the whole. She points to the experience of women, where often self-identity is formed not through opposition to others but through interconnection with them.[7]

The trinitarian theology developed above agrees with various forms of deep ecology and ecofeminism about the intrinsic value of all creatures. It is also in agreement with their critiques of exploitative and destructive human behavior. As opposed to some, however, it suggests that a commitment to the intrinsic value of all creatures can and must go hand and hand with a respect for the unique dignity of human persons.

In this theology the human person is understood as intersubjective and as interrelated with other creatures, which have their own ethical integrity. In this context the human person is understood as an individual in whom creation has come to consciousness, as one who stands before the free self-communication and forgiveness of God in grace, as one who is made in the image of God and is called into the family life of the trinitarian God as an adopted child of God. As Paul Santmire has written, "The human creature, created in community like all other creaturely beings, is unique in this respect: the human creature is called to enter into self-conscious communion with God, along with other humans, through confession of praise and acts of obedience."[8]

A Christian discipleship will need to recognize both the intrinsic value of all creatures and the unique dignity of human creatures. It will need to be committed to both ecology and justice. It will need to respect both the integrity of creation and the dignity of the human person. It supports a social ethics which combines ecological commitment with solidarity with the poor of the Earth. It sees economic oppression, sexism and the violation of the planet as radically interrelated. Social justice and care for the planet are not understood as competing options, but as part of one ethical stance. Action aimed at just economic and social conditions and action aimed at ecological sustainability are interrelated dimensions of the one praxis of discipleship. In the language of the World Council of Churches, discipleship involves a commitment to "justice, peace and the integrity of creation."

Reverence for Life

Reverence for all forms of life is a guiding norm for Christian praxis.

Albert Schweitzer argued that the basis for all ethics is the concept of "reverence for life." He based his understanding of ethical value on the idea that every living creature has a "will-to-live." He argued that right human conduct consists of giving the same reverence which a human being might give to his or her own life to each living creature and its will-to-live.

Schweitzer refused to make distinctions among different species in terms of their value. He admitted that, in the process of living, human beings do, in fact, have to kill other creatures. But, he argued, this should happen only when really necessary, and then it should be accompanied by an authentic compassion and a sense of moral responsibility for the life which has been sacrificed.

It was Albert Schweitzer's life's work to develop an ethic of love for all of creation. Just before his death in 1965, Rachel Carson dedicated her history-making *Silent Spring* to him, and the contemporary ecological movement began to gather public support.[9] I find Schweitzer's position wonderfully illustrated in his saying that the ethical person "shatters no ice crystal that sparkles in the sun, tears no leaf from its tree, breaks off no flower, and is careful not to crush any insect as he walks."[10]

Albert Schweitzer's ethic of respect for all forms of life remains a radical and needed challenge to contemporary culture. He writes that an absolute ethics of the will-to-live seeks to refrain from destroying any life, regardless of its type. An ethical person will not say of any instance of life, "This has no value."[11] I believe the attitude that every instance of life has value is the only one that is congruent with the view of God and creation that has emerged in this book.

At the same time, I will argue in a later section that we do need a principle of ethical discrimination—something that Schweitzer rejects. Lois Daly notes that in Schweitzer's work "there is no moral hierarchy that says that decisions to destroy infectious bacteria in human beings or other animals are the right decisions."[12] I believe that we do need a principle of discernment that can enable us to decide between the life of dangerous bacteria and a human life.

In a message for the World Day on Peace on 1 January 1990, John Paul II named two ethical principles as fundamental for a peaceful society: respect for life and respect for the integrity of creation.[13] In this message he names a number of specific issues that threaten life on Earth: the depletion of the ozone layer, the greenhouse effect, massive urban concentrations, industrial waste, the burning of fossil fuels, deforestation, dangerous herbicides, coolants and propellants, and the danger of submersion of low-lying lands. He finds that fundamental to all of these issues is the lack of respect for life—human life and the whole ecological balance of life on the planet. He points out how delicate ecological balances are upset by the uncontrolled destruction of plant and animal life and by the reckless exploitation of natural resources. He argues: "Respect for life, and above all the dignity of the human person, is the ultimate guiding norm for any sound economic or industrial or scientific progress."

It is self-evident that respect for life involves respect for the diversity of living species. Sean McDonagh has pointed out that "there has been no in-depth theological reflection on what extinction might mean for the community of the living and for God's sovereignty over creation."[14] The current massive extinction of living species is, in the main, the direct result of human beings destroying habitats and polluting environments.

In recent times scientists have become more aware of the series of mass extinctions that have eliminated many species. These include the extinctions at the beginning of the Cambrian period, 570 million years ago, and at the end of the Permian period, 245 million years ago. It is estimated that in these two extinctions most forms of life (perhaps 80-90 percent of species) were destroyed. The extinction we face at the end of the twentieth century is different in character to the mass extinctions of the past. They were caused by climactic and geological changes, and possibly, in some cases, by collisions between meteorites and the Earth. The extinction we face today has a moral character. It is the result of destructive human action and inaction. It is important to note that in the current human-made extinction, plant diversity is being destroyed.[15]

According to the theological vision of the trinitarian God as Persons-In-Mutual-Relationship and as a God of dynamic and ecstatic fecundity, the diversity of living creatures is the self-expression of divine fruitfulness. The human destruction of biodiversity is an act of contempt for the divine self-expression. It is not only unthinkably destructive, it is extreme hubris and an extreme form of human sin.

The way of conversion lies in the path of personal, cultural and political reverence for life. As the Presbyterian Eco-Justice Task Force says, "Keeping and healing the creation is God's work." Because it is God's work it is also the church's mission.[16] It is because individual forms of life are modes of divine self-communication that care for life is the work of discipleship.

The Biotic Community

A Christian ecological praxis recognizes the interdependence of living creatures and gives particular ethical weight to biological com-

*munities, from local ecosystems to the biological community of the
Earth.*

Respect for life cannot be restricted to individual animals or plants,
or even to species, but must extend to interacting ecosystems. Contemporary ecologists have been able to describe the food chains that link
diverse species and to show the delicate balances that hold together the
interconnecting web of life in specific biotic communities.[17]

I have already had reason to refer to Aldo Leopold's *A Sand County
Almanac*. In this classic statement of a holistic approach to ethics,
Leopold spells out what he calls "the land ethic." He sees all ethics as
resting on the premise that the individual is a member of a community
of interdependent parts. He sees the history of human ethics as a gradual
extension of the boundaries of community to include all people. Now it
has to include the land as well—"The land ethic simply enlarges the
boundaries of the community to include soils, waters, plants and animals, or collectively: the land."[18]

Human beings are called to treat the land with respect and to see
themselves as part of a land community. Leopold writes: "That land is
a community is the basic concept of ecology, but that land is to be
loved and respected is an extension of ethics."[19] Leopold offers a famous criterion for an ecological ethics: "A thing is right when it tends
to preserve the integrity, stability, and beauty of the biotic community.
It is wrong when it tends otherwise."[20]

As Ian Barbour notes, right action is here being defined in terms of
its consequences for the biotic community. The criterion is the good of
the whole ecosystem.[21] Barbour supports a holistic approach to ecological ethics, but he does not support a biocentric ethics that would
simply subsume the human under the biological. Such ethics provide
no grounds for decisions when the interests of diverse members of a
biotic community are in conflict. His own view is that "the integrity of
the ecosystem is important because it makes possible *the welfare of
interdependent individuals*, human and nonhuman."[22] In his view, ecological integrity is a precondition for other values, but it does not serve
as a definition of all value. Our goals need to be compatible with the
health of the ecosystem, but they need not be limited to it.

The relational view of God developed above, as Persons-In-Mutual-
Communion, and the relational metaphysics and relational understand-

ing of human beings that flow from it, lend support to Leopold's concept that the whole has ethical weight. The biotic community is an important source of moral value. But it also supports Barbour's argument that the good of the whole is not the only source of ethical value. It sees the whole and the individual as intrinsically interrelated. To be a human person is to be in relationship with other humans and interrelated in a biotic community. A relational ethics attributes value to the individual person, to the political and social, and to the biotic community.

In all kinds of decisions, whether they concern damming a river, building a road, or overturning a rock, we need to ask what effect our actions will have on the ecosystem involved. As John Paul II has said, "One cannot use with impunity the different categories of beings, whether animate or inanimate—animals, plants, the natural elements— simply as one wishes, according to one's own economic need." Rather, "One must take into account the nature of each being and its mutual connection in an ordered system, which is precisely the cosmos."[23] A trinitarian theology supports Aldo Leopold's conviction that the integrity of the biotic community is a basic principle for an ecological ethics, but it claims that there are also other basic principles.

A Criterion for Ethical Discernment

A criterion which may be used to discern between competing interests of different species of living creatures is that of the level of consciousness of the creatures involved.

It is often assumed when one argues for the *intrinsic* value of animals, plants and forests, that intrinsic value means *equal* value. Thus, if a cockroach and a human being both have intrinsic value, they must both have equal value. In fact, this view is adopted by some ecological advocates, but it is not the view that I am proposing.

I argue that a theological approach to this issue suggests that a cockroach and a human being do indeed both have intrinsic value, but they do not possess the same value. Because a cockroach has intrinsic value, it would be wrong to crush one arbitrarily and unnecessarily. But because human beings have a unique value as compared to a cockroach, they are justified in expelling cockroaches from their kitchens.

As Ian Barbour writes, "We need a *principle of discrimination* when the different forms of life conflict."[24] Such a principle of discrimination can be found in process theology, and it is articulated in the ecological work of John Cobb and Charles Birch. The criterion they suggest for distinguishing between the intrinsic value of different creatures is the richness, complexity and intensity of their experience.[25]

This criterion amounts to a human judgment about the level of feeling or consciousness a being has achieved. It means that we would give more ethical weight to the life of a chimpanzee than to a mosquito. It means that it is right to kill a disease-carrying mosquito in order to protect the health of a human family.

I differ from Charles Birch when he says that "only feeling confers intrinsic value."[26] Admittedly, he sees continuity in natural beings and some level of self-determination or feeling all the way down to electrons. For Birch and Cobb feeling is wider than what is usually meant by consciousness. For them, feeling and intrinsic value are extended to the components of all natural entities. However, some beings, such as rocks, are seen only as "aggregates," and the intrinsic value of a rock is only the sum of the intrinsic value of the molecules, atoms and electrons that compose it. In this book I have sought to go beyond this view of process theology and argue that we need a theocentric ecological ethics which attributes intrinsic value to creatures not because they have feeling (Birch and Cobb) or because they experience pain (Peter Singer), but because they are the divine self-expression.[27]

In my view rocks, mountain ranges, forests and ecosystems are not simply aggregates of creatures which have intrinsic value, but they also have intrinsic value in themselves because they are modes of divine presence and the expression of trinitarian fruitfulness.

While I do not want to *derive* the concept of intrinsic value from the richness of experience, I do believe, with Birch and Cobb, that an important criterion in ethical decisions is the level of consciousness of the creatures involved. I also agree with Peter Singer that part of the ethical task is to acknowledge a special place for those creatures that experience pain and to seek to reduce unnecessary suffering in the world.

Because I remain firmly committed to the value of the dignity of the human person, as creation come to consciousness and invited into family relationship with the trinitarian God, I argue for the equal value of all human beings before God. Furthermore, I have argued that in the

revelation of divine Wisdom in Jesus of Nazareth we are confronted
with God's priority for the poor and disabled. For these reasons I radically oppose using the criterion of the level of consciousness to discriminate between the relative value of human beings or to discriminate against those who might suffer from a disability or whose
consciousness might not be fully developed.

It is sometimes objected that the judgment about the "richness of
experience" or the degree of consciousness is made only from a human
perspective. But human ethical decisions only can be made from a limited human perspective. It is the only perspective we have, and we must
make the best judgments we can on the basis of what we can see and
understand as human beings. Sometimes it is said that this is a return to
anthropocentrism. But this is to confuse different meanings of the word
anthropocentrism. It is important to note again that the kind of
anthropocentrism that I have sought to overcome is the view that the
value of a tree or a forest comes only from its usefulness to humans.

In working out how to assess one intrinsic value over against another, we human beings have to use our human brains to discover ethical criteria with which we can guide our human acts. I argue, along
with Birch and Cobb, that our best perception of the level of consciousness of a creature, which admittedly will always be a limited human
judgment based on available information, is a useful and a necessary
criterion.

According to this criterion, primates and whales have ethical priority in relationship to flies and worms. In this framework it is justifiable
to destroy cancer cells in order to save human lives.

Ecological Sustainability

*A Christian praxis which respects the intrinsic value of all creatures
involves a commitment to an ecologically sustainable economic and
political system and to a lifestyle congruent with sustainability.*

If our theology commits us to respecting the intrinsic value of all
creatures, then Christian praxis needs to take a position on the sustainable use of resources.

One of the few theologians to tackle this urgent issue is John Cobb.
Cobb has shown how contemporary economics, with its commitment

to solving economic problems by growth of gross national product, can lead only to ecological and human disaster. Both in his own work and in his collaboration with the economist Herman Daly he has had the courage to envision an alternative economic strategy of ecological sustainability.[28] Because I believe that this vision of a sustainable and livable society is an urgently needed corrective to current thinking about economics, I will summarize some key elements of John Cobb's view.

Cobb envisions the cities of the future along the lines of the work done by Paolo Soleri.[29] Soleri calls his proposed cities architectural ecologies or arcologies. These cities would be not only energy efficient, but also free of dependence on fossil fuel, built to run on solar energy. They would be built so that there would be no need for private transport within the city. Housing, industry, shopping, recreation areas, and some food growing areas would all be included in an integrated unit, using solar energy in an efficient manner.

In agriculture, the recent trend away from family farms to agribusinesses would need to be reversed. Cobb points out that we have a growing numbers of examples of nearly sustainable organic farms and the long history of successful farms run by Amish families. This movement toward small family farms would need to go hand in hand with a gradual reduction in meat consumption, particularly the consumption of beef.

A fundamental element in John Cobb's vision of an ecologically sustainable future is the idea that economic policies would include all social and environmental costs in the price of goods. If we began to calculate the real costs of products—the damage to the atmosphere, pollution of rivers, or the loss of topsoil, as well as the cost of disposing of used products—then we would quickly move toward the production of more ecologically sustainable products. He argues that nations will need to decide what portion of proven reserves of minerals could be mined each year. This would be reflected in price and encourage frugality, recycling, and the development of more sustainable substitutes.[30]

In the arena of international politics Cobb argues against the idea that world hunger and poverty will be solved simply by a massive increase in Gross Global Product, which will be the result of unrestrained global free trade. Instead, he argues that poor countries need policies of redistribution of land, self-sufficiency in food production, appropriate technology, and policies that favor their own local industries and sustainable development from below. He points to the fact that within countries, human advances, like a just wage and a forty-hour week, have come about not through an increase in Gross National Product, but through political processes aimed at human welfare. At the global level there are not yet parallel political structures which can work effectively for human good, but only an economics of "free trade," which tends toward the maximum level of exploitation of workers and resources.

Cobb supports a concept of free trade among relatively self-sufficient nations, rather than a "free trade" where a poorer country is forced to specialize in one or very few commodities and becomes totally dependent on international economic institutions. His view of the global unity is of a "community of diverse and self-reliant peoples, not a standardized pool of labor working for subsistence together with globally homogenized consumerism."[31]

He argues that we need to think of large political entities as communities of smaller communities, and he wants the smaller communities to participate in the decisions that affect them. He wants nations to control economic institutions rather than being controlled by them— and governments to place human welfare above economic interest and unrestricted free trade.

At the heart of John Cobb's criticism of the prevailing economics is his understanding that "the breakdown of community that accompanies the growth of GNP is not coincidental."[32] Breakdown in community patterns, along with an ever-increasing use of resources and pollution of the Earth, is implicit in the view of endless economic progress. In Cobb's view all this is consistent with the individualism which is at the base of this kind of economic theory.

Cobb seeks to envision an economics for community which is also an economics of ecological sustainability. In my view, an alternative economic vision like Cobb's is required if we are to survive as a global biological community, and if we are to begin to become a global human community. A theology centered on trinitarian communion supports an economics geared to community and to sustainability.

To accept the concept of sustainability is to accept the idea of human and earthly finitude. It seems to me that it involves a thorough acceptance of a global ethical responsibility to limit the human population through education about appropriate and freely chosen family planning.

It is estimated that between 1990 and 2030 the Earth's population may jump by about 3.6 billion; food sources simply cannot keep pace.[33] There has been a leveling off in grain yields and in the ocean's seafood catch since 1984. We face a combination of falling grain output per person and a shrinking seafood catch per person. Lester Brown warns that the growing demand for food and the Earth's physical capacity to satisfy these demands may dominate the next four decades as much as ideological conflict dominated the four decades from 1950 to 1990.[34]

There is every reason to believe that there is a limit to how much food the Earth can provide for human consumption—and that we are perilously near that limit. Many in our global community already face starvation and malnutrition, because of many factors, including inequality in access to resources, exploitative practices by the wealthy and powerful, political instability, wars, expanding populations and degradation of land. We need to face the limited nature of the carrying capacity of our planet. The response called for seems to be one of commitment to global solidarity in the distribution of resources, along with commitment to a sustainable economics, a sustainable lifestyle, the empowering of women, and global education in responsible and freely chosen family planning.

Companions with Other Creatures in an Earth Community

The praxis of Christian discipleship involves the rediscovery for a new era of the Franciscan theology of companionship and family relationship between human beings and other creatures in the one Earth community.

I have been arguing that the praxis of Christian discipleship must take into account the intrinsic value of every creature; that it must involve a commitment to the praxis of reverence for life; that the intrinsic value of every creature needs to be held together with the value that is placed on human persons, so that a Christian life is understood as commitment to both ecology and justice; that where a principle of discernment is needed between competing life-forms, the level of a creature's consciousness can be used as one criterion; that systems as wholes, ecological wholes and biological communities, have ethical weight; and that a praxis of ecological sustainability is the only proper theological response to our current crisis.

All of this is suggesting that ethical imperatives for ecological praxis come from not just one or two sources but from a number of sources: the intrinsic value of a creature, reverence for life, the dignity of the human person, the level of consciousness of a creature, the ecological whole and sustainability.

This means that neither a simplistic ethical "egalitarianism," which refuses to discriminate among creatures in any circumstances, nor an absolute "hierarchy," which would place the needs of human beings above other creatures in every situation, is appropriate. There are times when the needs of human beings should take second place to the needs of the whole biological community—a clear example would be the choice to save the remaining rain forests of the Earth.

A Christian praxis that values the integrity of all creatures goes beyond specific ethical decisions. It is a matter of worldview, emotional commitment, conviction and lifestyle. It is a matter of spirituality, an abiding recognition that other creatures are companions before God in an Earth community, children of the universe.

Many peoples have had this sense of companionship or of family relationship with other creatures. Australian Aboriginal people see the land itself as Mother; they see themselves as in a communal relationship with other creatures through the "Dreaming." Patrick Dodson describes this Dreaming relationship:

> For Aboriginal people the creative and life giving forces are still very much alive. The land is full of the spirits, thoughts and deeds of the creative forces. The spirits of the ancestors of all human, plant and animal life are represented in the land forms. This extends to celestial forms such as the planets and the stars, the moon and the sun. There are stories and songs throughout the land which relate these things. Sites where events of great significance occurred are holy places—sacred sites. Some places are so important that their story can only be told by initiated people.[35]

George Tinker describes the Native American experience of kinship with other creatures. He writes of the Lakota prayer formula "*Mitakuye oyasin*," which is used often in the way "Amen" is used often in Christian circles. It means "for all my relations." Tinker writes that "every Lakota who prays this prayer knows that our relatives necessarily include the four-leggeds, the wingeds, and all the living, moving things on Mother Earth."[36] He says of the Native American understanding of creation that "it embraces all of life from trees and rocks to international relations." Its kinship view of creation informs all activities from hunting and dancing to administering government agencies. Tinker says that if we believe that we are all relatives in this world, then we must live together differently from the way we have been doing—"we will live together out of respect for each other, working toward the good of each other."[37]

Something like this traditional approach to creation is required by an ecological theology. What is needed, Sally McFague tells us, is a new "aesthetic sensibility" toward other creatures, which "values what is unselfishly, with a sense of delight in others for their own sakes." This is a necessary step in the movement from an anthropocentric to an ecological sensibility.[38] She writes that "to feel in the depths of our beings that we are part and parcel of the evolutionary ecosystem of our cosmos is a prerequisite for contemporary Christian theology."[39]

We are only at the beginning of the process of adopting this aesthetic sensibility.[40] I believe that a crucial part of this will be a recovery of the Christian mystical tradition. Matthew Fox has long been engaged in the project of developing a contemporary creation spirituality and showing the relevance of the Christian mystical tradition—as instanced in great figures like Hildegard of Bingen and Meister Eckhart—for contemporary ecological issues.[41]

I think it can be argued that, in spite of all neoplatonic distortions in the tradition, the great mystics have, by and large, all become lovers of the creatures that God loves. Sally McFague speaks of our invitation to become friends of the Friend of the universe.[42] To become friends with such a Friend is to share this Friend's delight in kangaroos and bougainvilleas. It seems to me that authentic mystics have come to recognize that, as Aldo Leopold once suggested, God "likes to hear birds sing and to see flowers grow."[43] Part of the process of union with God is coming to share in this divine enjoyment.

To be caught up in love for the exuberant trinitarian God is also to recognize the Beloved in the exuberant life of a bougainvillea.

Bonaventure would call this the grace of "contuition." This is a real contemplation, a real seeing—a capacity to gaze on a bougainvillea, to take great delight in its beauty, and, at the same time, to know it as the self-expression of divine Wisdom.

As I said earlier, much of Bonaventure's theology is an attempt to reflect on the insights that flowed from the mystical experience of Francis of Assisi. Francis was the great practitioner of "contuition," the great example of a Christian sense of companionship and family relationship with other creatures. For Francis, the sun, the moon, the stars, the wind, water, fire, and the Earth, who sustains and governs us, and even death itself, are brothers and sisters, companions and common creatures before God.

Roger Sorrell has shown how Francis's attitude to creation depends upon his biblical and medieval Christian heritage, but is at the same time profoundly original. He shows how Francis carefully crafted his great poem *The Canticle of Brother Sun*, writing it in a popular style and (unusual for Francis) in Italian, thus linking it with vernacular troubadour poetry and assuring its widespread transmission. Francis gave the poem to his friars so that they might pass it on to the whole community of the faithful. Francis saw the friars as God's troubadours and jongleurs. They were to take the poem to the world. As Sorrell says, this was a "medieval attempt to propagandize."[44] Its main purpose was "to inspire people and teach them how to think of creation with gratitude, appreciation and respect."[45]

Sorrell sees the *Canticle* not as an invocation directed toward creation, but as an exhortation directed toward humanity to value and to give thanks for creation.[46] He sees its purpose as appreciative and ecological. It is ecological "in that it explicitly rejects a view of creation that would objectify it and take it for granted as being worthless and irrelevant unless it proves serviceable for humanity." Francis emphasizes not only creation's usefulness to people, but also its "intrinsic qualities—its worth apart from humanity's needs, a worth gained from its specific divine endowment, which merits notice and respect."[47]

Sorrell shows how Francis's work goes beyond an objectifying "I—It" relationship with creation toward an "I—Thou" relationship of mutual community: "Francis's ideas, while certainly relating to typical medieval views of humankind and creatures in the chain of being, actually represent something profoundly new for the ascetic traditions of the high Middle Ages, in their emphasis on autonomy coupled with mutual service, respect and affection."[48] Francis's vision was of a "harmonious and interdependent community of creation."[49] Sorrell sees the *Canticle* as a *"tour de force* of medieval thought," which influenced not only religious life, but the artistic heritage of Giotto and the new values of realism and interest in the physical world of pre-Renaissance and Renaissance artists.

Francis, the patron saint of ecologists, challenges us today to a discipleship and a contemporary ecological praxis based upon the theological insight that we are sisters and brothers to other creatures, members of one community of creation.

> Be praised, my Lord, with all your creatures,
> Especially Sir Brother Sun,
> Who brings the day. You enlighten us through
>   him.
>
> How beautiful and radiant he is, with such
>   splendor!
> Of you, Most High, he bears the likeness.
>
> Be praised, my Lord, for Sister Moon and the
>   Stars.
> In heaven you have formed them, bright and
>   precious, and beautiful.
>
> Be praised, my Lord, for Brother Wind,
> And for Air, for Cloudy and Clear, and all
>   weather,
> By which you give sustenance to your creatures.
>
> Be praised, my Lord, for Sister Water,
> She is very useful, and humble, and precious,
>   and pure.
>
> Be praised, my Lord, for Brother Fire,
> By whom you light up the night,
> How beautiful he is, how happy, how powerful
>   and strong!

Be praised, my Lord, for our Sister, Mother
  Earth,
Who nourishes and governs us,
And produces different fruits with colored
  flowers and herbs.[50]

Notes

Introduction: Ecology and Theology

1. Haeckel spelled the word as *oecologie*. The modern spelling appeared in the 1890s along with the first sophisticated ecological monographs. See Roderick Nash, *The Rights of Nature: A History of Environmental Ethics* (Leichhardt, NSW: Primavera Press, 1990), 55.

2. Aldo Leopold, *A Sand County Almanac: With Essays on Conservation from Round River* (New York: Ballantine Books, 1949, 1966), xix.

3. Charles Taylor, *The Sources of the Self: The Making of the Modern Identity* (Cambridge, Mass.: Harvard University Press, 1989).

4. See Rosemary Radford Ruether's analysis in *Gaia and God: An Ecofeminist Theology of Earth Healing* (San Francisco: HarperSanFrancisco, 1992).

5. Sally McFague writes: "To put the matter in a nutshell, a third-world woman of color (as well as her first-world sister in the ghettoes of major cities) is the most impacted person on the planet. Her greatest ecological sin is probably ravaging denuded forests to gather firewood to cook her family's dinner. The most responsible person is a first-world, usually white, usually male, entrepreneur involved in a high energy, high profit business" (*The Body of God: An Ecological Theology* [Minneapolis: Fortress Press, 1993], 4).

6. For an accessible survey of the major issues facing the planet see Al Gore's *Earth in the Balance: Ecology and the Human Spirit* (New York: Penguin Books, 1992, 1993).

7. Lester Brown, "The New World Order," in *State of the World 1991*, 7. The loss of trees has led to a tragic shortage of fuelwood in poorer countries. Much of the world relies on wood or charcoal for energy. The world-wide fuelwood shortage has huge human and ecological costs. Ian Barbour, in *Ethics in an Age of Technology* (San Francisco: HarperSanFrancisco, 1993), 183, notes examples of reforestation policies which are helping to reverse these trends: in Nepal, villagers plant fodder grasses and fast-growing trees together on denuded slopes; in Kenya, the Greenbelt Movement has enlisted children in 670 communities in growing millions of seedlings for replanting; in Kerala, church groups, cooperatives and women's groups support a major replanting project, and the governments of India, China and the United States of America have major replanting programs. However, in the tropical rain forests trees are being cut down far faster than reforestation or nature can replace them,

and the rate of deforestation is increasing. See Sandra Postel and Lori Heise, *Reforesting the Earth: Worldwatch Paper 83* (Washington, D.C.: Worldwatch Institute, 1988). See also Sandra Postel and John C. Ryan, "Reforming Forestry," in Lester R. Brown (ed.), *State of the World 1991* (New York: W.W. Norton, 1988), 74ff.

8. Other remnants of rain forest can be found in Central America, the Atlantic coast of Brazil, sub-Sahara Africa, Madagascar, the Indian subcontinent, the Indochina peninsula, the Philippines, northern Australia, and on islands of the Pacific and Indian oceans.

9. John Terborgh, *Diversity and the Tropical Rain Forest* (New York: Scientific American Library, 1992), 187.

10. See Al Gore, *Earth in the Balance*, 117.

11. James Lockman, "Reflections on the Exploitation of the Amazon in the Light of Liberation Theology," in Carol Robb and Carl Casebolt, *Covenant for a New Creation: Ethics, Religion and Public Policy* (Maryknoll, N.Y.: Orbis Books, 1991), 170-71. For a theological reflection on the rain forests from the perspective of the Philippines see Sean McDonagh, *The Greening of the Church* (Scoresby, Vic.: Canterbury Press, 1990), particularly pp. 74-106.

12. Al Gore, *Earth in the Balance*, 120.

13. See Sandra Postel and Lori Heise, *Reforesting the Earth*, 41.

14. Philip Fearnside, *Human Carrying Capacity of the Brazilian Rainforest* (New York: Columbia University Press, 1986), 44.

15. Ibid. 46.

16. Al Gore, *Earth in the Balance*, 106-7.

17. See John Terborgh, *Diversity and the Tropical Rain Forest*, 3-4.

18. James Lockman, "Reflections," 173.

19. Ibid. 169.

20. John Terborgh, *Diversity and the Tropical Rain Forest*, 1-2.

21. Ibid. 5.

22. Ibid. 186. See John C. Ryan, "Conserving Biological Diversity," in Lester Brown (ed.), *State of the World 1992*, 9-26.

23. Thomas Berry, *The Dream of the Earth* (San Francisco: Sierra Club Books, 1988), 9.

24. Ian Barbour, *Ethics in an Age of Technology*, 184.

25. Ibid.

26. Norman Myers, *The Primary Source: Tropical Forests and Our Future* (New York: W.W. Norton, 1984), 189-293.

27. Postel and Heise note that the World Bank has been criticized for support of large-scale projects that destroy tropical forests and include migrations and resettlement of people in Brazil and Indonesia, and, in response, has set up a department charged with reviewing the environmental impact of all large projects (*Reforesting the Earth*, 14). On the relationship between economics and forests, see Alan Thein Durning, "Redesigning the Forest Economy," in Lester R. Brown (ed.), *State of the World 1994* (New York: W.W. Norton, 1994), 22-40.

28. See Sean McDonagh, *The Greening of the Church*, 9-37.

29. See, for example, G.F.R. Ellis and W. R. Stoeger, "Introduction to General Relativity and Cosmology," in Robert John Russell, Nancey Murphy and C. J. Isham (eds.), *Quantum Cosmology and the Laws of Nature* (Vatican City: Vatican Observatory Publications, 1993), 32-48. For further general introductions see John Barrow and Joseph Silk, *The Left Hand of Creation* (New York: Basic Books, 1983); Paul Davies, *Superforce: The Search for the Grand Unified Theory of Everything* (London: Unwin, 1984); *The Cosmic Blueprint* (London: Unwin, 1987); Paul Davies and John Gribbin, *The Matter Myth: Towards 21st-Century Science* (London: Penguin, 1991); Timothy Ferris, *Coming of Age in the Milky Way* (New York: William Morrow and Company, 1988); E. R. Harrison, *Cosmology* (Cambridge University Press, 1981); Stephen Hawking, *A Brief History of Time: From the Big Bang to Black Holes* (London: Bantam Press, 1988); Steven Weinberg, *The First Three Minutes: A Modern View of the Origin of the Universe* (New York: Bantam Books, 1977); *Dreams of a Final Theory* (New York: Pantheon Books, 1992).

30. Stephen Hawking, *A Brief History of Time*, 39.

31. Bruce Vawter, *This Man Jesus: An Essay Toward a New Testament Christology* (Garden City: Doubleday, 1973), 196-97.

32. Elizabeth A. Johnson, "Jesus, the Wisdom of God: A Biblical Basis for Non-Androcentric Christology," in *Ephemerides Theologicae Lovanienses* 61 (1985), 261-94. See also her *She Who Is: The Mystery of God in Feminist Theological Discourse* (New York: Crossroad, 1992).

33. In this it has much in common with Tony Kelly's creative treatment of theology's interaction with ecology and cosmology in his *An Expanding Theology: Faith in a World of Connections* (Newtown, NSW: E.J. Dwyer, 1993), although our approaches and methodologies are quite different. Another ecological theology which appeared while I was working on this text is John F. Haught's *The Promise of Nature: Ecology and Cosmic Purpose* (New York: Paulist Press, 1993). John Haught develops a processive and eschatological theology of creation.

1. The Wisdom of God in Biblical Tradition

1. *Sirach* and *The Wisdom of Solomon* are considered part of the canon for Roman Catholics and for the Orthodox, but not within Judaism and not in the Protestant tradition where they are understood as apocryphal books. On the importance of Wisdom literature and of personified Wisdom see Roland E. Murphy, "Wisdom Literature and Biblical Theology," in the *Biblical Theology Bulletin* 24 (Spring 1994), 4-7.

2. Kathleen M. O'Connor, *The Wisdom Literature* (Wilmington, Del.: Michael Glazier, 1988), 59. Kathleen O'Connor goes on to note that this theology of Sophia cannot be taken as overcoming gender biases in the biblical tradition, at least not without making some critical distinctions. She shows that both the Wisdom Woman and the Woman of Folly, or the "Strange

Woman," are "male projections of opposing aspects of the human condition onto female figures" (61). These stereotypical views of women, along with the misogynism of some Wisdom texts, mean that Wisdom literature must be approached with "critical caution." Nevertheless, O'Connor judges that "the figure of the Wisdom Woman ultimately transcends narrow female stereotypes to take on, in the texts and in our imaginations, a life of her own" (63). The picture of the Strange Woman falls away in the literature, while the Wisdom Woman "grows in importance, beauty and divinity." Thus "feminine stereotypes are potentially broken for us all" and the Wisdom Woman "brings with her a vision of reality filled with hope and promise for our fragmented, peaceless world" (63). See also Claudia V. Camp, "Woman Wisdom as Root Metaphor: A Theological Consideration," in K. G. Hoglund, E. F. Huwiler, J. T. Glass and R. W. Lee (eds.), *The Listening Heart: Essays in Wisdom and the Psalms in Honor of Roland E. Murphy* (Sheffield: JSOT Press, 1987), 45-76.

3. Roland E. Murphy, *The Tree of Life: An Exploration of Biblical Wisdom Literature* (New York: Doubleday, 1990), 146.

4. On the problems of dating Job, and on Job in general, see Norman Habel, *The Book of Job: A Commentary* (Philadelphia: Westminster, 1985), 40-42. See also Marvin H. Pope, *Job* (Garden City: Doubleday, 1965), xxx-xxxvi.

5. Roland Murphy, *The Tree of Life*, 135.

6. See J. Crenshaw, "Wisdom in the OT," *Interpreters Dictionary of the Bible Supplement* (Nashville: Abingdon Press, 1976), 954; Roland Murphy, *The Tree of Life*, 19.

7. John Hayes, *An Introduction to the Study of the Old Testament* (Nashville: Abingdon, 1979), 330.

8. Roland Murphy notes that "begot" = "created" according to the Septuagint. See *The Tree of Life*, 136.

9. On the various meanings of this word, see Bernhard Lang, *Wisdom in the Book of Proverbs: An Israelite Goddess Redefined* (New York: Pilgrim, 1986), 65.

10. Roland Murphy, *The Tree of Life*, 137.

11. Ibid. 138. Roland Murphy, in company with many other scholars, thus rejects as inadequate Gerhard von Rad's earlier position that Sophia was simply a personification of world order or the "self-revelation of creation." See Gerhard von Rad, *Wisdom in Israel* (Nashville: Abingdon, 1972), 144-76.

12. Kathleen O'Connor, *The Wisdom Literature*, 137.

13. Roland Murphy, *The Tree of Life*, 139.

14. Kathleen O'Connor, *The Wisdom Literature*, 145.

15. David Winston argues for a date around the reign of Gaius "Caligula" (37-41 C.E.). See "Solomon, Wisdom Of," in the *Anchor Bible Dictionary* 6 (New York: Doubleday, 1992), 122. On what follows see also his *The Wisdom of Solomon: Anchor Bible 43* (Garden City: Doubleday, 1979).

16. Roland Murphy, *The Tree of Life*, 84.

17. David Winston, "Solomon, Wisdom Of," 123.

18. Roland Murphy, *The Tree of Life*, 88.

19. Ibid. 144.

20. C. L. Larcher, *Études sur le livre de la Sagesse* (Paris: Gabalda, 1969), 391.

21. David Winston, "Solomon, Wisdom Of," 125.

22. Ibid.

23. Kathleen O'Connor, *The Wisdom Literature*, 178.

24. See Elizabeth Johnson, "Jesus, the Wisdom of God," 268. See also David Winston, "Solomon, Wisdom Of," 124-25. Aretalogies of Isis (Greek doxologies, in which the goddess praises herself) show her universal sovereignty: she is creator of the universe, and the founder of civilization under its aspects of law, morality, craft and social relationships. She controls sexual union, childbirth, family life and fate. It seems clear that in Wisdom 6-9 there are real connections with the praises of Isis. The author has skillfully adapted the Isis aretalogies for the purpose of praising Wisdom. See James M. Reese, *Hellenistic Influence on the Book of Wisdom and Its Consequences* (Rome: Biblical Institute Press, 1970), 36-50; Burton Mack, *Logos und Sophia* (Gottingen: Vandenhoeck & Ruprecht, 1973). See also Hans Conzelmann, "The Mother Of Wisdom," in James Robinson (ed.), *The Future of Our Religious Past: Essays in Honour of Rudolph Bultmann* (New York: Harper and Row, 1971), 230-43; John Kloppenborg, "Isis and Sophia in the Book of Wisdom," *Harvard Theological Review* 75 (1982), 57-84.

25. See Elizabeth Johnson, "Jesus, the Wisdom of God" (271-75), in which she surveys five types of answer to this question: 1. Wisdom is the personification of cosmic order (Gerhard von Rad); 2. Wisdom is the personification of the wisdom sought and learned in Israel's wisdom schools (Bernhard Lang); 3. Wisdom is the poetic personification of a divine attribute—God's wisdom (R. N. Whybray); 4. Wisdom is a hypostasis (Helmer Ringren); 5. Wisdom is a personification of God's own self in creative and saving involvement with the world. Each of the five positions can be supported by appeal to certain texts. Elizabeth Johnson argues that the fifth option is the best explanation of at least a number of texts. Personifications, like Sophia and Logos, are ways of asserting the transcendent God's nearness. She cites, in support of the fifth view, scholars such as Raymond Brown, James Dunn, C. Larcher, Roland Murphy, Virginia Mollenkott, and Pierre Bonnard. In any case, scholars who hold other views, like Von Rad and Ringren, admit the functional equivalence of Sophia with Yahweh, in the equivalence between the deeds of Sophia and those of the biblical God.

26. Roland Murphy, *The Tree of Life*, 147.

27. Ibid. Emphasis added.

28. Kathleen O'Connor, *The Wisdom Literature*, 83.

29. Elizabeth Johnson, "Jesus, the Wisdom of God," 275.

30. See James Dunn's *Christology in the Making* (London: SCM, 1980). My own approach to biblical Wisdom Christology owes much to Dunn's work and to Elizabeth A. Johnson's "Jesus, the Wisdom of God." I have already mentioned Bruce Vawter's *This Man Jesus*. See also James M. Reese, "Christ as Wisdom Incarnate: Wiser than Solomon, Loftier than Lady Wisdom," *Biblical Theology Bulletin* 11 (1981), 44-47; Leo G. Perdue, "The Wisdom Say-

ings of Jesus," *Forum* 2 (1986), 3-35; Robert M. Grant, "The Christ at the Creation," in R. Hoffmann and G. Larue (eds.), *Jesus in History and Myth* (Buffalo: Prometheus, 1986), 157-67; William Gray, "Wisdom Christology in the New Testament: Its Scope and Relevance," *Theology* 89 (1986), 448-59; Pheme Perkins, "Jesus: God's Wisdom," *Word and World* 7 (1987), 273-80; Bernard B. Scott, "Jesus as Sage: An Innovative Voice in Common Wisdom," in J. Gammie (ed.), *The Sage In Israel* (Winona Lake, Ind.: Eisenbrauns, 1990), 399-425. An important work in this whole area is M. Jack Suggs's *Wisdom, Christology and Law in Matthew's Gospel* (Cambridge, Mass.: Harvard University Press, 1970). Other longer studies include Wilfred Knox, *St. Paul and the Church of the Gentiles* (London: Cambridge University Press, 1939, 1961); Pierre Bonnard, *La Sagesse en personne, annoncée et venue: Jésus Christ* (Paris: 1966); A. Feuillet, *Le Christ, Sagesse Dieu d'après les épîtres pauliennes* (Paris: Gabalda, 1966); Felix Christ, *Jesus Sophia: Die Sophia Christologie bei den Synoptikern* (Zurich: Zwingli-Verlag, 1970); Jack T. Sanders, *The New Testament Christological Hymns: Their Historical Religious Background* (London: Cambridge University Press, 1971); R. G. Hamerton-Kelly, *Pre-Existence, Wisdom, and the Son of Man: A Study of the Idea of Pre-Existence in the New Testament* (London: Cambridge University Press, 1973); Fred W. Burnett, *The Testament of Jesus Sophia: A Redaction-Critical Study of the Eschatological Discourse in Matthew* (Washington, D.C.: University of America Press, 1981).

31. These are the texts considered by Jack T. Sanders in *The New Testament Christological Hymns*. On these hymns see also R. G. Hamerton-Kelly, *Pre-Existence, Wisdom, and the Son of Man*; James Dunn, *Christology in the Making*; Elisabeth Schüssler Fiorenza, "Wisdom Mythology and the Christological Hymns of the New Testament," in Robert Wilkens (ed.), *Aspects of Wisdom in Judaism and Early Christianity* (Notre Dame, Ind.: University of Notre Dame Press, 1975), 17-41.

32. Bruce Vawter, *This Man Jesus*, 153-54.

33. Cf. Jack T. Sanders, *The New Testament Christological Hymns*, 24-25.

34. Myles M. Bourke, "The Epistle to the Hebrews," in Raymond Brown, Joseph Fitzmyer and Roland Murphy (eds.), *The New Jerome Biblical Commentary* (Englewood Cliffs, N.J.: Prentice Hall, 1990), 922-23.

35. Bruce Vawter, *This Man Jesus*, 159.

36. Myles M. Bourke, "The Epistle to the Hebrews," 923.

37. William L. Lane, *Word Biblical Commentary: Volume 47a: Hebrews 1-8* (Dallas: Word Books, 1991), 12.

38. Elizabeth Johnson, "Jesus, the Wisdom of God," 279.

39. Eduard Schweizer, *The Letter to the Colossians: A Commentary* (Minneapolis: Augsburg Publishing House, 1982), 246.

40. Other influences include the prophetic word, the Torah and the Memra (Aramaic for "word") of the Jewish Targums. See Raymond Brown, *The Gospel According to John (i-xii)* (Garden City, N.Y.: Doubleday, 1966), 519-24.

41. Ibid. 523.

42. Elizabeth Johnson, *She Who Is*, 98. The references are: E. Schweizer, "Aufnahme und Korrectur jüdischer Sophiatheologie im Neuen Testament," in *Hören und Handeln: Festschrift für E. Wolf* (Munich: C. Kaiser, 1962), 33f.; F. Braun, "Saint Jean, La Sagesse et L'Histoire," in *Neotestamentica et Patristica* (Leiden: Brill, 1962), 123; W. Knox, *Paul and the Church of the Gentiles* (London: Cambridge University Press, 1939), 84.

43. James D.G. Dunn, in "Christology (NT)," in *The Anchor Bible Dictionary* 1 (New York: Doubleday, 1992), writes: "The concept 'Word' is given preference over 'Wisdom,' perhaps simply because the masculine concept seemed more appropriate, but probably mainly because 'Word' was the more serviceable concept to provide a bridge of communication between Jewish monotheism and Greek religious philosophy (as with Philo)" (987).

44. Elizabeth Johnson, "Jesus, the Wisdom of God," 277. Recent writing in this area includes: Robin S. Barbour, "Creation Wisdom and Paul," in R. McKinney (ed.), *Creation, Christ and Culture* (Edinburgh: Clark, 1976), 22-42; Richard A. Horsley, "Wisdom of Words and Words of Wisdom in Corinth," *The Catholic Biblical Quarterly* 39 (1977), 224-39; James M. Reese, "Paul Proclaims the Wisdom of the Cross: Scandal and Foolishness," *Biblical Theology Bulletin* 9 (1979), 147-53; Robin S. Barbour, "Wisdom and the Cross in 1 Corinthians 1 and 2," in C. Andressen (ed.), *Theologia crucis—signum crucis* (Tubingen: Mohr, 1979), 57-71; Celine Mangan, "Christ the Power and the Wisdom of God: The Semitic Background to 1 Cor 1:24," *Proceedings of the Irish Biblical Association* 4 (1980), 21-34; Vincent P. Branick, "Source and Redaction Analysis of 1 Corinthians 1-3," *Journal of Biblical Literature* 101 (1982), 251-69; James Davis, *Wisdom and Spirit: An Investigation of 1 Cor 1:18-3:20 Against the Background of Jewish Sapiential Traditions in the Greco-Roman Period* (Lanham, Md.: University Press of America, 1984); Gail P. Corrington, "Paul and the Two Wisdoms: 1 Corinthians 1:18-31 and the Hellenistic Mission," *Proceedings Estn Gt Lakes and Midwest Bibl. Soc* 6 (1986), 72-84; Victor P. Furnish, "Theology in 1 Corinthians: Initial Soundings," *Society of Biblical Literature; 1989 Seminar Papers* (1989), 246-64; Peter Lampe, "Theological Wisdom and the 'Word about the Cross'; The Rhetorical Scheme in 1 Corinthians 1-4," *Interpretation* 44 (1990), 117-31.

45. Elizabeth Johnson, "Jesus, the Wisdom of God," 278. Johnson mentions, as supporting this view, Pierre Bonnard, W. D. Davies, James Dunn, A. Feuillet, Ulrich Wilckens, H. Conzelmann, Wilfred Knox and Eduard Schweizer.

46. James Dunn, *Christology in the Making*, 212. See also 1 Corinthians 10:1-4, where Paul identifies the rock from which the Jewish people drank in the desert as Christ. Dunn sees this as a parallel between the rock then and Christ now, rather than a clear reference to pre-existence (183-84). See also 2 Corinthians 4:4; Romans 10:6-10; Philippians 2:6-11.

47. Joseph A. Fitzmyer, *The Gospel According to Luke (X-XXIV)* (Garden City, N.Y.: Doubleday, 1985), 950.

48. Joseph A. Fitzmyer, *The Gospel According to Luke (I-IX)* (Garden City, N.Y.: Doubleday, 1981), 679.

49. M. Jack Suggs, *Wisdom, Christology and Law in Matthew's Gospel*, 97. See also William Beardslee, "The Wisdom Tradition and the Synoptic Gospels," *Journal of the American Academy of Religion* (1967), 231-40; Felix Christ, *Jesus Sophia*; Fred Burnett, *The Testament of Jesus-Sophia*; James M. Robinson, "Jesus as Sophos and Sophia: Wisdom Tradition and the Gospels," in R. Wilken (ed.), *Aspects of Wisdom in Judaism and Christianity* (Notre Dame, Ind.: University of Notre Dame Press, 1975), 1-16; John S. Kloppenborg, "The Formation of Q and Antique Instructional Genres," *Journal of Biblical Literature* 105 (1986), 443-62; "Symbolic Eschatology and the Apocalypticism of Q," *The Harvard Theological Review* 80 (1987), 287-306; "The Formation of Q Revisited: A Response to Richard Horsley," *Society of Biblical Literature: 1989 Seminar Papers* (1989), 204-15; Betty J. Lilly, "Matthew's Wisdom Theology: Old Things and New," *Proceedings, Estn Gt Lakes and Midwest Bibl Soc* (1989), 124-37; R. S. Sugirtharajah, "Wisdom, Q, and a Proposal for a Christology," *The Expository Times* 102 (1990), 42-46; Celia Deutsch, "Wisdom in Matthew: Transformation of a Symbol," *Novum Testamentum* 32 (1990), 13-47; Russell Pregeant, "The Wisdom Passages in Matthew's Story," *Society of Biblical Literature: 1990 Seminar Papers* (1990), 469-93; Michael Trainor, "The Begetting of Wisdom: The Teacher and the Disciples in Matthew's Community," *Pacifica* 4 (1991), 148-64.

50. M. Jack Suggs, *Wisdom, Christology and Law in Matthew's Gospel,* 130.

51. Ibid. 59.

52. John P. Meier, *Matthew* (Wilmington, Del.: Michael Glazier, 1980), 128.

53. See John P. Meier, *The Vision of Matthew: Christ, Church, and Morality in the First Gospel* (New York: Paulist Press, 1979), 78, note 57, for Meier's comment on M. J. Suggs, F. Christ, M. Johnson and E. Schweizer.

54. John Meier, *Matthew*, 127; idem, *The Vision of Matthew*, 80.

55. John Meier, *The Vision of Matthew*, 80.

56. Raymond Brown, *The Gospel According to John, I-XII* (Garden City, N.Y.: Doubleday, 1966), cxxii. In the next few paragraphs, I will be relying on this work of Brown's, particularly pages cxxii-cxxviii.

57. Ibid. cxxiii. Brown notes, "In particular, John iii 13 is very close to Bar iii 29 and Wis ix 16-17."

58. Ibid. cxxiv.

2. Jesus the Wisdom of God

1. I have attempted to explore this issue in the light of Karl Rahner's theology in *Jesus and the Cosmos* (New York: Paulist Press, 1991).

2. Monika Hellwig has developed a Christology built on the theme of compassion. See her *Jesus: The Compassion of God* (Wilmington, Del.: Michael Glazier, 1983).

3. C. H. Dodd, *The Parables of the Kingdom* (Glasgow: Collins, 1961), 21.

4. See Elisabeth Schüssler Fiorenza, *In Memory of Her: A Feminist Theological Reconstruction of Christian Origins* (London: SCM, 1983), 119ff.

5. Edward Schillebeeckx, *Jesus: An Experiment in Christology* (New York: Seabury Press, 1979), 200-29.

6. Elisabeth Schüssler Fiorenza, *In Memory of Her*, 148.

7. See Proverbs 1:7. Roland Murphy points out: "The positioning of this verse (echoed in 9:10; 15:33; Job 28:28; Ps 111:10) is important. It is the seventh verse, following upon the introduction, and it is repeated in 9:10, at the end of the first collection. Fear of the Lord also appears in 31:30, as a kind of conclusion to the book" (*The Tree of Life*, 16).

8. Gerhard von Rad, *Wisdom in Israel*, 67.

9. Kathleen O'Connor, *The Wisdom Literature*, 52-53.

10. See for example Thomas Aquinas, *Summa Theologiae* 1.43.5 ad 2, and 2-2.45.2. See Denis Edwards, *Human Experience of God* (New York: Paulist Press, 1983), 105-8. On medieval theologians and Sophia, see Barbara Newman, "Some Medieval Theologians and the Sophia Tradition," *The Downside Review* 108 (1990), 111-30.

11. See H. Jaeger, "The Patristic Conception of Wisdom in the Light of Biblical and Rabbinical Research," in *Studia Patristica*, F. Cross (ed.) (Berlin: Akademie Verlag: 1961), 4:90-106; Robert Grant, "The Book of Wisdom at Alexandria," in *After the New Testament* (Philadelphia: Fortress Press, 1967), 70-82.

12. See J. A. Lyons, *The Cosmic Christ in Origen and Teilhard de Chardin: A Comparative Study* (Oxford: Oxford University Press, 1982), 121.

13. Origen, *De Principiis*, 1.2.2. I am using the translation of G. W. Butterworth, *Origen: On First Principles* (New York: Harper and Row, 1966), 16.

14. Ibid. 1.2.4 (Butterworth, 17).

15. Ibid. 1.4.5 (Butterworth, 42).

16. Ibid. 2.6.2 (Butterworth, 109).

17. Athanasius, *Contra Gentes*, 42 (*P.G.* 25, 84-85).

18. Athanasius, *De Decretis* 27 (*P.G.* 25, 465).

19. Leo I, *Ep.* 28 (*PL* 54, 762-3), emphasis added.

20. Leo I, *Ep.* 31 (*PL* 54, 791), emphasis added. This text is read as part of the Liturgy of the Hours during Advent. See *The Divine Office: The Liturgy of the Hours According to the Roman Rite* (London: Collins, 1974), 1, 120.

21. *The Divine Office* 1, 549.

22. Ibid. 124

23. See Elizabeth Johnson, "Jesus, The Wisdom of God," 291-92.

24. Ibid. 292.

25. *De Ordine*, 1.2.16.

26. *DS* 806.

27. For the debate on this issue see John Hick (ed.), *The Myth of God Incarnate* (London: SCM, 1976); Michael Green (ed.), *The Truth of God Incarnate*

(Grand Rapids: Eerdmans, 1977); Michael Goulder (ed.), *Incarnation and Myth: The Debate Continued* (Grand Rapids: Eerdmans, 1979).

28. Karl Rahner points out that in the light of the necessity of defending Jesus' human subjectivity (his "person" in the modern sense) against a contemporary monophysitism or monothelitism, the point of unity in the hypostatic union remains "very formal and indetermined." See *Foundations of Christian Faith* (New York: Seabury, 1978), 292. For Rahner's defense of Jesus' human subjectivity see his "Reflections on the Knowledge and Self-consciousness of Christ," in *Theological Investigations V* (London: Darton, Longman and Todd, 1966), 193-215, and "The Position of the Christology in the Church between Exegesis and Dogmatics," in *Theological Investigations XI* (London: Darton, Longman and Todd, 1974), 198.

29. Walter Kasper, *Jesus the Christ* (New York: Paulist Press, 1976), 248.

30. Edward Schillebeeckx, *Jesus*, 667.

31. Elizabeth Johnson, "Jesus, The Wisdom of God," 261-94. See also her *She Who Is*, particularly chapter 8, 150-69.

32. Elizabeth Johnson, "Jesus, The Wisdom of God," 291.

33. Ibid. 294.

34. Ibid.

35. It is a common mistake to think that a foundation for social justice teaching is to be found in the prophetic literature, but not in the Wisdom teachings. Social justice is at the heart of Wisdom literature. See Bruce Malchow, "Social Justice in the Wisdom Literature," *Biblical Theology Bulletin* 12 (Oct. 82), 120-24. For the relationship between wisdom and the social construction of reality see Leo Perdue, "Cosmology and the Social Order in the Wisdom Tradition," in J. G. Gammie and L. Perdue (eds.), *The Sage in Israel and the Ancient Near East* (Winona Lake: Eisenbrauns, 1990), 457-78.

36. I am mindful here of the way David Tracy distinguishes between theologies of manifestation, proclamation and prophetic historical action (*The Analogical Imagination: Christian Theology and the Culture of Pluralism* [London: SCM, 1981], 371-445). Of course, as he points out, every adequate theology eventually needs to include all of these dimensions. I would see a Wisdom Christology as inclusive of all these dimensions, although at first glance it appears as a theology of manifestation.

37. Thomas Aquinas, *Summa Theologiae* 1.43.5 ad 2.

38. Ibid. 2-2.45.2.

39. Raimundo Panikkar, *The Unknown Christ of Hinduism* (Maryknoll, N.Y.: Orbis Books, 1988). This is a revised edition of his 1964 book and shows some developments in Panikkar's thought, including more reluctance to accept any complete identity between Christ and Jesus of Nazareth.

40. John Hick, *God and the Universe of Faiths* (New York: St. Martin's Press, 1973), 148-59; "Jesus and the World Religions," in John Hick (ed.), *The Myth of God Incarnate* (London: SCM, 1971). See also his *An Interpretation of Religion: Human Responses to the Transcendent* (New Haven: Yale University Press, 1988).

41. Paul F. Knitter, *No Other Name? A Critical Survey of Christian Attitudes Toward the World Religions* (Maryknoll, N.Y.: Orbis Books, 1985).

42. I agree with Knitter when he writes: "In boldly proclaiming that God has indeed been defined in Jesus, Christians will also humbly admit that God has not been confined to Jesus" (204). But I do not agree with him when he wants to speak of "*other incarnations*, other individuals who achieved or were granted the same fullness of God-human unity realized in Jesus" (191). It seems to me that this does compromise the uniqueness of Jesus, because incarnation is precisely Christian language which describes its central unique doctrine, a doctrine which, as far as I know, is not claimed in this way by any other traditions. It also seems unnecessary and unhelpful to approach interreligious dialogue with a prior Christian theology of incarnation that is to be applied to other founding figures. It seems far better to let each tradition speak for itself, rather than to speak of "multiple incarnations."

43. Roland Murphy, *The Tree of Life*, 126. See also Bruce V. Malchow, "Wisdom's Contribution to Dialogue," *Biblical Theology Bulletin* 13 (1983), 111-15.

44. Edward Schillebeeckx, *Church: The Human Story of God* (New York: Crossroad, 1990), 159-86. Schillebeeckx seeks to go beyond both "exclusive" and "inclusive" claims for Christianity, and to go beyond both "absolutism" and "relativism," by stressing both the universal meaning of Jesus and the historical limits of Jesus. See also his "The Religious and Human Ecumene," in Marc H. Ellis and Otto Maduro (eds.), *The Future of Liberation Theology: Essays in Honor of Gustavo Gutierrez* (Maryknoll, N.Y.: Orbis Books, 1989), 177-88.

45. The Second Vatican Council already speaks of those who are not Christians as sharing in the life of grace and as being offered a share in the paschal mystery of Christ (*Gaudium et Spes*, 22, see *Lumen Gentium*, 16) and speaks of other religious faiths as reflecting rays of that truth which enlightens all people (*Nostra Aetate*, 1).

46. A clear example of this for me, as an Australian theologian, is the invitation to Australian Christians to listen to the teaching of Aboriginal religious traditions concerning the sacredness of the land. It seems to me that here an Australian Christian has to be in apprenticeship to the Aboriginal religious view of the land, listening to hear a word of divine Wisdom, not clearly revealed in the Christian scriptures. I have developed this argument in the first chapter of *Called to Be Church in Australia* (Homebush, NSW: St. Paul Publications, 1987).

47. Edward Schillebeeckx, *Church: The Human Story of God*, 167.

48. Karl Rahner, "On Angels," *Theological Investigations* 19 (New York: Seabury Press, 1983), 235-74.

49. I have not used the word *incarnation* because such creatures may be constituted very differently from us—it is possible that they do not have our kind of flesh at all. On the subject of incarnation on other planets, Karl Rahner writes: "It cannot be proved that a multiple incarnation in different histories

of salvation is absolutely unthinkable." I would argue that, based on what we know through God's self-revelation in Wisdom, it is likely. For Rahner's comments see "Natural Science and Reasonable Faith," *Theological Investigations* 21 (New York: Seabury Press, 1988), 51, and *Foundations of Christian Faith* (New York: Seabury Press, 1978), 445-46.

3. Jesus—Wisdom and Ecology

1. This theme of the transformation of all things in Christ appears also in other texts, such as Romans 8:18-22, where the redemption of creation is seen in the context of Paul's Adam-Christ Christology. On this see Brendan Byrne, *Inheriting the Earth: The Pauline Basis of a Spirituality for Our Time* (Homebush, NSW: St. Paul Publications, 1990).

2. See Roland Murphy, *The Tree of Life*, 118. The saying can be attributed to W. Zimmerli. See his "The Place and the Limit of Wisdom in the Framework of the Old Testament Theology," in J. L. Crenshaw (ed.), *Studies in Ancient Israelite Wisdom* (New York: KTAV, 1976), 316. Zimmerli's concern is to explain how this "creation theology" fits within what he sees as typical biblical theology.

3. Roland Murphy, *The Tree of Life*, 135, 138.

4. As I noted above, the translation of the word *'āmôn* in Proverbs 8:30 is difficult; it can have various meanings including "craft worker" and "little child." However, in Wisdom 7:22 and 8:6, Wisdom is seen as a craft worker (*technitis*). In Mark (6:3) a form of this word is applied to Jesus. See Michael Trainor, "Wisdom in Mark," *Word in Life* 40:1 (February 1992), 18.

5. On wisdom and continuous creation see C. Larcher, *Études sur le livre de la Sagesse* (Paris: Gabada, 1969), 391.

6. Karl Rahner, *Foundations of Christian Faith* (New York: Seabury Press, 1978), 197. Rahner is not developing an explicitly Wisdom Christology, but, in my view, his theology of incarnation is compatible with a Wisdom theology.

7. C. K. Barrett, *A Commentary on the First Epistle to the Corinthians* (London: Adam and Charles Black, 1968), 54.

8. Ibid. 56.

9. Jerome Murphy-O'Connor, *1 Corinthians* (Wilmington, Del.: Michael Glazier, 1979), 14.

10. F. F. Bruce, *1 and 2 Corinthians* (London: Oliphants, 1971), 36.

11. Hans Conzelmann, *1 Corinthians: A Commentary on the First Epistle to the Corinthians* (Philadelphia: Fortress Press, 1975), 48.

12. Karl Rahner, "Immanent and Transcendent Consummation of the World," in *Theological Investigations* 11 (New York: Seabury Press, 1974), 289.

13. John D. Sinclair, *The Divine Comedy of Dante Alighieri, with Translation and Comment: III Paridiso* (New York: Oxford University Press, 1939, 1961), 492.

14. William F. Orr and James Arthur Walther, *The Anchor Bible: 1 Corinthians* (Garden City, N.Y.: Doubleday, 1976), 159.

15. Eduard Lohse, *Colossians and Philemon: A Commentary on the Epistles to the Colossians and to Philemon* (Philadelphia: Fortress Press, 1971), 42. Most modern commentators agree with Lohse. C.F.D. Moule is an example of a scholar who is unconvinced. See his *The Epistles of Paul the Apostle to the Colossians and to Philemon* (Cambridge: University Press, 1958), 61-62.

16. I am following Lohse, *Colossians and Philemon*, 42, and Eduard Schweizer, *The Letter to the Colossians: A Commentary* (Minneapolis, Minn.: Augsburg Publishing House, 1982), 55-81, in working with the hymn in terms of these two strophes. Most commentators accept this division, but some supplement it by dividing off a further connecting strophe in verses 17 and 18a, and some then speak of three strophes. See, for example, F. F. Bruce, *The Epistles to the Colossians, to Philemon, and to the Ephesians* (Grand Rapids: Eerdmans, 1984), 54; Petr Pokorny, *Colossians: A Commentary* (Peabody, Mass.: Hendrickson, 1991), 58-59; Ralph P. Martin, *Ephesians, Colossians, and Philemon* (Atlanta: John Knox Press, 1991), 105-6.

17. See, for example, Lohse, *Colossians and Philemon*, 42-43, Schweizer, *The Letter to the Colossians*, 82-88, and Martin, *Ephesians*, 105-10.

18. Bruce Vawter, *This Man Jesus*, 155-56.

19. Ibid. 158. If the author wanted to get rid of all cosmic references he could have done it by further editorial changes, by omitting the hymn, or by positively disagreeing with it. In agreeing with Vawter, I am disagreeing completely with Lohse and Schweizer, who both use the apparent fact of editorial interpolation as a basis for denying the theological import of the hymn. I can see no exegetical grounds for this at all. Eduard Schweizer argues from the evidence of interpolations to his own position that while the cosmic references to Christ may be appropriate for hymns, they are inappropriate for doctrine (*The Letter to the Colossians* 87, 273-77, 290-302). He fears that a doctrinal interpretation of Christ's cosmic role would lead to a situation where Christ would become a possession which could be placed at our disposal. It seems clear that this *a priori* position has a significant influence on Schweizer's reading of the text. I argue that Colossians 1:15-20, along with such texts as Ephesians 1:10, Hebrews 1:1-3 and John 1:1-18, allow and impel us to develop an appropriate cosmic Christology. In any case, a cosmic Christology need not, and absolutely must not, become a "possession placed at our disposal." Paul Santmire is surely right when he says that we must assume that "there is a certain critical continuity between the original hymn and the Pauline theology of Colossians" (*The Travail of Nature* [Philadelphia: Fortress Press, 1985], 264-66).

20. C.F.D. Moule, *The Epistles of Paul the Apostle*, 58-59.

21. Eduard Schweizer, *The Letter to the Colossians*, 246.

22. C.F.D. Moule, *The Epistles of Paul the Apostle*, 67.

23. Joseph Sittler, "Called to Unity," *The Ecumenical Review* 14 (1961-62), 177-78. Again, I disagree with Lohse's negative comment on Sittler's work, and with his argument, which is similar to Schweizer's (see note 16 above), that the "correction" of the hymn (the addition of the reference to the cross in

verse 20) "arrests all attempts to utilize the hymn for the purposes of a natural or cosmic theology" (*Colossians and Philemon*, 60-61, note 211). The hymn is an important source for a Christological theology of nature and for a Christological cosmic theology (it is certainly not the basis for a "natural theology"). There is no contradiction between the reference to the "blood of the cross" and a theology of God's action in creation, but a profound inner unity. Jürgen Moltmann is highly appreciative of Sittler's interpretation of the hymn in Colossians. See *The Way of Jesus Christ: Christology in Messianic Dimensions* (San Francisco: HarperSanFrancisco, 1990), 276-78.

24. Joseph Sittler, "Called to Unity," 178.

25. Ibid.

26. Philo calls Sophia the "beginning," the "image" and "the vision of God" (*Leg. All.* 1.43). These are also names for the Logos in Philo. See Lohse, *Colossians and Philemon*, 56.

27. See Lohse, *Colossians and Philemon*, 51, where he refers to texts from 2 Enoch: "And I saw there (i.e., in the seventh heaven) a very great light, and fiery troops of great archangels, incorporeal forces, and dominions and orders and governments, cherubim and seraphim, thrones and many-eyed ones, nine (ten) regiments" (2 Enoch 20:1); "all the hosts of heaven, and all the holy ones above, and the host of God, the Cherubim, Seraphim and Ophannim, and all the angels of power, and all the angels of principalities, and the Elect One, and all the other powers on the earth (and) over the water" (2 Enoch 61:10).

28. See the comment on "Principalities, Powers, and All Things" by Markus Barth in his *Ephesians: Introduction, Translation, and Commentary on Chapters 1-3* (Garden City, N.Y.: Doubleday, 1974), 170-83.

29. Markus Barth, *Ephesians*, 175. Barth is assuming that Paul is the author of Ephesians—this is a disputed question.

30. Eduard Lohse, *Colossians and Philemon*, 52.

31. Karl Rahner, *On the Theology of Death* (New York: Herder and Herder, 1962), 66.

32. I have developed this line of thought at greater length in *Jesus and the Cosmos*, 99-109.

33. These images are used by Karl Rahner in his rejection of the idea that the material world will become superfluous to human beings who are taken into the life of God. See his "Christianity and the 'New Man,' " in *Theological Investigations* 5, 147 and 148.

34. Ilya Prigogine and Isabelle Stengers, *Order Out of Chaos* (London: Heinemann, 1984), 200. On the new paradigm of the creative universe see Paul Davies, *The Cosmic Blueprint* (London: Unwin Hyman, 1987, 1989).

35. On this see Gabriel Daly, *Creation and Redemption* (Dublin: Gill and Macmillan, 1988), 100, where he points out that the word "new" in "new creation" does not mean the abolition of the old but its transformation.

4. The God of Mutual Love and Ecstatic Fecundity

1. Books 9 to 15 of Augustine's *De Trinitate* are devoted to analogies for the Trinity taken from the psychology of the human person. The triads, *mens-notitia-amor* and *memoria-intelligentia-voluntas*, are the most important. They have also been extremely influential in the trinitarian thinking of the West.

2. Catherine Mowry LaCugna, *God for Us: The Trinity and Christian Life* (San Francisco: HarperSanFrancisco, 1991).

3. Jürgen Moltmann has been an important figure in the development of a communal and social doctrine of the Trinity. See his *The Trinity and the Kingdom of God: The Doctrine of God* (San Francisco: Harper and Row, 1981) and *The Spirit of Life: A Universal Affirmation* (Minneapolis: Fortress Press, 1992). See also Leonardo Boff, *Trinity and Society* (Maryknoll, N.Y.: Orbis Books, 1988); Wolfhart Pannenberg *Systematic Theology 1* (Grand Rapids: Eerdmans, 1991); Joseph Bracken, *The Triune Symbol: Persons, Process and Community* (Lanham: University Press of America, 1985) and *Society and Spirit: A Trinitarian Cosmology* (Cranbury, N.Y.: Associated University Presses, 1991), and Ted Peters, *God as Trinity: Relationality and Temporality in Divine Life* (Louisville: Westminster, 1993). Three important general contemporary works on the Trinity which bring out the relational dimensions of trinitarian theology are Walter Kasper's *The God of Jesus Christ* (London: SCM, 1983), William J. Hill's *The Three-Personned God: The Trinity as a Mystery of Salvation* (Washington, D.C.: The Catholic University of America Press, 1982) and Anthony Kelly's *The Trinity of Love: A Theology of the Christian God* (Wilmington, Del.: Michael Glazier, 1989). A very significant contribution to a relational theology of the Trinity from an Orthodox perspective is John Zizioulas's *Being as Communion* (Crestwood, N.Y.: St. Vladimir's Seminary Press, 1985). Two recent feminist theologies which open up new insights on relational and communal approaches to the trinitarian God are Catherine Mowry LaCugna's *God for Us: The Trinity and Christian Life* and Elizabeth Johnson's *She Who Is: The Mystery of God in Feminist Theological Discourse*.

4. Augustine, *De Trinitate* VIII.X 14.

5. Zachary Hayes, *Saint Bonaventure's Disputed Questions on the Mystery of the Trinity: An Introduction and a Translation* (St. Bonaventure, N.Y.: The Franciscan University, 1979), 15.

6. Michael Schmaus, *Der liber propugnatorius des Thomas Angelicus und die Lehrunterschiede zwischen Thomas von Aquin und Duns Scotus*, vol. 2, *Die trinitärischen Lehrunterschiede* (Munster: Aschendorff, 1930). See William J. Hill, *The Three-Personned God*, 226.

7. William J. Hill, *The Three-Personned God*, 227.

8. The leading members of the Abbey of St. Victor were Hugh (d.1141), Achard (d.1171), Richard (d.1173), Walter, Adam, Godfrey and Andrew.

9. Richard justifies his appeal to experience by referring often to Romans 1:20: "Ever since the creation of the world his eternal power and divine nature, invisible though they are, have been understood and seen through the

things he has made." Congar notes at least ten instances in his *I Believe in the Holy Spirit* III (New York: Seabury Press, 1983), 106. Richard's discussion of friendship clearly presupposes experience, and in *De Trinitate* 111.3 he makes explicit appeal to experience: "Let each person examine his consciousness; without doubt and without contradiction he will discover that just as nothing is better than charity, so nothing is more pleasing than charity."

10. See Thomas Aquinas, *Summa Theologiae* 1.32.1 ad.2, where he criticizes this approach. Aquinas's opposition is to the idea that reason can demonstrate the Trinity. He is not opposed to Richard's argument as an explanation of faith. See 1 *Sent.*2.1.4. In the *Commentary on the Sentences* Aquinas makes use of this analogy, but avoids it in the *Summa Theologiae*. For critical comments on Richard see Theodore de Regnon, *Études de théologie positive sur la Sainte Trinité*, 4 vols. (Paris: Retaux, 1892-98), in II, 52-53, and John Bligh, "Richard of St. Victor's *De Trinitate*: Augustinian or Abelardian?" in the *Heythrop Journal* 1 (1960), 118-39.

11. See the comments of Yves Congar, *I Believe in the Holy Spirit* III, 103-8, and of William Hill, *The Three-Personned God*, 225-32. William Hill is rightly critical of any tendency in Richard to demonstrate the Trinity by reason, but then writes: "There is no reason why Richard of St. Victor's grounding of the Trinity in divine love cannot be purged of its apologetic element and made to function analogously to Aquinas' grounding of the Trinity in the dynamism of divine knowing and loving" (230). It is not clear that Richard really did have an apologetic intent in the modern sense. His whole argument is centered in the presumption of an intense Christian faith. He certainly maintains great respect for the incomprehensibility of God (see *De Trinitate* III.10 and IV.3). The problem is that he leaves himself open to the charge of attempting to prove the doctrine of the Trinity from reason by his use of the Anselmian language of "necessary reasons." Ewert Cousins deals with this and many other issues very helpfully in his "A Theology of Interpersonal Relations," *Thought* 45 (1970), 56-82. He shows that Richard's method must be situated within the context of faith, a metaphysics of exemplarism and an epistemology of illumination.

12. See Congar, *I Believe in the Holy Spirit* III, 106, n.1, and the book to which he refers, Jean Leclercq's *Monks and Love in Twelfth-Century France* (Oxford: Oxford University Press, 1979).

13. See Brian Patrick McGuire, *Friendship and Community: The Monastic Experience, 350-1250* (Kalamazoo, Mich.: Cistercian Publications, 1988), particularly 231-338.

14. Ewert Cousins, "A Theology of Interpersonal Relations," 59-60. In this paragraph I am following Cousins's line of thought.

15. Bernard of Clairvaux, *Sermones in Cantica Canticorum, PL* 183, 785-1198; *Liber de Diligendo Deo, PL* 182, 973-1000. Richard also wrote a commentary on the Canticle of Canticles—*In Cantica Canticorum Explicatio, PL* 196, 405-524; Aelred of Rievaulx, *Speculum Caritatis, PL* 195, 501-620; *De*

Spirituali Amicitia, PL 195, 659-702; William of St. Thierry, *De Natura et Dignitate Amoris, PL* 184, 379-408.

16. See *De Trinitate* 111.2 (*PL* 196, 916-917). For a critical text see Jean Ribaillier, *Richard de Saint-Victor, De Trinitate, texte critique avec introduction, notes et tables* (Paris: Vrin, 1958). Book III has been translated by Grover A. Zinn in *Richard of St. Victor: The Twelve Patriarchs, the Mystical Ark, Book Three of the Trinity* (New York: Paulist Press, 1979). In further quotations from Book III, I will follow this translation.

17. *De Trinitate* III.3 (Grover Zinn, *Richard of St. Victor*, 376).

18. *De Trinitate* III.4.

19. Ewert Cousins, "A Theology of Interpersonal Relations," 69-70.

20. *De Trinitate*, III.6 (Grover Zinn, *Richard of St. Victor,* 379).

21. *De Trinitate*, III.7 (Grover Zinn, *Richard of St. Victor*, 380).

22. *De Trinitate*, III.8.

23. Ibid. (Grover Zinn, *Richard of St. Victor*, 381).

24. Ewert Cousins, "A Theology of Interpersonal Relations," 78.

25. Ibid.

26. *De Trinitate*, III.15.

27. *De Trinitate*, III.19 (Grover Zinn, *Richard of St. Victor*, 392).

28. *De Trinitate*, III.20.

29. Ibid. (Grover Zinn, *Richard of St. Victor*, 393).

30. *De Trinitate*, III.22 (Grover Zinn, *Richard of St. Victor*, 394).

31. *De Trinitate*, III.23 (Grover Zinn, *Richard of St. Victor*, 395-96).

32. *De Trinitate*, V.16 and 19. In V:19 Richard writes: "*Constat namque, quia in uno ex tribus est amor summus et solum gratuitus. In altero vero sic summus, ut sit solum debitus. In tertio autem sic summus, ut sit ex uno debitus, ex altero omnino gratuitus.*" In Richard's Latin terminology as well as the triad of *amor gratuitus, amor debitus et gratuitus* and *amor debitus*, we find *amor privatus, amor mutuus* or *caritas*, and *amor consummata*, as well as love for oneself (*se*), love for the other (*condignus*) and love for a third who is mutually loved (*condilectus*). In fact it is these processions of love, combined with insight into the divine simplicity, which rule out any question of a "fourth" in God. See *De Trinitate*, V.20. In the last section of *De Trinitate* (VI) Richard discusses the procession of the Son (*genitus*) from the Father (*ingenitus*) by way of generation, and the Spirit's procession without generation (see VI.16).

33. See Congar, *I Believe in the Holy Spirit* III, 105. Richard is not totally opposed to the Augustinian approach to the Trinity, as is evident in his response to a question put to him about it. See his *Quomodo Spiritus Sanctus Est Amor Patris Et Filii* (*PL* 196, 1011-1O12), in J. Ribaillier, *Richard De Saint-Victor: Opuscules Théologiques: Texte Critique avec Introduction, Notes et Tables* (Paris: Libraire Philosophique J. Vrin, 1967), 164-66. As Ribaillier points out (160), the two approaches are not contradictory.

34. It is consistent with Richard's interest in the personal nature of trinitarian life that he rejects Boethius's classic definition of a person: "*Persona est*

naturae rationalis individualis substantia." Richard redefines person as "*naturae rationalis incommunicabilis existentia*" (*De Trinitate* IV. 24). A person is one who exists in himself or herself alone, according to a mode of reasonable existence, and who is distinguished from all others by a property that cannot be communicated. Richard is interested in the personal "who" and not simply the "what" of personal life. See *De Trinitate* IV.7. On this issue see Congar, *I Believe in the Holy Spirit*, 104-5.

35. *De Trinitate*, VI.15.

36. "*Nulla in Trinitate differentia est amoris, vel dignitatis*" (*De Trinitate*, V.24).

37. William Hill, *The Three-Personned God*, 226.

38. Catherine Mowry LaCugna uses this language and develops this kind of a theology in *God for Us: The Trinity and Christian Life*. She argues successfully for a proper understanding of the inner relationship between *oikonomia* and *theologia*, for a relational understanding of the Trinity, and for the Trinity as a practical doctrine. There are times when she seems to suggest that it is illegitimate to make *any* theological statements at all about the Trinity in itself. I would argue that while such statements must be based upon God's self-revelation in the economy, they can and ought be made.

39. John Zizioulas, *Being as Communion*, 44, and also "Human Capacity and Human Incapacity: A Theological Exploration of Personhood," in *The Scottish Journal of Theology* 28 (1975), 409. See Catherine Mowry LaCugna, *God for Us*, 260.

40. The quotation is from Stephen Hawking, *A Brief History of Time,* 174.

41. Unfortunately, Richard's insights into mutual love did not free him from the medieval cultural assumption of male superiority. Later in *De Trinitate* he asks whether it is appropriate in the Trinity to refer to one person as Father and the another as Son, in the light of the fact that both fathers and mothers are involved in human generation. He replies first that there is no sex in the divine nature. But, granted this, when we want to speak of generation in the Trinity it is appropriate to use names from the more worthy (*dignior*) sex. While this second assertion is revelatory of the depths of patriarchy's hold on medieval theology, the first is still extremely important and is not attended to enough: "*In divina autem natura, ut in commune novimus, omnino nullus est sexus*" (*De Trinitate* VI. 4). Although Richard thought this was "commonly known" in his day, it is clear that it is still not common knowledge in many circles today. Richard is quite clear that male language for God is not essential. It needs justification, and his justification is explicitly patriarchal.

42. Ewert Cousins, "A Theology of Interpersonal Relations," 80.

43. Ewert H. Cousins, "St. Bonaventure, St. Thomas, and the Movement of Thought in the 13th Century," in Robert W. Shahan and Francis J. Kovach (eds.), *Bonaventure and Aquinas: Enduring Philosophers* (University of Oklahoma Press, 1976), 16. This tradition has been widely ignored not only by process thinkers but also by representatives of "classical theism."

44. See Zachary Hayes, *Disputed Questions*, 32-33. My approach to Bonaventure depends on Zachary Hayes's scholarly work on Bonaventure's trinitarian theology.

45. *Itinerarium Mentis in Deum*, 5.2. For the Latin text with translation, see Philotheus Boehner (trans.), *Saint Bonaventure's Itinerarium Mentis in Deum: With an Introduction, Translation and Commentary* (Saint Bonaventure, N.Y.: The Franciscan Institute, 1956).

46. Ibid. 6.2.

47. Ibid. The translation in this case is my own.

48. See 1 *Sent.*, d.27, p.1, a.u., q.2.

49. Ewert Cousins, "St. Bonaventure, St. Thomas, and the Movement of Thought in the 13th Century," 18.

50. Zachary Hayes explains: "While the nature is the primary principle in the generation of the Son (*natura est principium concomitante voluntate*), the will is a real principle in the generation of the Spirit (*voluntas est principium concomitante natura*). Since it is the fecundity of the nature and the will from which the emanations flow, and since the intellect precisely as intellect is not fecund, Bonaventure always uses the term *per modum naturae* to designate the first procession. The Augustinian tradition of an intellectual emanation is this subsumed within this dominant framework." See Zachary Hayes, *Disputed Questions*, 34.

51. Zachary Hayes, *Disputed Questions*, 36. Bonaventure takes as his point of departure the fact that the first person is innascible, understood positively as the fullness of the source: "*Innascibilitas dicit in Patre plenitudinem fontalitatis sive fontalem plenitudinem*" (I *Sent.* d.29, dub.1). This *plenitudo fontalis* is related to Bonaventure's understanding of the first person as the "*principium*": "*Pater est principium totius deitatis*" (Ibid.). He states as a principle of fecund primacy: "The more primary a thing is, so the more fecund it is, and the principle of others" (1 *Sent.* d.2, a.u., q.2). Because the first person is innascible, then this person is also first, the source of fecundity, and the Father. This primacy means that the first person is self-communicating and the only *auctor* of the trinitarian processions. The fullness of the source cannot be communicated, so only the first person is *auctor* of the Holy Spirit. Thomas Aquinas does not agree with giving such positive content or priority to the concept of innascibility (*Summa Theologiae* 1.32.3; 1.33.4 ad 1).

52. Zachary Hayes writes of these two arguments: "Bonaventure's argument is constructed around two poles which reflect both the Dionysian and the Victorine concern. Neither of these poles can be reduced to the other since each provides only a limited vision of the mystery of God. The same bipolar argumentation appears again in the *Itinerarium*, but with a certain priority given to the Dionysian pole. In his final work, which we may see as his mature thought on the matter, the two poles are in fact presented as two parallel arguments, thus confirming the view that there is a basic distinction between the argument from the good and the argument from love" (*Disputed Ques-*

tions, 35). His references are to *Itin.* 6,2 and *Hexaemeron*, 11,11 and 12. For a discussion of the sources of Bonaventure's thought and its relationship to Richard and Pseudo-Dionysius, see Hayes, *Disputed Questions*, 13-24.

53. 1 *Sent.* d.2, a.u., q.4, fund.1.

54. 1 *Sent.* d. 11, a.u., q.2, resp.

55. I *Sent.* d.10, a.2, q.1, resp.; I *Sent.* d.18, a.u., q.4, resp.; I *Sent.* d.10, a.2., q.2, resp.

56. *Itinerarium Mentis in Deum*, 6.2. The translation is my own.

57. See 1 *Sent.* d.19, p.1, a.u., q.4. Peter Lombard wrote on this subject without using the word. The term *perichoresis* was used by the Greek theologian John Damascene in *De fide orthodoxa*, 8.

58. Yves Congar, *I Believe in the Holy Spirit* III, 114.

59. *Summa Theologiae*, 1.42.5. On *perichoresis* and its meaning see Catherine LaCugna, *God for Us*, 270-78. She writes: "Effective as a defense against tritheism and Arian subordinationism, *perichoresis* expressed the idea that the three divine persons mutually inhere in one another, draw life from one another, 'are' what they are by relation to one another. *Perichoresis* means being-in-one-another, permeation without confusion. No person exists by him/herself or is referred to him/herself; this would produce number and therefore division within God. Rather, to be a divine person is to be so *by nature* in relation to other persons" (270-71).

60. See 1 *Sent.* d.31, p.2, dub.7.

61. I *Sent.* d.31, p.2, a.1, q.2, resp.; *Comment.in Joan.* c.1, p.1, q.1. See Zachary Hayes comments in *Disputed Questions*, 51, and also in his "Incarnation and Creation in the Theology of St. Bonaventure," in Romano Stephen Almagno and Conrad L. Harkins (eds.), *Studies Honoring Ignatius Charles Brady, Friar Minor* (St. Bonaventure, N.Y.: The Franciscan Institute, 1976), 313-14.

62. 1 *Sent.* d.35, a.u., q.4, conc; *Breviloquium* 1,8.7. See Leonard Bowman, "The Cosmic Exemplarism of Bonaventure," *The Journal of Religion* 55 (1975), 182-83.

63. Zachary Hayes points out that Bonaventure distinguishes two ways in which a procession of exemplarity can be understood: "The first way refers to the *exemplatum* in the proper sense; that is, it refers to a being which is truly other than and distinct from the original which it resembles. Understood in this way, it is the created world that is the *exemplatum* proceeding from God as from its exemplar. The second way refers to the very *ratio exemplandi*, that is, to the very basis in God Himself of all exemplarity. This refers to the emanation of the Son who is the Word of God's self-expression in whom God disposes all things" (*Disputed Questions*, 47). See 1 *Sent.* d.6, a.u., q.1-3.

64. I *Sent.* d.6, a.u., q.3, resp.; *Breviloquium* 1, 8; *Hexaemeron*, 1. Augustine had used this expression in his *De Trinitate* (VI.X 11).

65. 1 Sent. d.6, a.u., q.3, ad 4. See Hayes, *Disputed Questions*, 47.

66. Leonard Bowman uses this expression in "The Cosmic Exemplarism of Bonaventure," 183. He borrows it from Alexander Gerkin, *La Theologie du verbe: La relation entre l'Incarnation et la Creation selon S. Bonaventure*, trans. Jacqueline Greal (Paris: Editions Franciscaines, 1970), 132. Bonaventure takes for granted the scholastic doctrine that God is present to creation by way of "essence, power and presence" (1 *Sent*. d.37, p.1, a.3, q.2, resp.; *Breviloquium*, 1, 5) and builds on this.

67. 1 *Sent*. d.7, a.u., dub.2.

68. *"Unde creatura non est nisi quoddam simulacrum sapientiae Dei, et quoddam sculptile"* (*Hexaemeron*, 12).

69. *"Omnis enim creatura ex natura est illius aeternae sapientiae quaedam effigies et simultudo"* (*Itinerarium* 2.12).

70. See Etienne Gilson, *The Philosophy of St. Bonaventure* (London: Sheed and Ward, 1938), p. 215. See Bonaventure, II *Sent*. d.16, a.u., q.2, where he says that it cannot be an accident in a creature to be a vestige.

71. *Breviloquium*, 2.12. Trans. Jose de Vinck, *The Works of Bonaventure II: The Breviloquium* (Paterson, N.J.: St. Anthony Guild, 1963), 104. I have added the emphasis. Bonaventure can also mention the shadow (*umbra*) of God, which is the most elementary and general reflection of God in creation. It reflects God as one, whereas the trace or vestige reflects the three persons. Bonaventure's chief interest is not in the shadow, but in the vestige, image and likeness.

72. Ibid. See also *Hexaemeron*, 2.

73. Leonard Bowman, "The Cosmic Exemplarism of Bonaventure," 187.

74. On all of this see Leonard Bowman, "The Cosmic Exemplarism of Bonaventure," 190-94. The patterns characteristic of the vestige appear in triads which echo triple causality as efficient, exemplary and final: one, true, good; mode, species, order; measure, number, weight. But Bonaventure's interest is in the middle member of each triad, as this is where a creature's form expresses the divine Art. For the sake of clarity I deal with only the middle members of the triads in the text.

75. *Itinerarium*, 2.10 (trans. Boehner, 59).

76. Bowman points out that number refers to a broader concept than our arithmetic notions: "It also refers to all ratios, harmonies, proportions, and even rhythms. Hence number is the foundation of proportion" ("The Cosmic Exemplarism of Bonaventure," 193).

77. *Breviloquium*, 2.11.2. Etienne Gilson speaks of the image of God in the creatures as "the analogy which the generating act imprints upon the being that it has engendered" (*The Philosophy of St. Bonaventure*, 220).

78. *Itinerarium*, 1.15 (trans. Boehner, 29). Bonaventure has a developed theory of knowledge, which I cannot discuss in detail, of the presence of the eternal Art to the intellect, as a light which gives guidance and direction to human knowing.

79. Zachary Hayes, "Disputed Questions on the Mystery of the Trinity," 32.

80. Zachary Hayes, "Incarnation and Creation in the Theology of St. Bonaventure," 315.

81. Bonaventure's understanding of "seminal principles" is clearly dated biologically, but it reveals the openness in his system of thought to an emergent kind of thinking. Leonard Bowman writes: "The seminal principles are active and positive potentialities which are inserted by God into matter. They are the essences or forms of all things which can be produced out of matter ... The actuation of a seminal form is analogous to the blooming of a rose from a bud; what is already there implicitly is made explicit; what is there in repose is awakened. Bonaventure's concept of matter is therefore a dynamic and positive one: matter is not a passive potentiality, but is pregnant with a multiplicity of positive possibilities and bears within itself a kind of dim mirror image of the Eternal Art" ("The Cosmic Exemplarism of Bonaventure," 195). There is a tendency in matter to rise to even higher forms. There are, then, some links between the thought of Bonaventure and that of Teilhard de Chardin. See Ewert H. Cousins, "Teilhard de Chardin et Saint Bonaventure," *Études Franciscanes* 19 (1969), 175-86.

82. In the *Breviloqium* (7.4.7) he writes: "Since vegetative and sensate beings do not have the power of perpetual life and eternal duration which belongs to the higher state, their whole substances are consumed; yet in such a way that they are preserved as ideas; and in a certain sense they survive also in their image, the human being, who is akin to creatures of every kind. It may be said then, that all things are to be renewed and, so to speak, rewarded, in the renewal and glorification of the human being." Bonaventure saw the elements and the heavenly bodies (the sun, the moon and the stars) as surviving, but in a state of repose, having reached their goal.

83. See Karl Rahner, "Christianity and the 'New Man,'" *Theological Investigations* 5, 147; "The Resurrection of the Body," *Theological Investigations* 2, 212-13; "The Festival of the Future of the World," *Theological Investigations* 7, 183.

84. Ewert Cousins, "St. Bonaventure, St. Thomas, and the Movement of Thought in the 13th Century," 19.

85. *Hexaemeron*, 13,14.

5. An Ecological Theology of the Trinity

1. In fact, I believe that on the basis of trinitarian mutuality, equality and *perich½r¶sis*, it is important to reject not only subordination in the Trinity, but also the use of monarchical language. In the tradition of the early church, the First Person (the unoriginate and unbegotten one) is seen as the sole principle (arche) and source of divine life in the Trinity. I would certainly want to respect this insight. I am not advocating a rejection of the economic missions of the Word and Spirit, nor of the idea of the Fountain Fullness as unoriginate origin of Word and Spirit, but only of the value-laden language of monarchy. This language can legitimate oppressive monarchical structures between hu-

man beings and betray the very meaning of the Trinity as a doctrine which challenges us to relationships and structures of mutuality and participation. The traditional distinctions, such as those Bonaventure makes between the Fountain Fullness, the Word and the Bond of Love, need not be understood or described in the language of monarchy. The description of the Fountain Fullness in the tradition as the "unoriginate origin" must be understood as a human attempt to describe the structure of trinitarian relationships based on what is revealed to us in the missions of Word and Spirit. Although there is clearly a sense in which the First Person is understood by the scriptures as the origin of the missions, and is understood by the tradition as the origin in terms of trinitarian relations, the One who is Unoriginate Origin is *not* prior in time, in power or in importance to the Word or the Spirit. All are equally eternal, and equally original, each united with the others in mutual *perichoresis*. The concept of the Fountain Fullness as Unoriginate Origin needs to be held together with radical mutuality and interdependence.

2. Aldo Leopold, "The Land Ethic," in *A Sand County Almanac*, 239.

3. Ibid. 253.

4. On these developments see Roderick Nash, *The Rights of Nature: A History of Environmental Ethics* (Leichhardt, NSW: Primavera Press, 1989), 55-86.

5. Catherine LaCugna, *God for Us*, 248-49.

6. Ibid. 248.

7. Tony Kelly, *An Expanding Theology: Faith in a World of Connections*, 158.

8. Walter Kasper, *The God of Jesus Christ*, 310. See also page 290, where Kasper traces this line of thought in the work of J. Ratzinger.

9. Thomas Berry, *The Dream of the Earth*, 11.

10. Simone Weil, "Forms of the Implicit Love of God," in *Waiting For God* (New York: Harper & Row, 1973), 208. See Elizabeth Johnson, *She Who Is*, 218.

11. Elizabeth Johnson, *She Who Is,* 219.

12. *Lumen Gentium*, 1.

13. In my view it would be helpful to find alternative language for what is called in Roman Catholic circles the "hierarchical constitution" of the church, because of the ambiguity of this language in our culture. I would certainly want to acknowledge the importance of structure and authority in the church and of the role of ordained ministry, above all as an "effective symbol" of the church's *communio*. I have developed this last line of thought in *Called to Be Church in Australia*. This line of thought raises the important issue of democratic participation in the church, which I cannot take up further here. On this, see Edward Schillebeeckx, *Church: The Human Story of God* (New York: Crossroad, 1991).

14. On the proper role of the persons in the economy of salvation see Karl Rahner, *The Trinity* (New York: Herder and Herder, 1970), 27. On the Holy Spirit, see David Coffey, "A Proper Mission for the Holy Spirit," *Theological*

Studies 47 (1986), 227-50 and "The 'Incarnation' of the Holy Spirit in Christ," *Theological Studies* 45 (1984), 466-80.

15. Lateran IV (1215) affirmed the Augustinian view that the world was created by the divine essence. This teaching can coexist with a proper role of the trinitarian persons in creation.

16. "Eucharistic Prayer for Masses of Reconciliation II."

17. Jürgen Moltmann, *The Spirit of Life.* See also Elizabeth A. Johnson, *Women, Earth and Creator Spirit* (New York: Paulist Press, 1993), 41-60.

18. *Summa Theologiae*, 1.45.6.

19. Ibid. 1.45.7.

20. Ibid. 1.45.6; 1.45.7 ad 1. What distinguishes the trinitarian persons for Thomas is opposition of relations, which he would not see as coming into play in creation.

21. See *1 Sent.* d.6, a.u., q.3, ad 4. When Bonaventure considers the hypothetical question of whether the Father or the Spirit could have become incarnate, he agrees with Anselm and Thomas Aquinas and finds that it cannot be excluded. See *III Sent.* d.1, a.1, q.4. In this I think he is inconsistent with his own system. But for a context for this see Zachary Hayes, "Incarnation and Creation in the Theology of St. Bonaventure," 309-12.

22. Karl Rahner, *Foundations of Christian Faith*, 197.

23. See Joseph M. Hallman, *The Descent of God: Divine Suffering and Human History* (Minneapolis: Fortress Press, 1991), chapters 1-5. Hallman not only traces the powerful impact of Greek philosophy in the patristic interpretation of biblical texts concerned with divine emotions, but also documents signs of resistance to the Greek view of divine immutability in the patristic sources.

24. For a summary of Augustine's reasons, see Hallman, *The Descent of God*, 110-11.

25. Jewish scholars have had a great influence on Christian theology at this point. See Abraham Heschel, *The Prophets* (New York: Harper & Row, 1962); Elie Wiesel, *Night* (New York: Bantam Books, 1982). Jürgen Moltmann has led the way in Christian theology on this issue. See his *The Crucified God: The Cross of Christ as the Foundation and Criticism of Christian Theology* (New York: Harper & Row, 1973), *The Trinity and the Kingdom* and *The Way of Jesus Christ.* Although I am in admiration of Moltmann's work, I differ from his position that there was a real abandonment of Jesus by God and from his view that "on the cross the Father and the Son are so widely separated that the direct relationship between them breaks off" (*The Way of Jesus Christ*, 174). I believe that this goes beyond any biblical evidence, and that it is not congruent with the view of God that we find in the preaching and praxis of Jesus. On the contrary, the resurrection tells us that although Jesus experienced apparent abandonment, God in reality remained faithfully with Jesus on the cross, overcoming death and bringing liberation. Process thinkers have long addressed

the issue of suffering in God. See, for example, Alfred North Whitehead, *Process and Reality: An Essay in Cosmology* (New York: Macmillan, 1929); Charles Hartshorne, *Omnipotence and Other Theological Mistakes* (Albany: State University of New York, 1984). See also Bernard Loomer, "Two Conceptions of Power," *Process Studies* 6 (1976), 5-32. I have found much to learn from in the process understanding of relational power, particularly from Loomer's work, but I differ from the general process view on God and creation, particularly because my view is strongly trinitarian, and also because I stress God's freedom and transcendence in creation, arguing that creation is a free act of love.

26. For a strong analysis and theological argument along these lines see particularly the last chapter of Elizabeth Johnson, *She Who Is*, "Suffering God: Compassion Poured Out," 246-72. For a treatment from a feminist and a process perspective from within the Reform tradition see Anna Case-Winters, *God's Power: Traditional Understandings and Contemporary Challenges* (Louisville: Westminster/John Knox Press, 1990).

27. Ted Peters, *God—The World's Future: Systematic Theology for a Postmodern Era* (Minneapolis: Fortress Press, 1992), 201.

28. Elizabeth Johnson, *She Who Is*, 265.

29. *Summa Theologiae*, 1.13.7; 1.28.1; 1.45.3 ad 1. A key problem for Aquinas was that in Aristotelian thought, relation is classified as an accident, and no accident can inhere in the divine being. On this, see Anthony Kelly, "God: How Near a Relation?" *Thomist* 34 (1970), 191-229; William Hill, "Does the World Make a Difference to God?" *Thomist* 38 (1974), 146-64; John Wright, "Divine Knowledge and Human Freedom: The God Who Dialogues" *Theological Studies* 38 (1977), 450-77; Catherine LaCugna, "The Relational God: Aquinas and Beyond," *Theological Studies* 46 (1985), 647-63.

30. See Jürgen Moltmann, *Trinity and the Kingdom*, 108-11; William Hill, *The Three-Personned God*, 76, n.53.

31. Walter Kasper, *The God of Jesus Christ*, 194-95.

32. John Polkinghorne, *Reason and Reality: The Relationship Between Science and Theology* (London: SPCK, 1991), 84. See his *Science and Providence* (London: SPCK, 1989), 66-67.

33. W. H. Vanstone, *Love's Endeavour, Love's Expense* (London: Darton, Longman and Todd, 1977), 63. See Polkinghorne, *Reason and Reality*, 83.

34. Edward Schillebeeckx, *Church: The Human Story of God*, 91.

35. For a summary of positions on these issues see C. J. Isham and J. C. Polkinghorne, "The Debate over the Block Universe," in *Quantum Cosmology and the Laws of Nature*, 135-44.

36. John Polkinghorne, *Reason and Reality*, 83.

37. Arthur Peacocke, *God and the New Biology* (London: J.M. Dent, 1986), 97-98 (emphasis added). For another important contribution on the issue of theology and chance, see D. J. Bartholomew, *God of Chance* (London: SCM, 1984).

38. As Bach did at the court of Frederick the Great in Potsdam in 1747. See Arthur Peacocke, *Theology for a Scientific Age: Being and Becoming—Natural and Divine* (Oxford: Basil Blackwell, 1990), 175.

39. Ibid.

6. Human Beings and Other Creatures

1. Charles Taylor, *Sources of the Self: The Making of the Modern Identity* (Cambridge, Mass.: Harvard University Press, 1989).

2. See R. Descartes, *Discourse on the Method of Rightly Conducting the Reason*, in E. S. Haldane and G.R.T. Ross (trans.), *The Philosophical Works of Descartes* (Cambridge: Dover, 1955), I, 119.

3. Ian Barbour, *Religion in an Age of Science* (San Francisco: HarperSanFrancisco, 1990), 205.

4. Ibid.

5. Jürgen Moltmann, *The Spirit of Life*, 24.

6. Ibid. 33.

7. See Karl Rahner, "Reflections on the Unity of the Love of Neighbor and the Love of God," *Theological Investigations* VI (New York: Seabury Press, 1969), 231-49.

8. See Rosemary Radford Ruether, *Gaia and God,* particularly 116-42, and 171-201.

9. Karl Rahner, *On the Theology of Death* (New York: Herder and Herder, 1962), 19. In his more recent work Rahner argues that because death is an entrance into the eternity of God, there may be no "intermediate state" between death and the resurrection of the body. See "The Intermediate State," *Theological Investigations* XVII (New York: Crossroad, 1981), 119.

10. John F. Haught, *The Promise of Nature*, 138.

11. Karl Rahner, "The Body in the Order of Salvation," *Theological Investigations* XVII, 71-89.

12. Ibid. 87.

13. 10^{80} is equivalent to writing the number 1 followed by 80 zeros. According to Paul Davies and John Gribben, *The Matter Myth: Towards 21st Century Science* (London: Viking, 1991), "in scarcely more than a billion-trillion-trillionth of a second the Universe would have swelled in volume by a factor of 10^{80}. The region of space visible to us today increased in radius during that tiny time interval from 10^{-26} cm to about 10 cm" (160).

14. Stephen Hawking, *A Brief History of Time*, 118.

15. Paul Davies, *Superforce*, 181. For a helpful description of this process and the story of its discovery see Timothy Ferris, *Coming of Age in the Milky Way*, 255-82.

16. Robert John Russell, "Finite Creation Without a Beginning: The Spiritual and Theological Significance of Stephen Hawkings' Quantum Cosmology," in *The Way* (October 1992), 268.

17. See G. Nicholis and I. Prigogine, *Self-Organization in Non-Equilibrium Systems* (New York: Wiley, 1977); I. Prigogine and I. Stengers, *Order Out of Chaos* (London: Heinemann, 1984); M. Eigen and P. Schuster, *The Hypercycle* (Heidelberg: Springer-Verlag, 1979). On this whole area see Paul Davies, *The Cosmic Blueprint* ((London: Unwin, 1987).

18. Carl Sagan, *Cosmos* (New York: Ballantine Books, 1980), 286.

19. Arthur Peacocke, *God and the New Biology*, 91. See also p. 126.

20. Pierre Teilhard de Chardin, *The Phenomenon of Man* (London: William Collins, 1959), 243.

21. Paul Davies, *Superforce*, 204.

22. On this see Karl Rahner, "Christology Within an Evolutionary View of the World," in *Theological Investigations* V (London: Darton, Longman and Todd, 1966), 161-63.

23. Sally McFague, *The Body of God: An Ecological Theology*, 171.

24. Ibid. These themes are developed in an important book that appeared after I had written this text. See Philip Hefner, *The Human Factor: Evolution, Culture and Religion* (Minneapolis: Fortress Press, 1993).

25. Ibid. 174.

26. Ibid. 197.

27. See Denis Edwards, *What Are They Saying About Salvation?* (New York: Paulist Press, 1986). See also "Sin and Salvation in the South Land of the Holy Spirit," in Peter Malone (ed.), *Discovering an Australian Theology* (Homebush, NSW: St. Paul Publications, 1988), 89-102.

28. Paul Davies, *God and the New Physics* (London: Penguin, 1983), 204.

29. Ibid. 205.

30. Steven Weinberg, *The First Three Minutes: A Modern View of the Origin of the Universe*, 144.

31. Steven Weinberg, *Dreams of a Final Theory: The Search for the Fundamental Laws of Nature*, 256.

32. Karl Rahner, "Natural Science and Reasonable Faith," *Theological Investigations* XXI (New York: Crossroad, 1988), 53.

33. John Polkinghorne, *Science and Creation: The Search for Understanding* (London: SPCK, 1988), 65. See also his *Science and Christian Belief* (London: SPCK, 1994), 162-75.

34. Ilya Prigogine and Isabelle Stengers write that "in spite of the important progress made by Hawking and others, our knowledge of large-scale transformations in our universe remains inadequate" (*Order Out of Chaos*, 117). Freeman Dyson and Frank Tipler have both offered adventurous alternatives to mainstream cosmology on the future of human beings and the universe. See Freeman Dyson, "Time Without End: Physics and Biology in an Open Universe," *Reviews of Modern Physics* 51: 447-60, and his *Infinite in All Directions* (New York: Harper & Row, 1988); and F. J. Tipler, "The Omega Point Theory: A Model of an Evolving God," in R. J. Russell and W. R. Stoeger (eds.), *Physics, Philosophy and Theology* (Vatican: Vatican Observatory, 1988); and J. D. Barrow and F. J. Tipler, *The Anthropic Cosmological Principle* (Ox-

ford: Clarendon Press, 1986). For a critical theological response to these speculations see Willem B. Drees, *Beyond the Big Bang: Quantum Cosmologies and God* (La Salle, Ill.: Open Court, 1990), 117-54.

35. See Karl Rahner, "The Resurrection of the Body," *Theological Investigations* II (Baltimore: Helicon Press, 1963), 212.

36. See Gustavo Gutiérrez, *A Theology of Liberation: History, Politics and Salvation*, revised edition (Maryknoll, N.Y.: Orbis Books, 1973, 1988), 83-105.

37. Paul VI, *Evangelii Nuntiandi*, 33. The Sacred Congregation for the Doctrine of the Faith in its two Instructions (1984 and 1986) has entered into dialogue with liberation theology, raised some critical questions, and affirmed some fundamental insights of this theology.

38. Edward Schillebeeckx, *Christ: The Christian Experience in the Modern World* (London: SCM, 1980), 734-43.

39. Jürgen Moltmann, *The Way of Jesus Christ*, 274-341.

40. John Polkinghorne, *Reason and Reality*, 102. Polkinghorne sees the New Creation as the fruit of the coming to be of a new, less independent relationship between God and the universe: "The good that is possible in the new creation is a different good, for it is based on the coming-to-be of a different relationship between God and the world. In the astounding symbol of the Cosmic Christ (especially in Colossians 1:15-20) we have the image of a reconciliation of universal scope, so that the new creation comes about—in a way unimaginable to us in mystery—through a relinquishment of the gift of independence and a return, through Christ, to a more intimate relationship with the Father of all. Involved here is the concept of the eventual solidarity of all that is in the Cosmic Christ" (102-3).

41. John Paul II, *Redemptor Hominis*, 48.

7. Ecological Praxis

1. James M. Gustafson, *Ethics from a Theocentric Perspective: Volume One, Theology and Ethics* (Chicago: University of Chicago Press, 1981), 113.

2. Thomas Berry, *The Dream of the Earth*.

3. Arne Naess, *Ecology, Community and Life-Style: Outline of an Ecophilosophy* (Cambridge University Press, 1987); Bill Devall and George Sessions (eds.), *Deep Ecology: Living As If Nature Mattered* (Salt Lake City: Peregrine Books, 1985).

4. J. Baird Callicott, "Animal Liberation: A Triangular Affair," *Environmental Ethics* 2 (Winter 1980), 324-37.

5. Thomas Berry, *The Dream of the Earth*, 209.

6. See, for example, Ariel Kay Salleh, "Deeper than Deep Ecology: The Eco-Feminist Connection," *Environmental Ethics* (Winter 1984), 339-45. For a recent example of a wide range of ecofeminist theological views see Carol J. Adams (ed.), *Ecofeminism and the Sacred* (New York: Continuum, 1993).

7. Marti Kheel, "Ecofeminism and Deep Ecology: Reflections on Identity and Difference," in Carol S. Robb and Carl J. Casebolt, *Covenant for a New Creation: Ethics, Religion and Public Policy*, 141-64.

8. H. Paul Santmire, "Healing the Protestant Mind: Beyond the Theology of Human Dominion," in Dieter T. Hessel (ed.), *After Nature's Revolt: Eco-Justice and Theology* (Minneapolis: Fortress Press, 1992), 74.

9. Rachel Carson's *Silent Spring* (Cambridge, Mass.: Riverside Press, 1962) made a wide audience aware of the chemical poisoning of the Earth.

10. Albert Schweitzer, *Civilization and Ethics: Philosophy of Civilization Part II* (London: A. and C. Black, 1923), 254. See also his *My Life and Thought: An Autobiography* (New York: George Allen and Unwin, 1933), 183-92.

11. Albert Schweitzer, *Indian Thought and Its Development* (Boston: Beacon Press, 1960), 187-88. See also his *The Teaching of Reverence for Life* (New York: Holt, Rinehart and Winston, 1965).

12. Lois K. Daly, "Ecofeminism, Reverence for Life, and Feminist Theological Ethics," in Charles Birch, William Eakin and Jay B. McDaniel (eds.), *Liberating Life: Contemporary Approaches to Ecological Theology* (Maryknoll, N.Y.: Orbis Books, 1990), 99.

13. John Paul II, *The Ecological Crisis: A Common Responsibility* (Washington D.C.: United States Catholic Conference, 1991).

14. Sean McDonagh, *The Greening of the Church*, 182. See also his *To Care for the Earth: A Call to a New Theology* (Santa Fe: Bear & Company, 1986), 189-91.

15. Sean McDonagh, *The Greening of the Church*, 180. For an overview of the place of extinctions in the history of evolution, see Robert M. Gascoigne, *The History of the Creation: A Christian View of Inorganic and Organic Evolution* (Sydney: Fast Books, 1993). See also Stephen J. Gould, *Wonderful Life: The Burgess Shale and the Nature of History* (London: Hutchinson, 1990).

16. *Keeping and Healing the Creation: A Resource Paper Prepared by the Presbyterian Eco-Justice Task Force* (Louisville, Ky.: Presbyterian Church, 1989). Issued by the Committee on Social Witness Policy, Presbyterian Church (U.S.A.).

17. For an overview of environmental ethics, see Roderick Frazier Nash, *The Rights of Nature: A History of Environmental Ethics* (Leichardt, NSW: Primavera Press, 1990).

18. Aldo Leopold, *A Sand County Almanac*, 239.

19. Ibid. xix.

20. Ibid. 262.

21. Ian Barbour, *Ethics in an Age of Technology*, 61.

22. Ibid. 63.

23. John Paul II, *On Social Concerns*, 34.

24. Ian Barbour, *Ethics in an Age of Technology*, 70.

25. Charles Birch and John B. Cobb, *The Liberation of Life: From the Cell to the Community* (New York: Cambridge University Press, 1981). See also

Charles Birch, *On Purpose* (Kensington, NSW: New South Wales University Press, 1990).

26. Charles Birch, "Christian Obligation for the Liberation of Nature," in Charles Birch, William Eakin and Jay B. McDaniel, *Liberating Life*, 59. John Cobb also argues that "intrinsic value is correlative to feeling." See his *Sustainability: Economics, Ecology and Justice* (Maryknoll, N.Y.: Orbis Books, 1992), 97.

27. For Peter Singer's views see *Animal Liberation: A New Ethic for Our Treatment of Animals* (London: Jonathon Cape, 1976).

28. See John B. Cobb, *Sustainability*, and Herman E. Daly and John B. Cobb, *For the Common Good: Redirecting the Economy toward Community, the Environment, and a Sustainable Future* (Boston: Beacon Press, 1989).

29. See John Cobb, *Sustainability*, 38-42.

30. Ibid. 56-65.

31. Ibid. 51.

32. Ibid. 74.

33. See Lester R. Brown, "Facing Food Insecurity," in *State of the World 1994*, 178.

34. Ibid. See also Sandra Postel, "Earth's Carrying Capacity," in *State of the World 1994*, 3-21.

35. Patrick Dodson, "The Land Our Mother, the Church Our Mother," *Compass* 22 (Autumn/Winter, 1988), 1.

36. George M. Tinker, "Creation as Kin: An American Indian View," in *After Nature's Revolt*, 148.

37. Ibid. 152-53.

38. Sally McFague, *Models of God: Theology for an Ecological, Nuclear Age*, 11.

39. Ibid. 9.

40. For examples of attempts at a new sensibility and a new story of creation see Brian Swimme and Thomas Berry, *The Universe Story: From the Primordial Flaring Forth to the Ecozoic Era: A Celebration of the Unfolding of the Cosmos* (HarperSanFrancisco, 1992), and Fritjof Capra and David Steindl-Rast, with Thomas Matus, *Belonging to the Universe: New Thinking About God and Nature* (London: Penguin, 1992).

41. See Matthew Fox, *Original Blessing: A Primer in Creation Spirituality* (Santa Fe: Bear and Co., 1983); *The Coming of the Cosmic Christ* (Melbourne: CollinsDove, 1988); *Creation Spirituality: Liberating Gifts for the Peoples of the Earth* (New York: HarperCollins, 1991).

42. Sally McFague, *Models of God*, 172.

43. Aldo Leopold, "Some Fundamentals of Conservation in the Southwest," *Environmental Ethics* 1 (Summer 1979), 140-41.

44. Roger D. Sorrell, *St. Francis of Assisi and Nature: Tradition and Innovation in Western Attitudes Toward the Environment* (Oxford: Oxford University Press, 1988), 114.

45. Ibid. 124.

46. There are various opinions about how to translate Francis's "*per*," as when he writes "*per sor Luna*." One view is to translate this as "by" or "through sister Moon." Here creation is seen as the agent of praise. The other view, which is Sorrell's, translates it as "for sister Moon." Here Francis is exhorting humankind to join him in praise of God because of creation's beauty. See Roger Sorrell, *St. Francis of Assisi and Nature*, 115-24.

47. Ibid. 123.

48. Ibid. 133.

49. Ibid. 134.

50. This is my own translation of these verses of the *Canticle*, but I have followed some of the phrasing of Roger Sorrell. See *St. Francis of Assisi*, 100-1.

Index

Also in the Ecology and Justice Series